RAYMOND BRIGGS

Ethel & Ernest

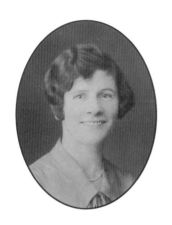 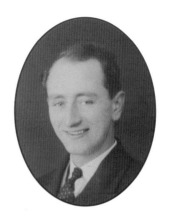

JONATHAN CAPE
London

For my Mother & Father

First published 1998

3 5 7 9 10 8 6 4

© 1998 Raymond Briggs

Raymond Briggs has asserted his right
under the Copyright, Designs and Patents Act, 1988
to be identified as the author of this work

First published in the United Kingdom in 1998 by Jonathan Cape
Random House, 20 Vauxhall Bridge Road, London SW1V 2SA

Random House Australia (Pty) Limited
20 Alfred Street, Milsons Point, Sydney
New South Wales 2061, Australia

Random House New Zealand Limited
18 Poland Road, Glenfield
Auckland 10, New Zealand

Random House South Africa (Pty) Limited
Endulini, 5a Jubilee Road,
Parktown 2193, South Africa

Random House UK Limited Reg No 954009
A CIP catalogue record for this book
is available from the British Library

ISBN 0 224 04662 4

Printed and bound in Singapore
by Tien Wah Press (Pte) Ltd

Ethel & Ernest

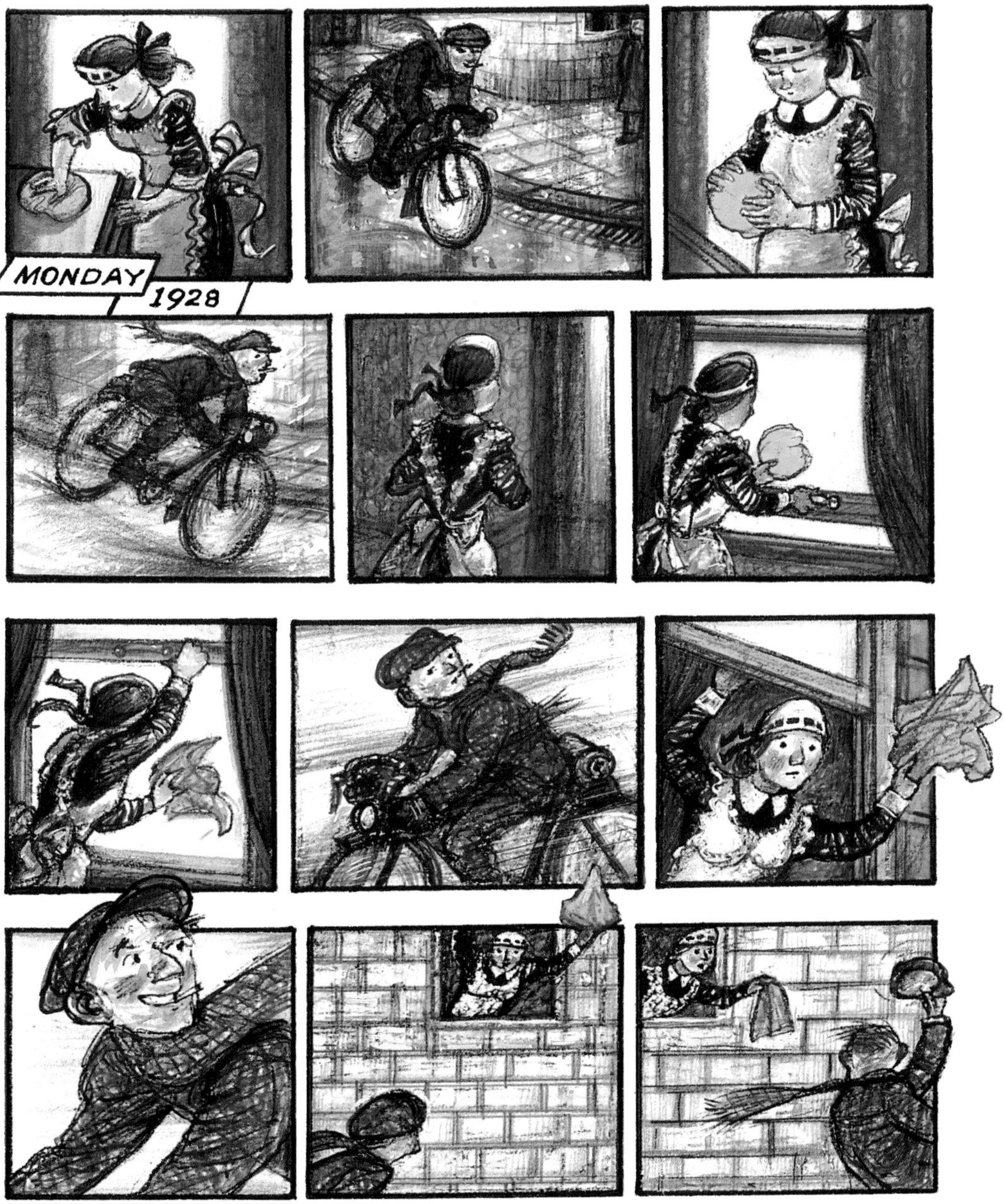
MONDAY
1928

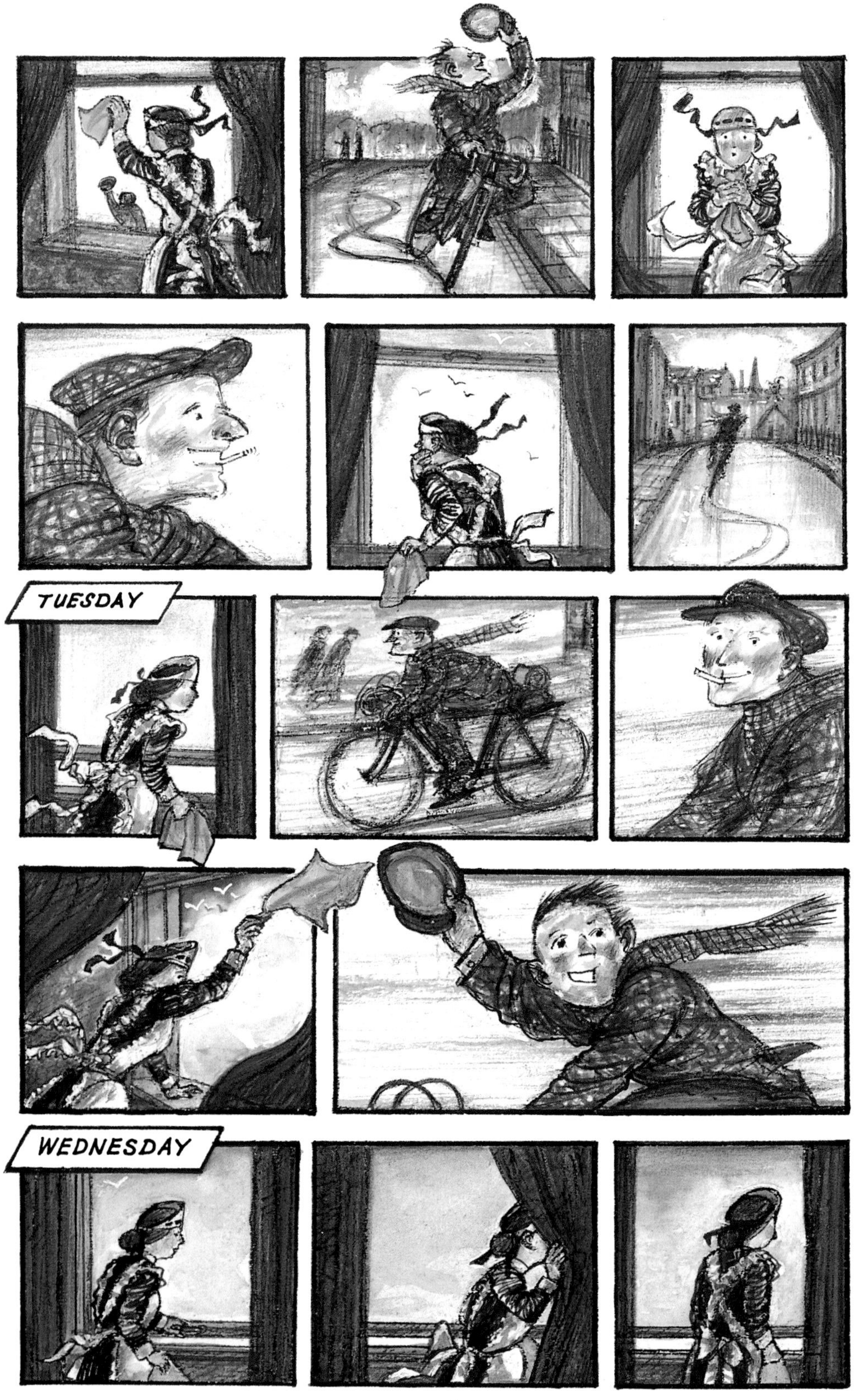
TUESDAY
WEDNESDAY

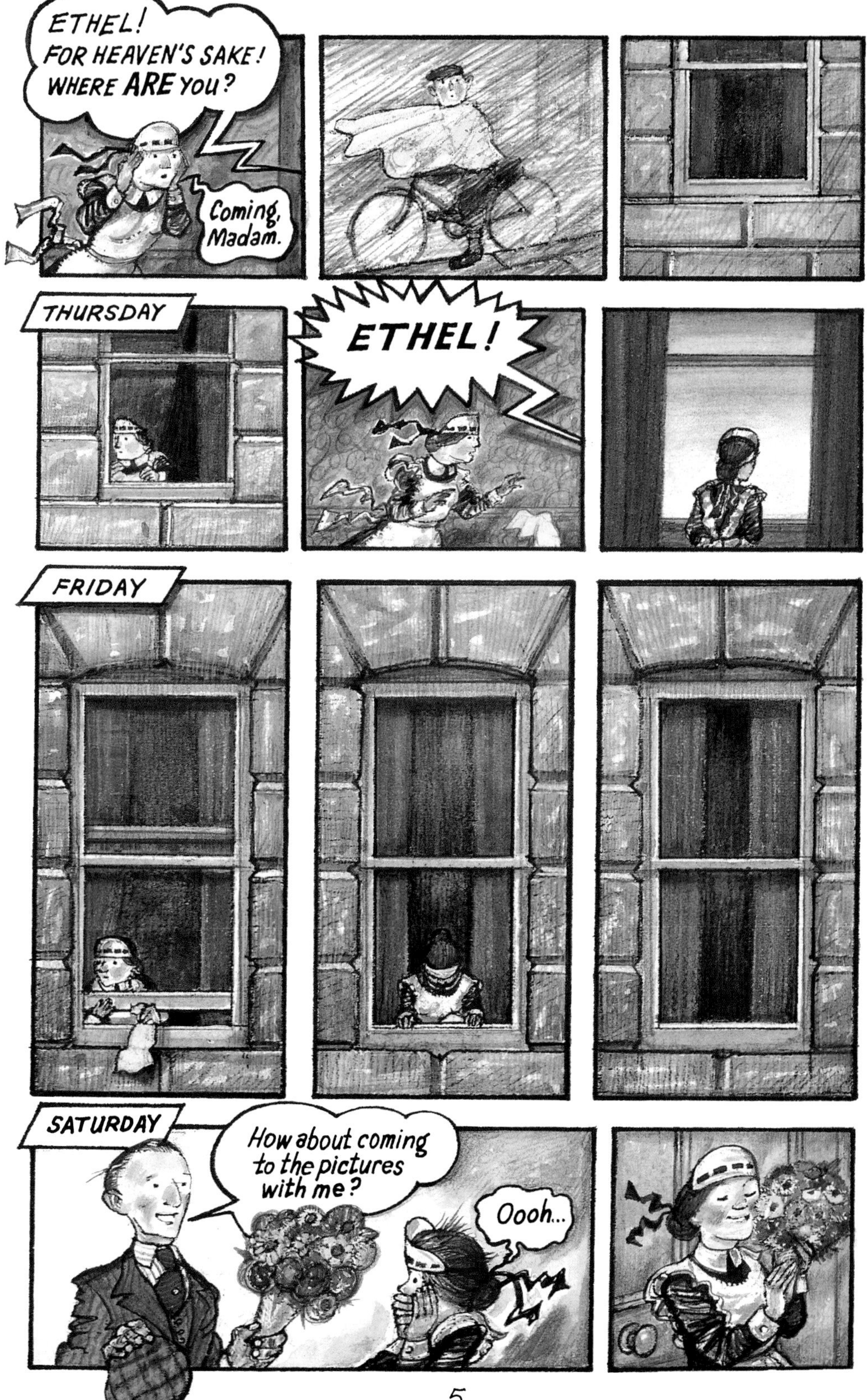
ETHEL! FOR HEAVEN'S SAKE! WHERE ARE YOU?
Coming, Madam.
THURSDAY
ETHEL!
FRIDAY
SATURDAY
How about coming to the pictures with me?
Oooh...

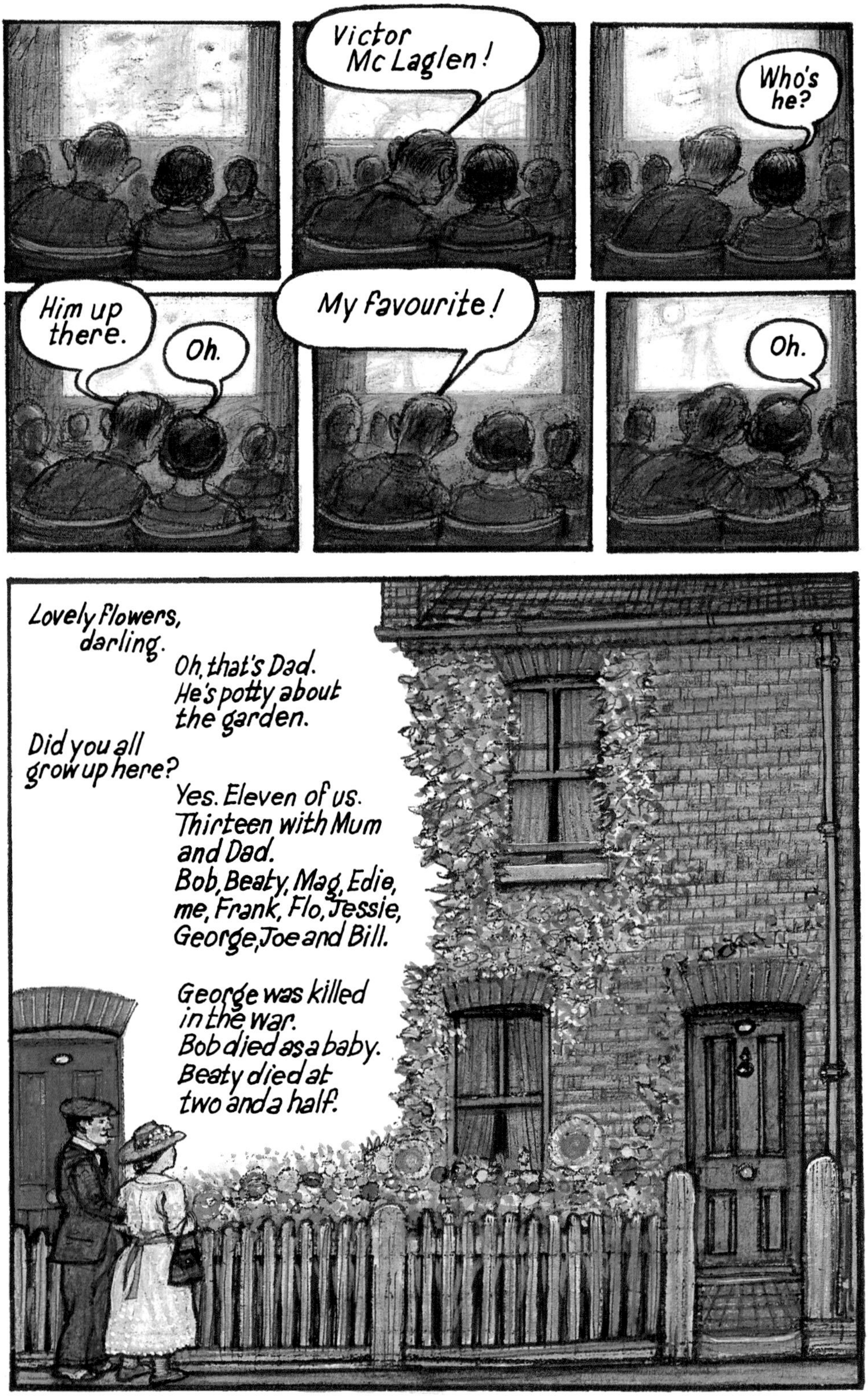
Victor McLaglen!
Who's he?
Him up there.
Oh.
My favourite!
Oh.
Lovely flowers, darling.
Oh, that's Dad. He's potty about the garden.
Did you all grow up here?
Yes. Eleven of us. Thirteen with Mum and Dad. Bob, Beaty, Mag, Edie, me, Frank, Flo, Jessie, George, Joe and Bill.
George was killed in the war. Bob died as a baby. Beaty died at two and a half.

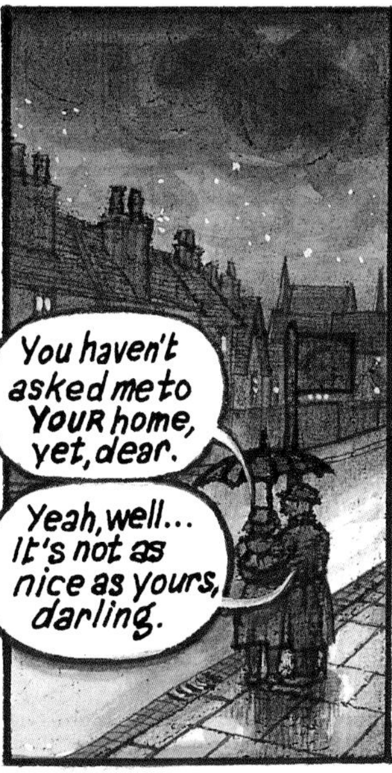
You haven't asked me to YOUR home, yet, dear.
Yeah, well... It's not as nice as yours, darling.

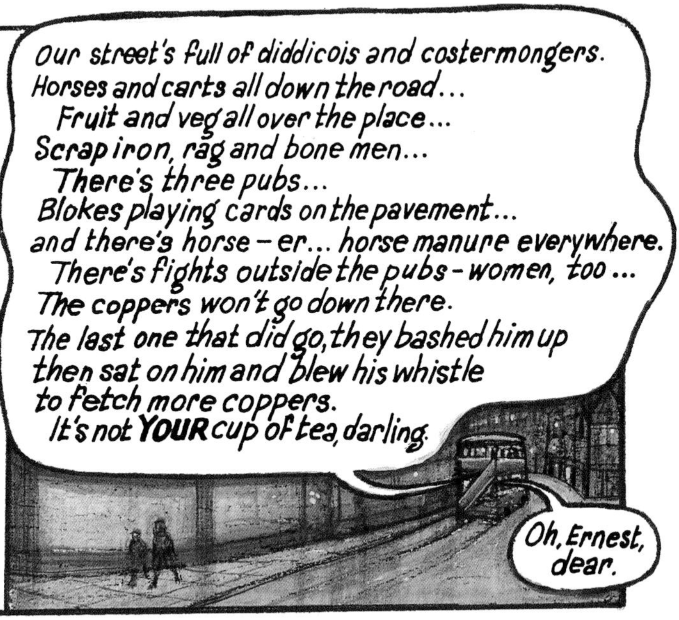
Our street's full of diddicois and costermongers. Horses and carts all down the road... Fruit and veg all over the place... Scrap iron, rag and bone men... There's three pubs... Blokes playing cards on the pavement... and there's horse – er... horse manure everywhere. There's fights outside the pubs – women, too... The coppers won't go down there. The last one that did go, they bashed him up then sat on him and blew his whistle to fetch more coppers. It's not YOUR cup of tea, darling.
Oh, Ernest, dear.

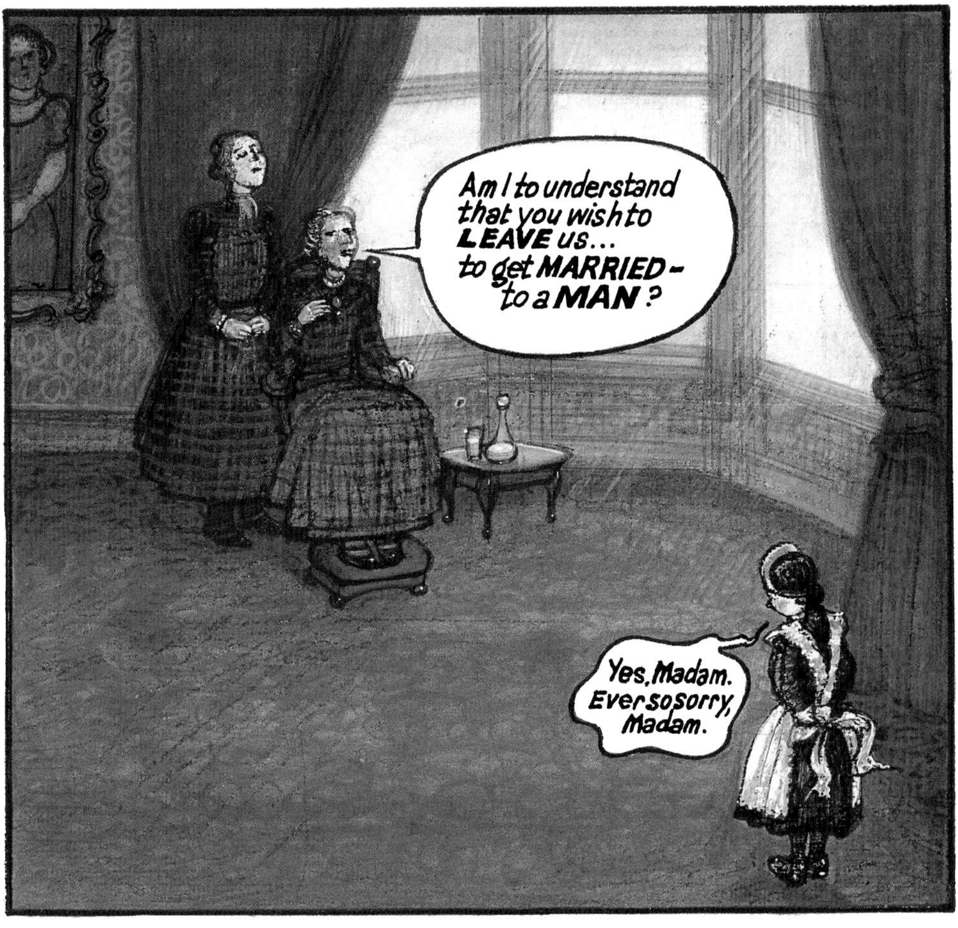
Am I to understand that you wish to LEAVE us... to get MARRIED – to a MAN?
Yes, Madam. Ever so sorry, Madam.

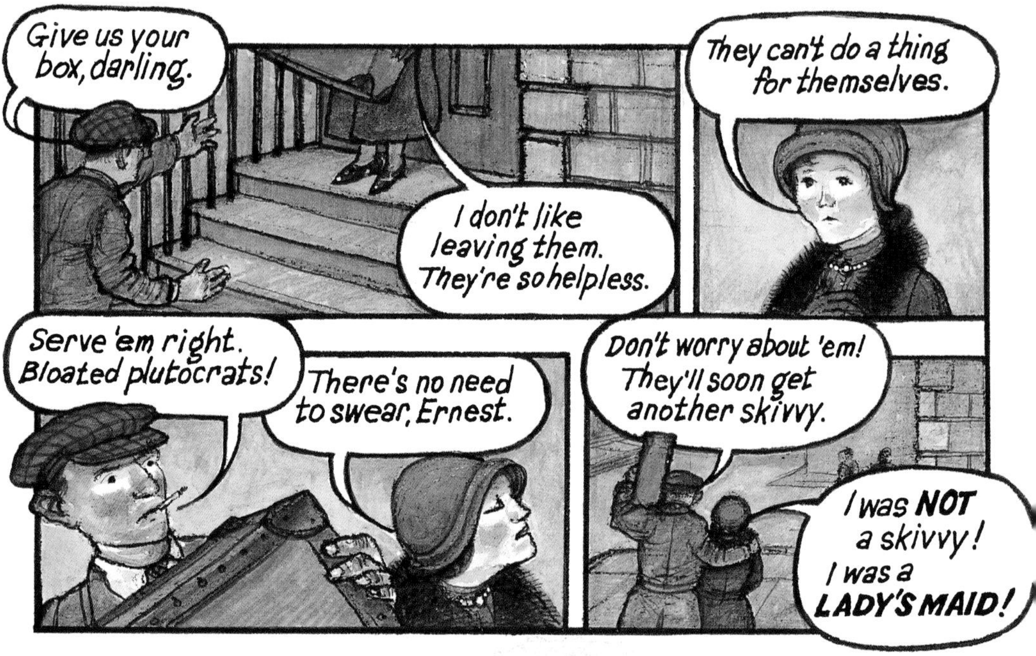
Give us your box, darling.
I don't like leaving them. They're so helpless.
They can't do a thing for themselves.
Serve 'em right. Bloated plutocrats!
There's no need to swear, Ernest.
Don't worry about 'em! They'll soon get another skivvy.
I was NOT a skivvy! I was a LADY'S MAID!

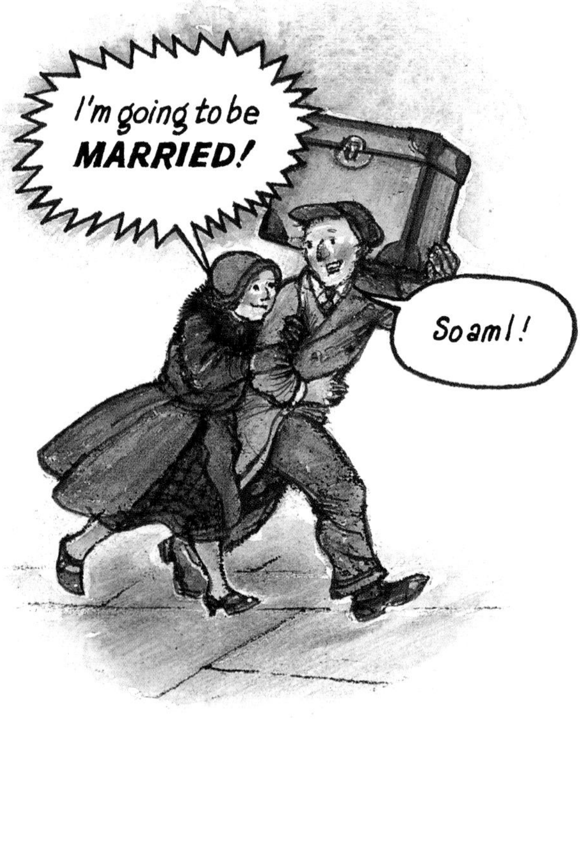
I'm going to be MARRIED!
So am I!

1930
~
1940

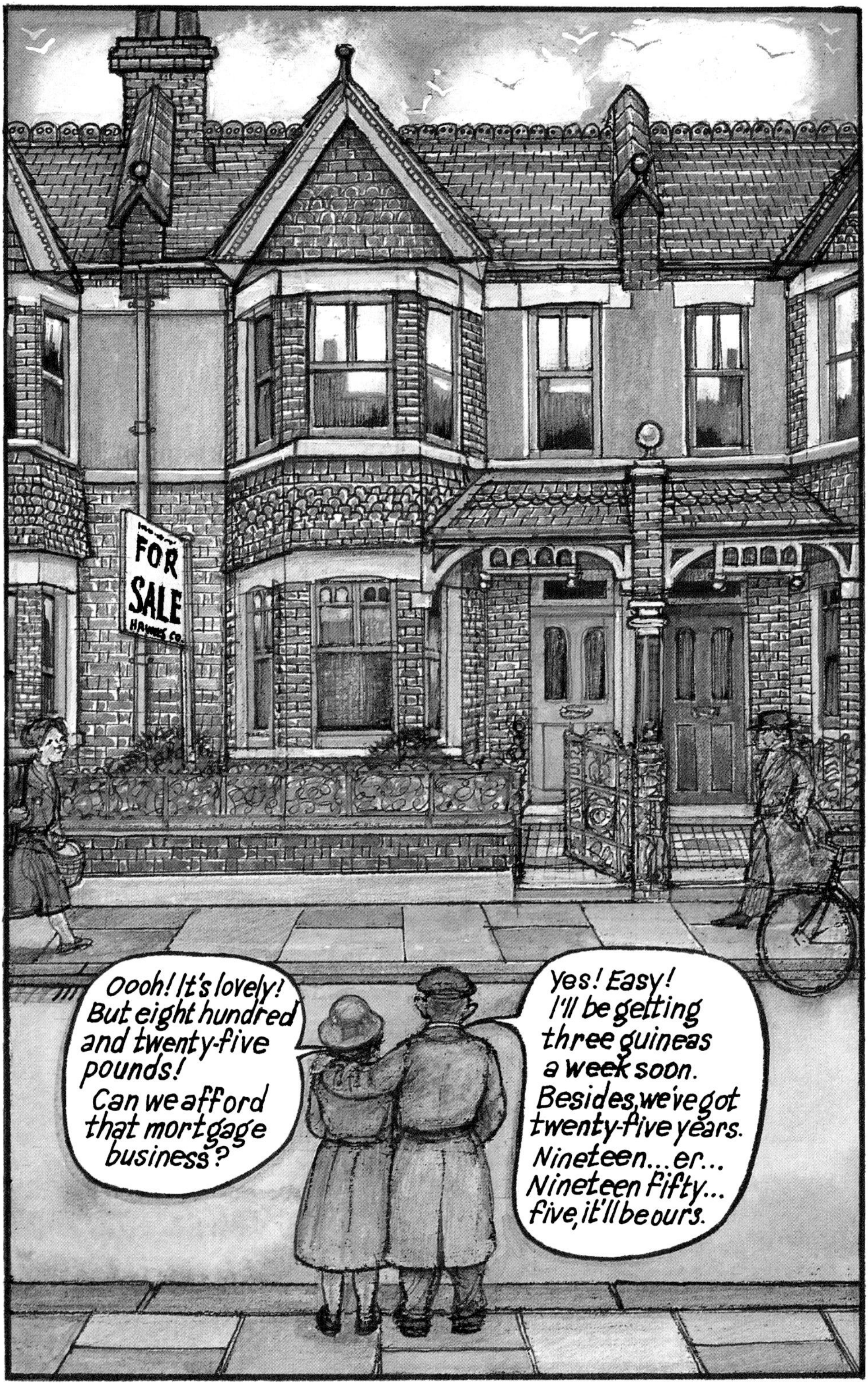
FOR SALE
Oooh! It's lovely! But eight hundred and twenty-five pounds! Can we afford that mortgage business?
Yes! Easy! I'll be getting three guineas a week soon. Besides, we've got twenty-five years. Nineteen... er... Nineteen fifty... five, it'll be ours.

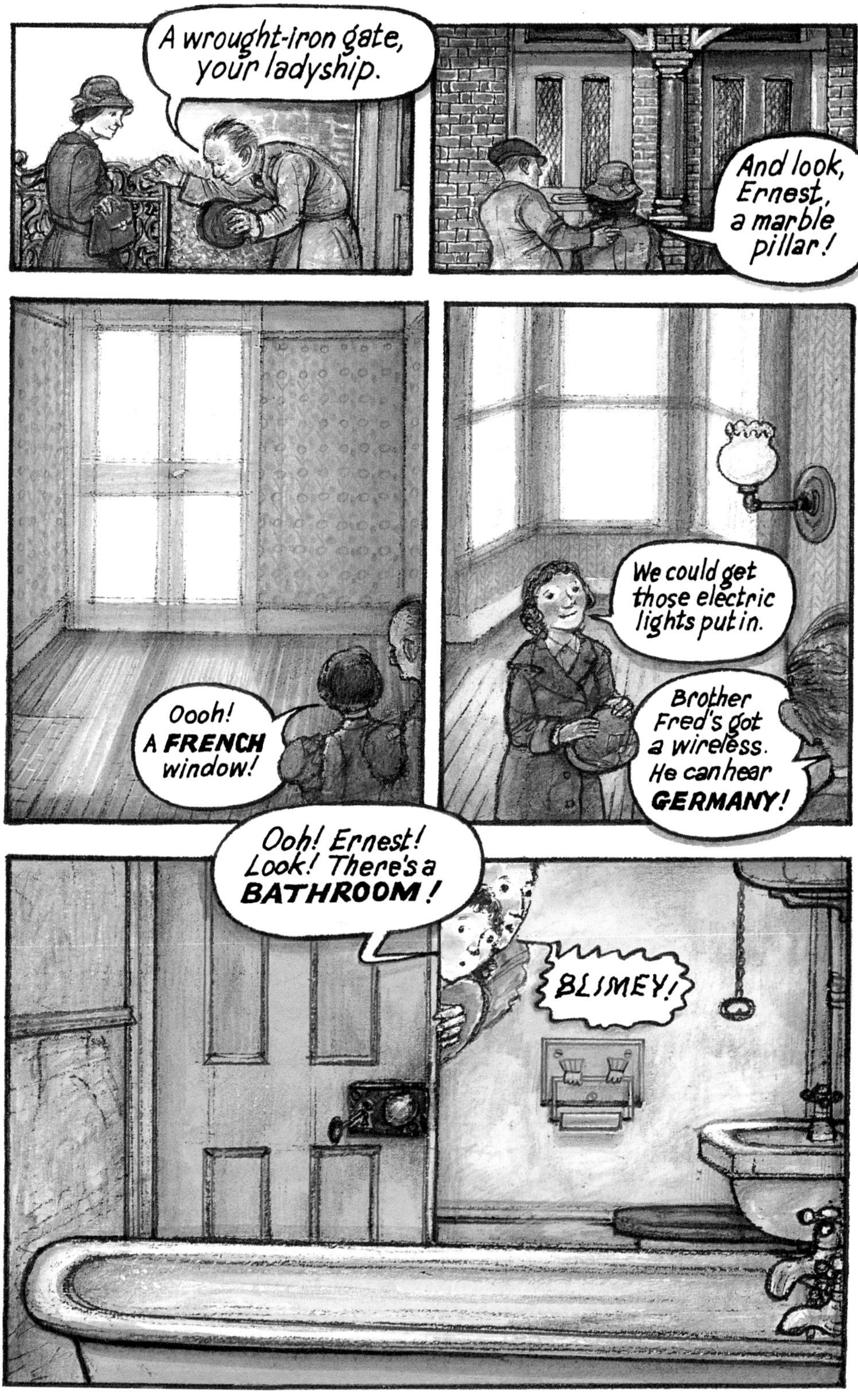
A wrought-iron gate, your ladyship.
And look, Ernest, a marble pillar!
Oooh! A **FRENCH** window!
We could get those electric lights put in.
Brother Fred's got a wireless. He can hear **GERMANY**!
Ooh! Ernest! Look! There's a **BATHROOM**!
BLIMEY!

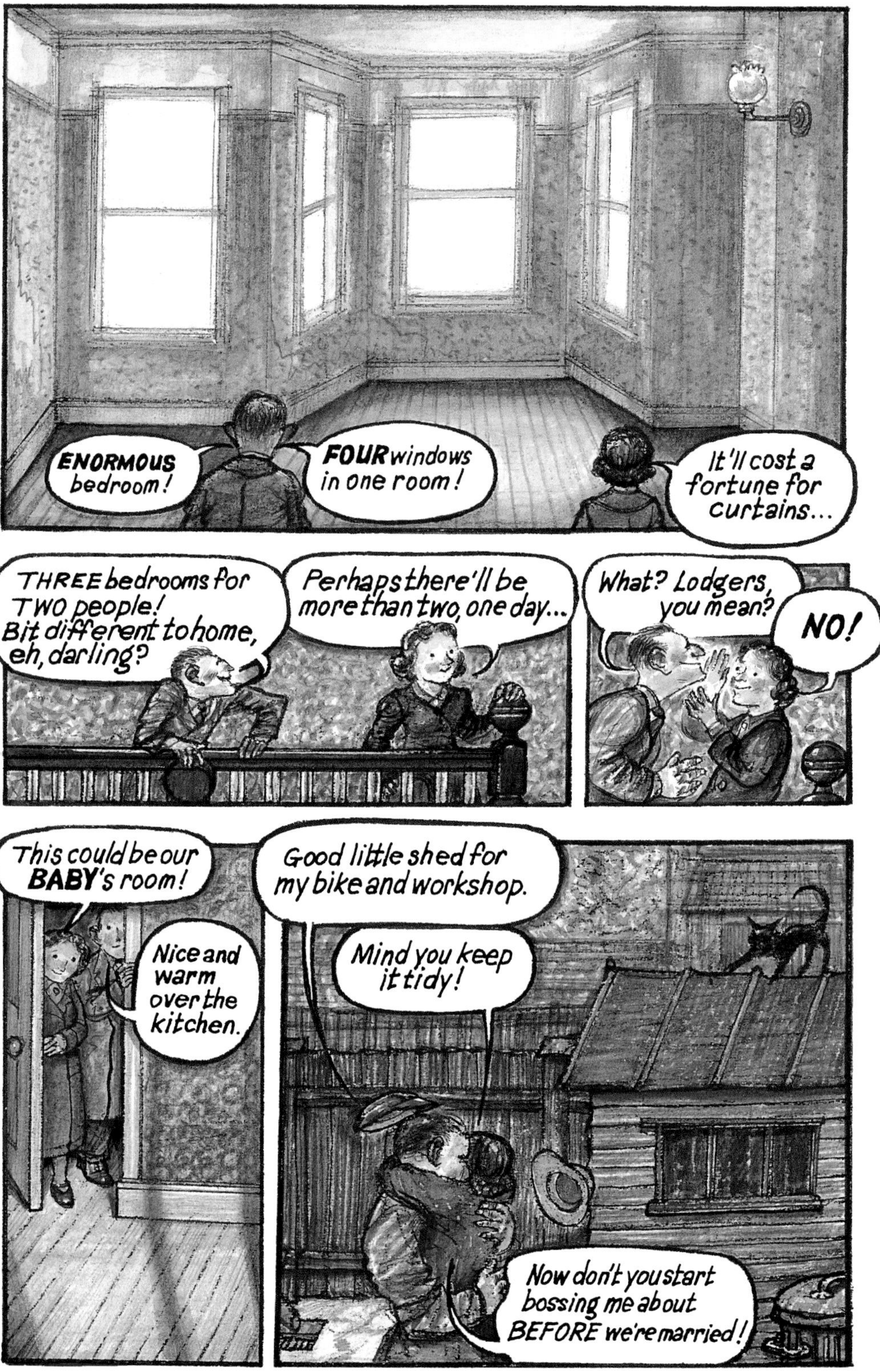
ENORMOUS bedroom!
FOUR windows in one room!
It'll cost a fortune for curtains...
THREE bedrooms for TWO people! Bit different to home, eh, darling?
Perhaps there'll be more than two, one day...
What? Lodgers, you mean?
NO!
This could be our BABY's room!
Nice and warm over the kitchen.
Good little shed for my bike and workshop.
Mind you keep it tidy!
Now don't you start bossing me about BEFORE we're married!

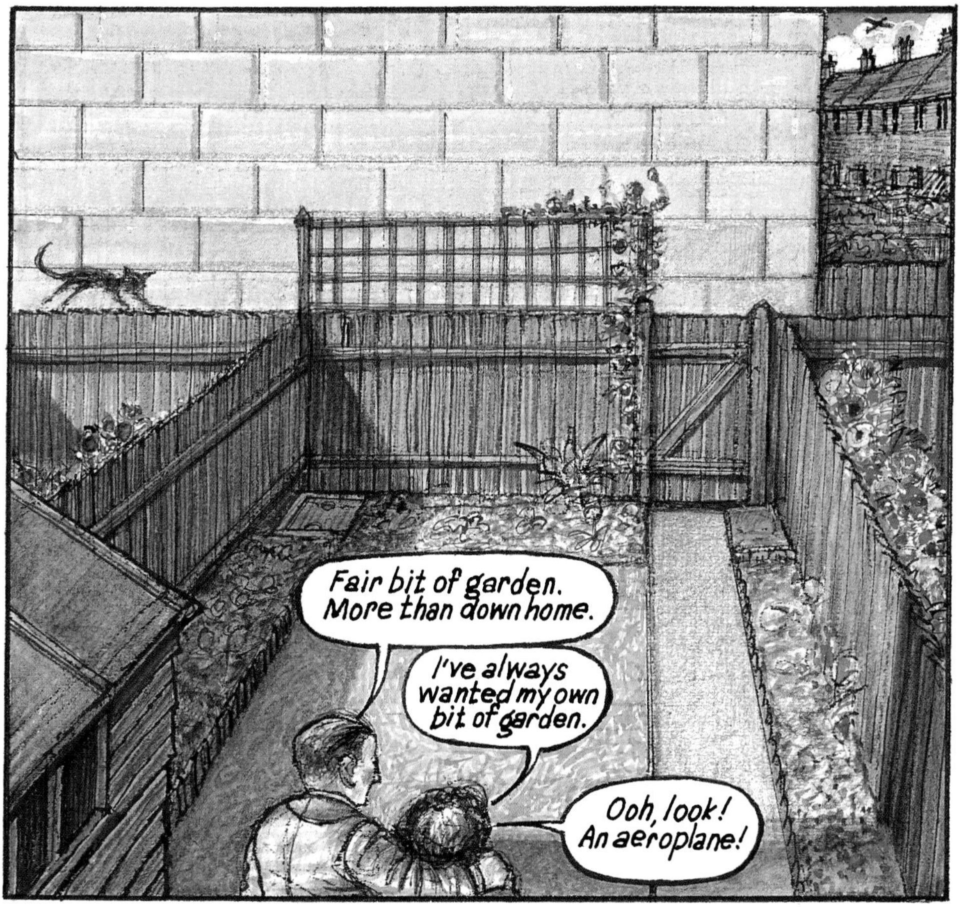
Fair bit of garden. More than down home.
I've always wanted my own bit of garden.
Ooh, look! An aeroplane!

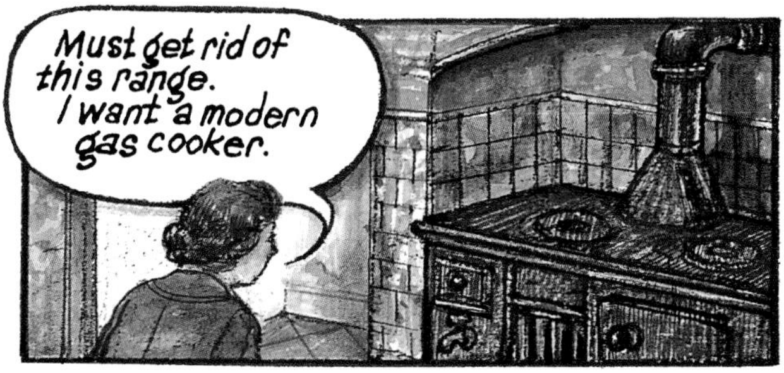
Must get rid of this range. I want a modern gas cooker.

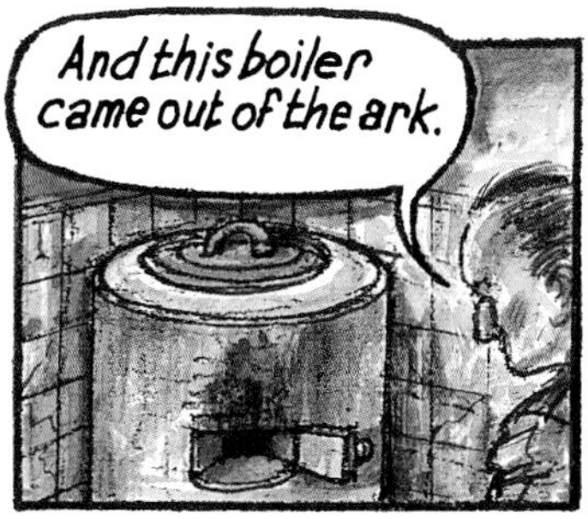
And this boiler came out of the ark.

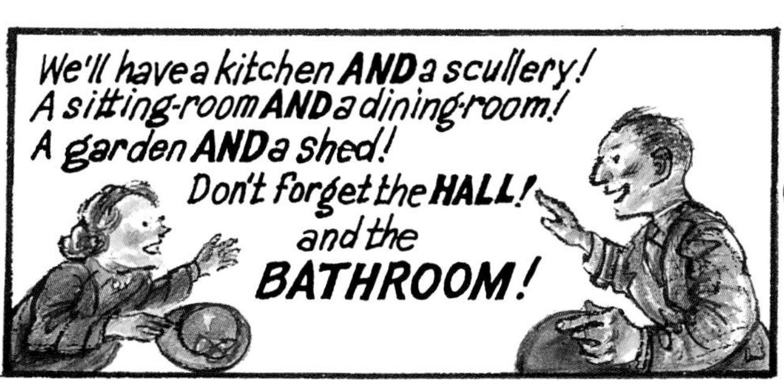
We'll have a kitchen AND a scullery!
A sitting-room AND a dining-room!
A garden AND a shed!
Don't forget the HALL! and the BATHROOM!

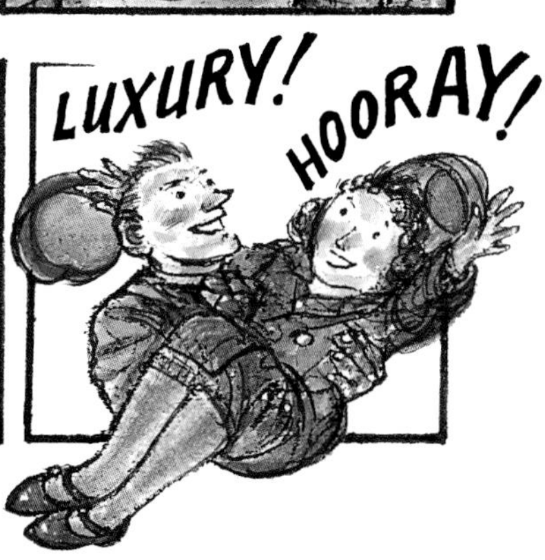
LUXURY!
HOORAY!

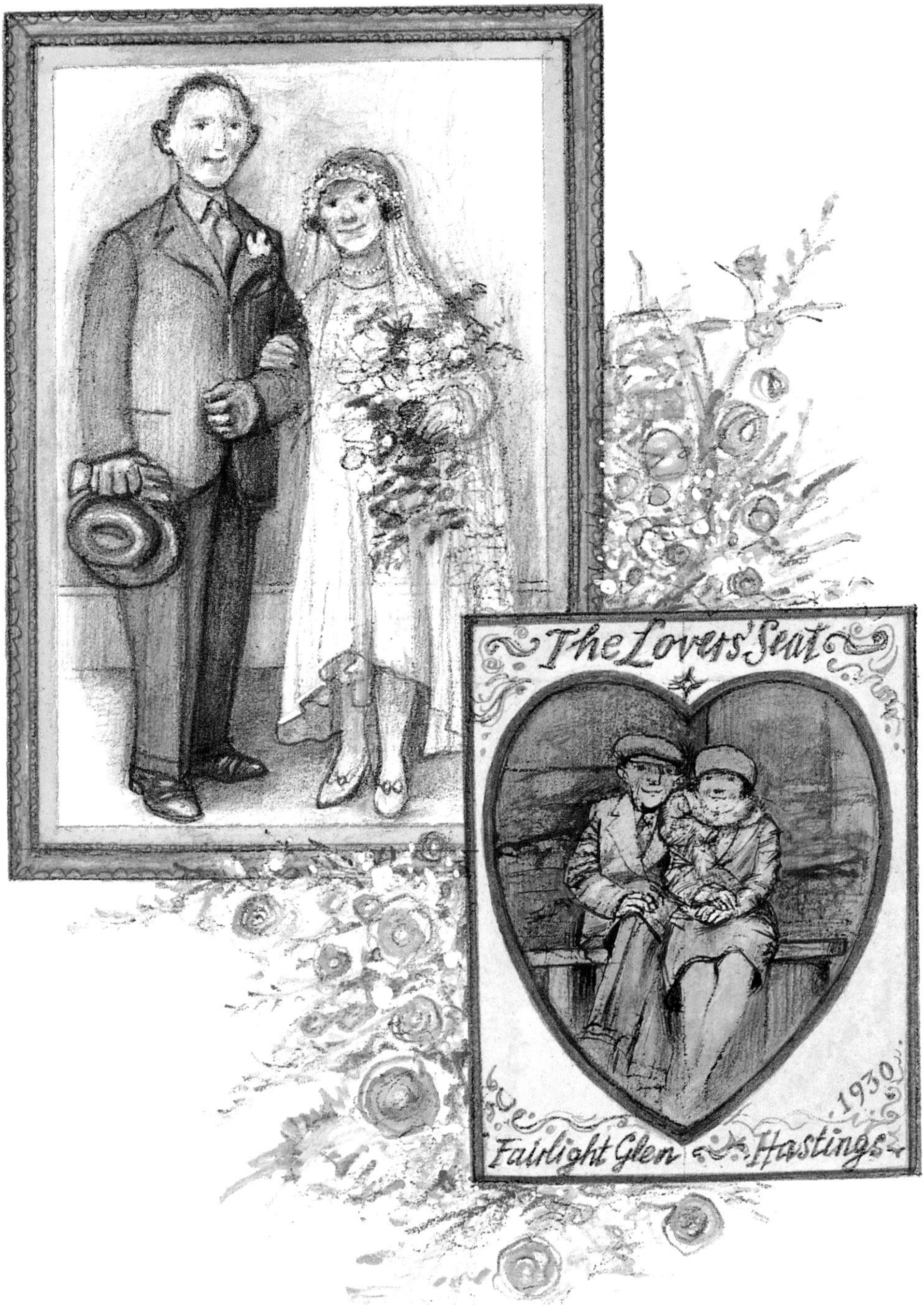
The Lovers' Seat
1930
Fairlight Glen
Hastings

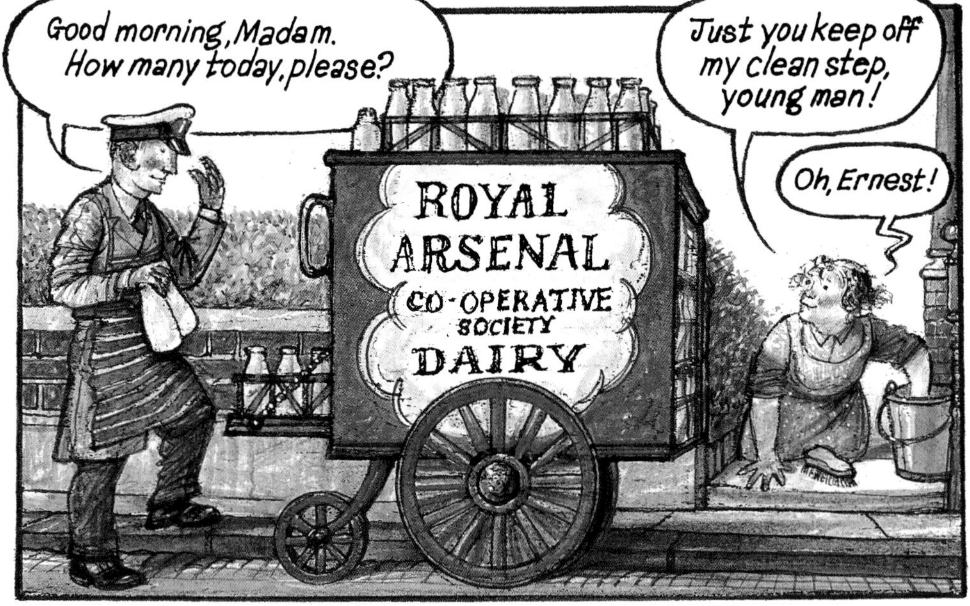
Good morning, Madam. How many today, please?
Just you keep off my clean step, young man!
Oh, Ernest!
ROYAL ARSENAL CO-OPERATIVE SOCIETY DAIRY

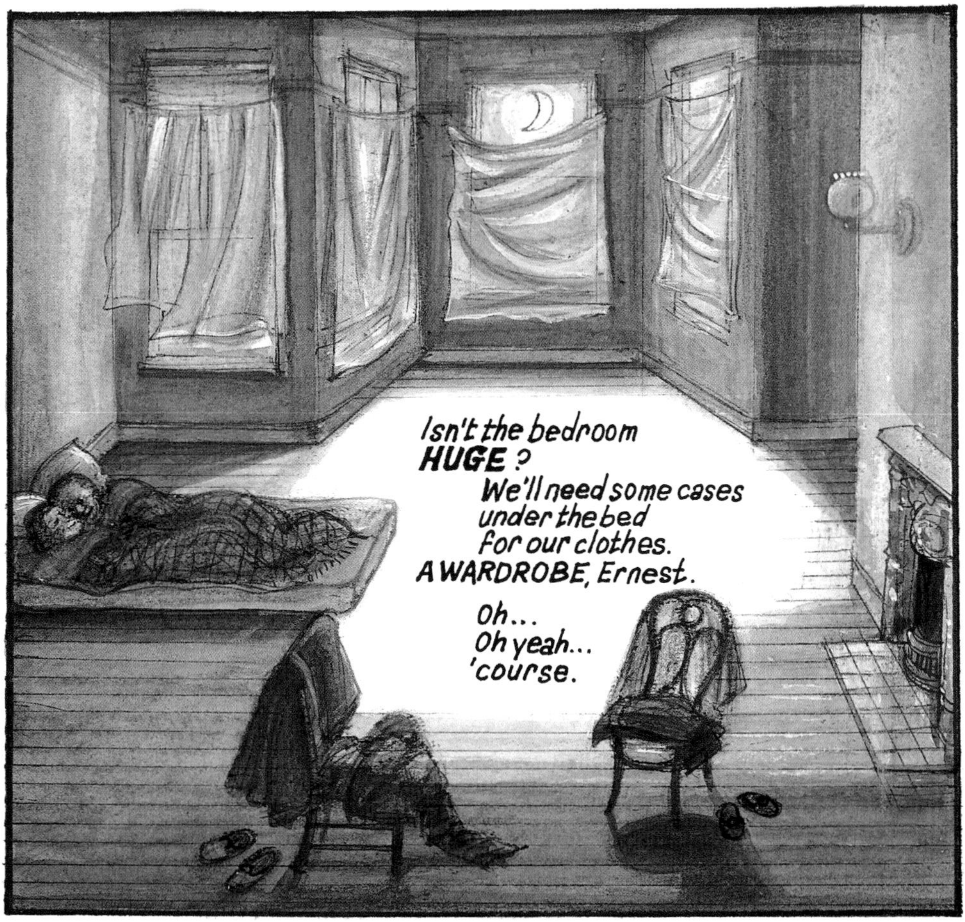
Isn't the bedroom HUGE?
We'll need some cases under the bed for our clothes.
A WARDROBE, Ernest.
Oh... Oh yeah... 'course.

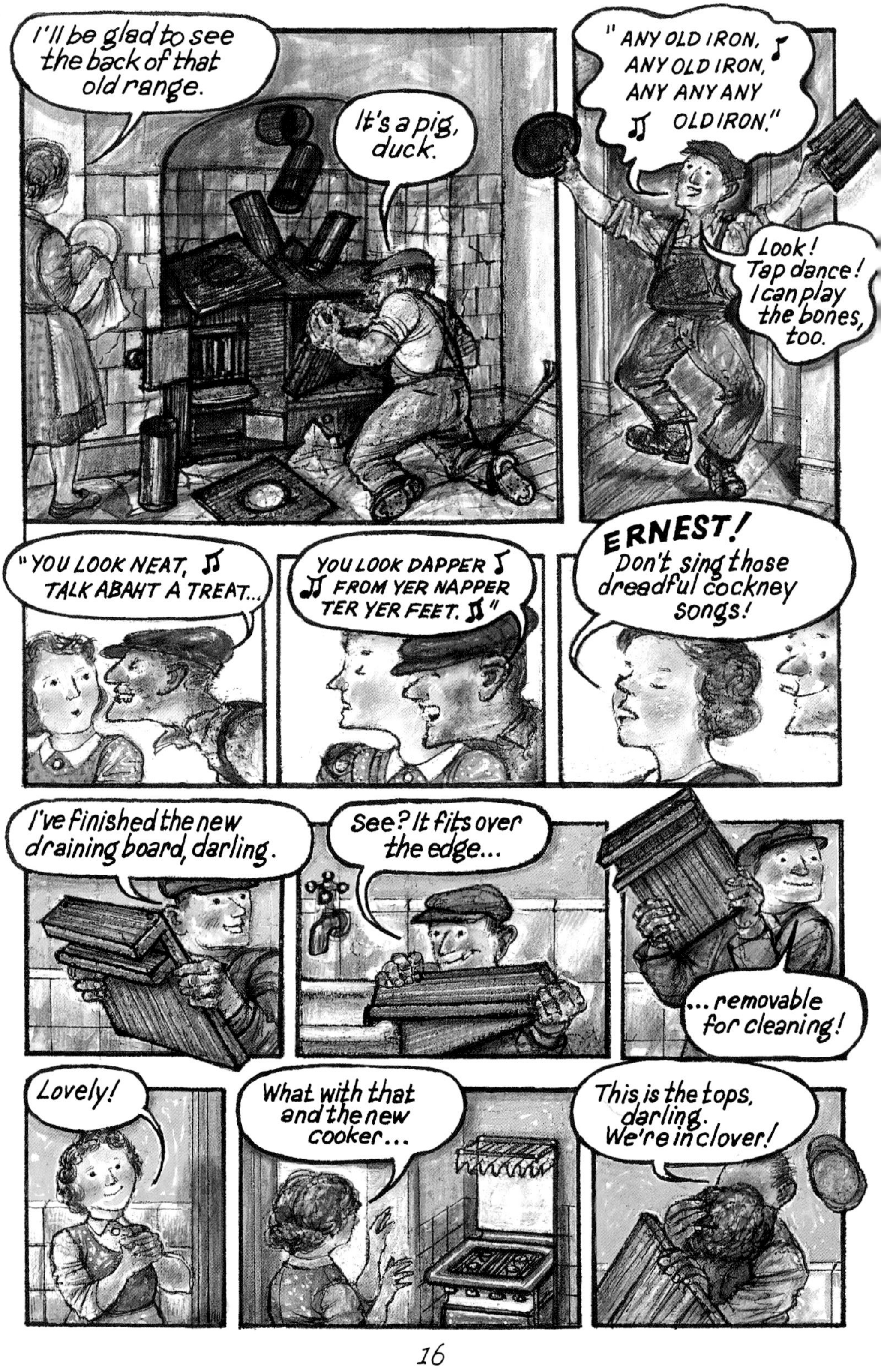
I'll be glad to see the back of that old range.
It's a pig, duck.
"ANY OLD IRON, ANY OLD IRON, ANY ANY ANY OLD IRON."
Look! Tap dance! I can play the bones, too.
"YOU LOOK NEAT, TALK ABAHT A TREAT...
YOU LOOK DAPPER FROM YER NAPPER TER YER FEET."
ERNEST! Don't sing those dreadful cockney songs!
I've finished the new draining board, darling.
See? It fits over the edge...
...removable for cleaning!
Lovely!
What with that and the new cooker...
This is the tops, darling. We're in clover!

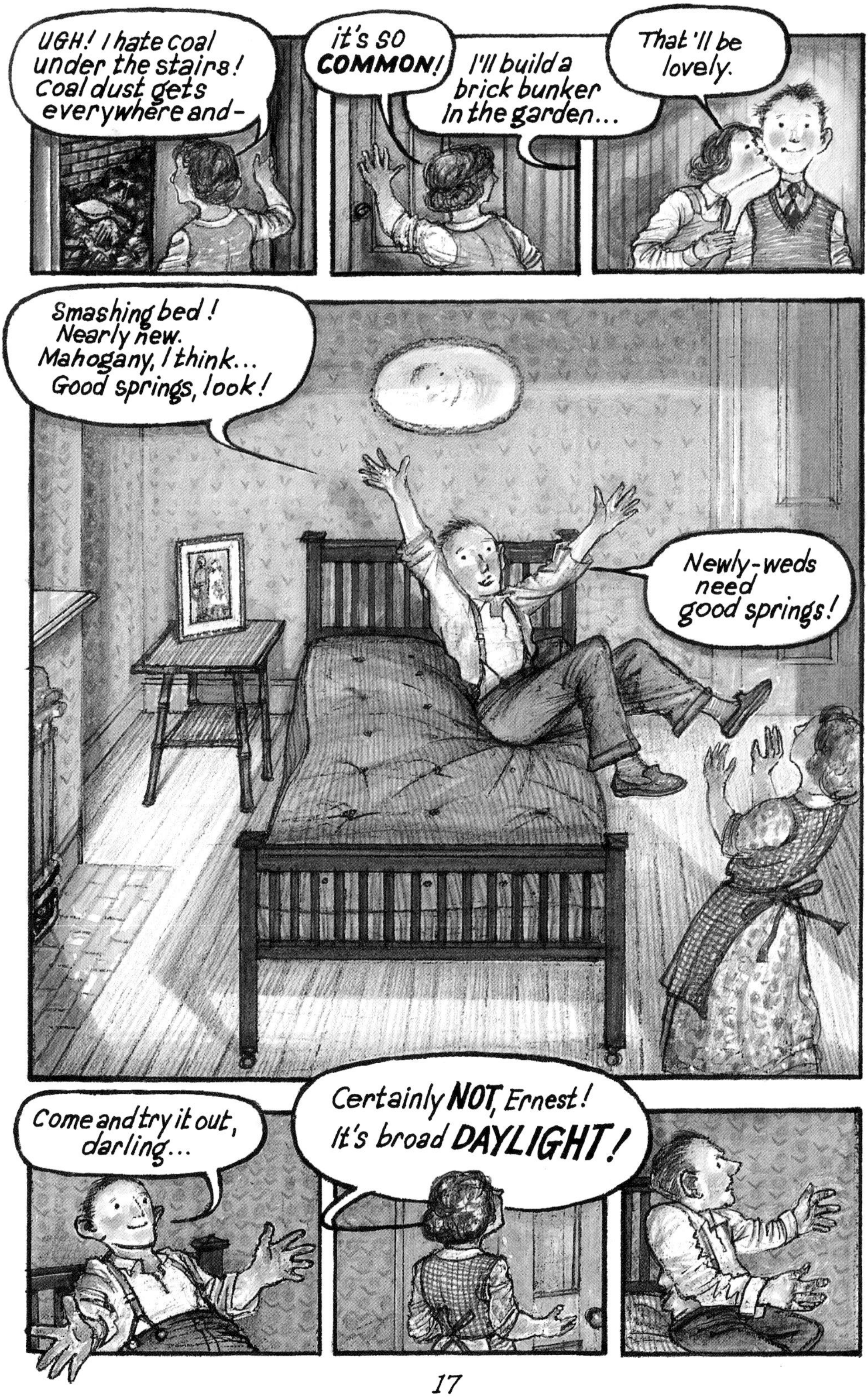
UGH! I hate coal under the stairs! Coal dust gets everywhere and-
it's so COMMON!
I'll build a brick bunker in the garden...
That'll be lovely.
Smashing bed! Nearly new. Mahogany, I think... Good springs, look!
Newly-weds need good springs!
Come and try it out, darling...
Certainly NOT, Ernest! It's broad DAYLIGHT!

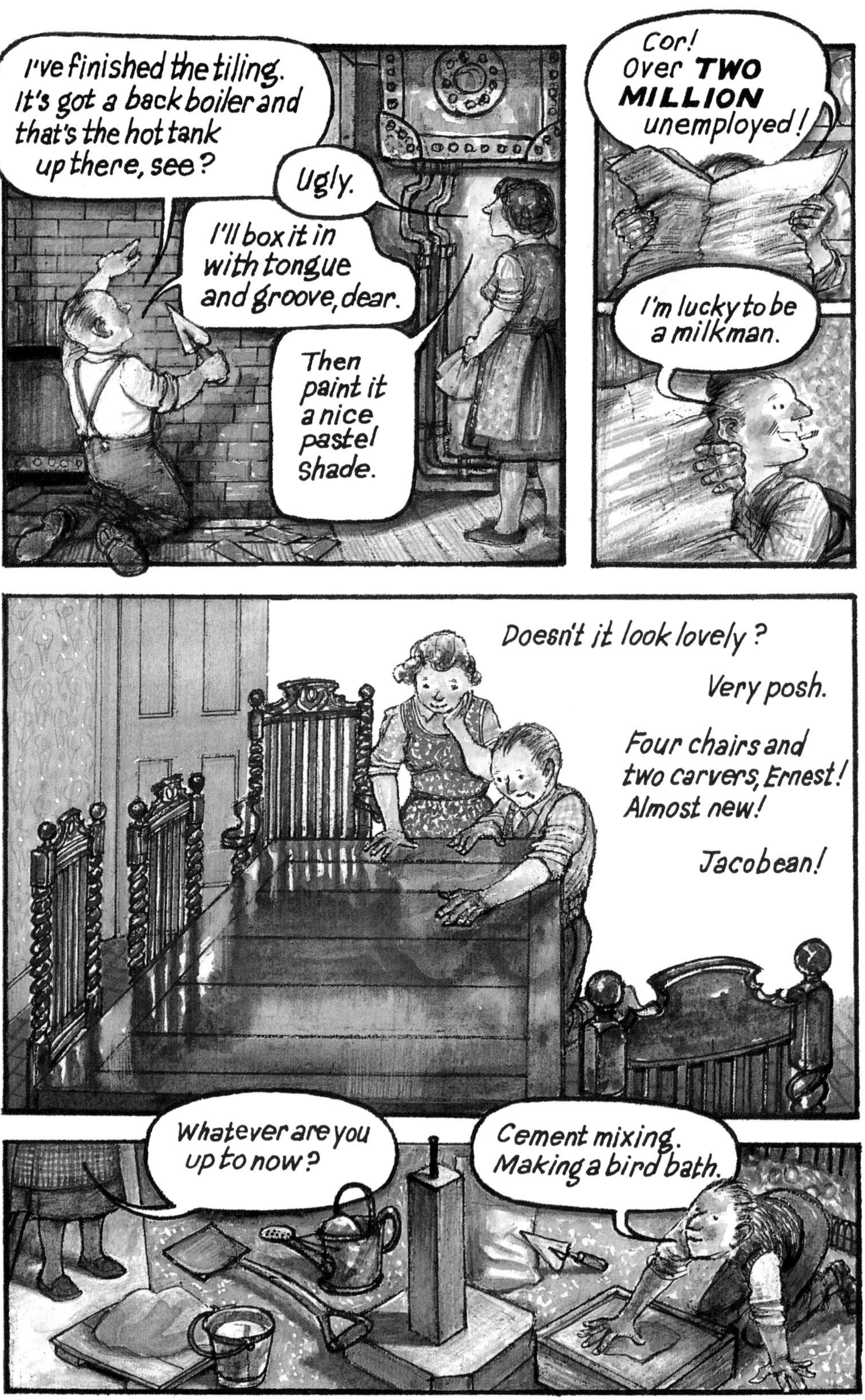
I've finished the tiling. It's got a back boiler and that's the hot tank up there, see?
Ugly.
I'll box it in with tongue and groove, dear.
Then paint it a nice pastel shade.
Cor! Over TWO MILLION unemployed!
I'm lucky to be a milkman.
Doesn't it look lovely?
Very posh.
Four chairs and two carvers, Ernest! Almost new!
Jacobean!
Whatever are you up to now?
Cement mixing. Making a bird bath.

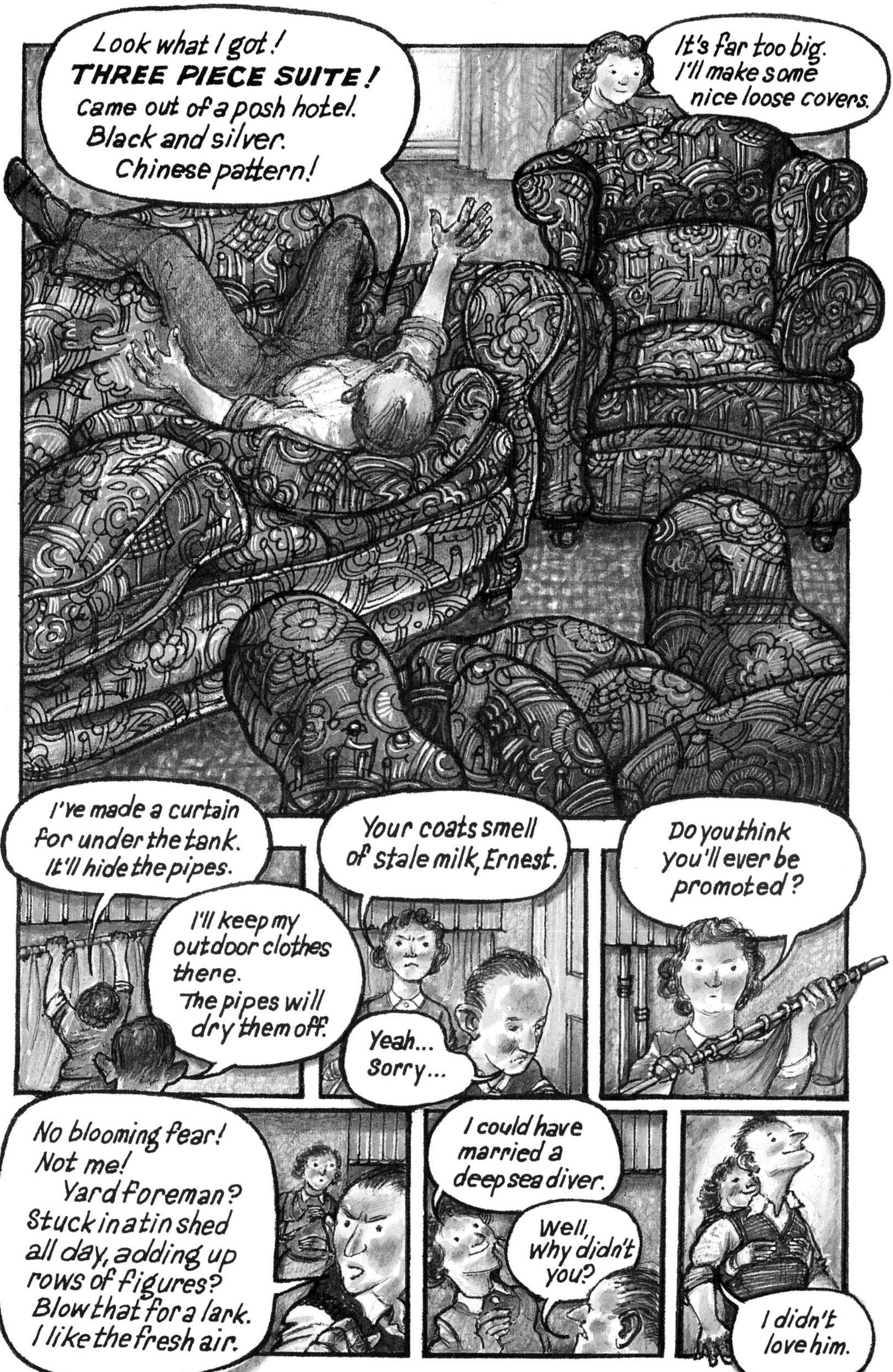
Look what I got! THREE PIECE SUITE! Came out of a posh hotel. Black and silver. Chinese pattern!
It's far too big. I'll make some nice loose covers.
I've made a curtain for under the tank. It'll hide the pipes.
I'll keep my outdoor clothes there. The pipes will dry them off.
Your coats smell of stale milk, Ernest.
Yeah... Sorry...
Do you think you'll ever be promoted?
No blooming fear! Not me! Yard foreman? Stuck in a tin shed all day, adding up rows of figures? Blow that for a lark. I like the fresh air.
I could have married a deep sea diver.
Well, why didn't you?
I didn't love him.

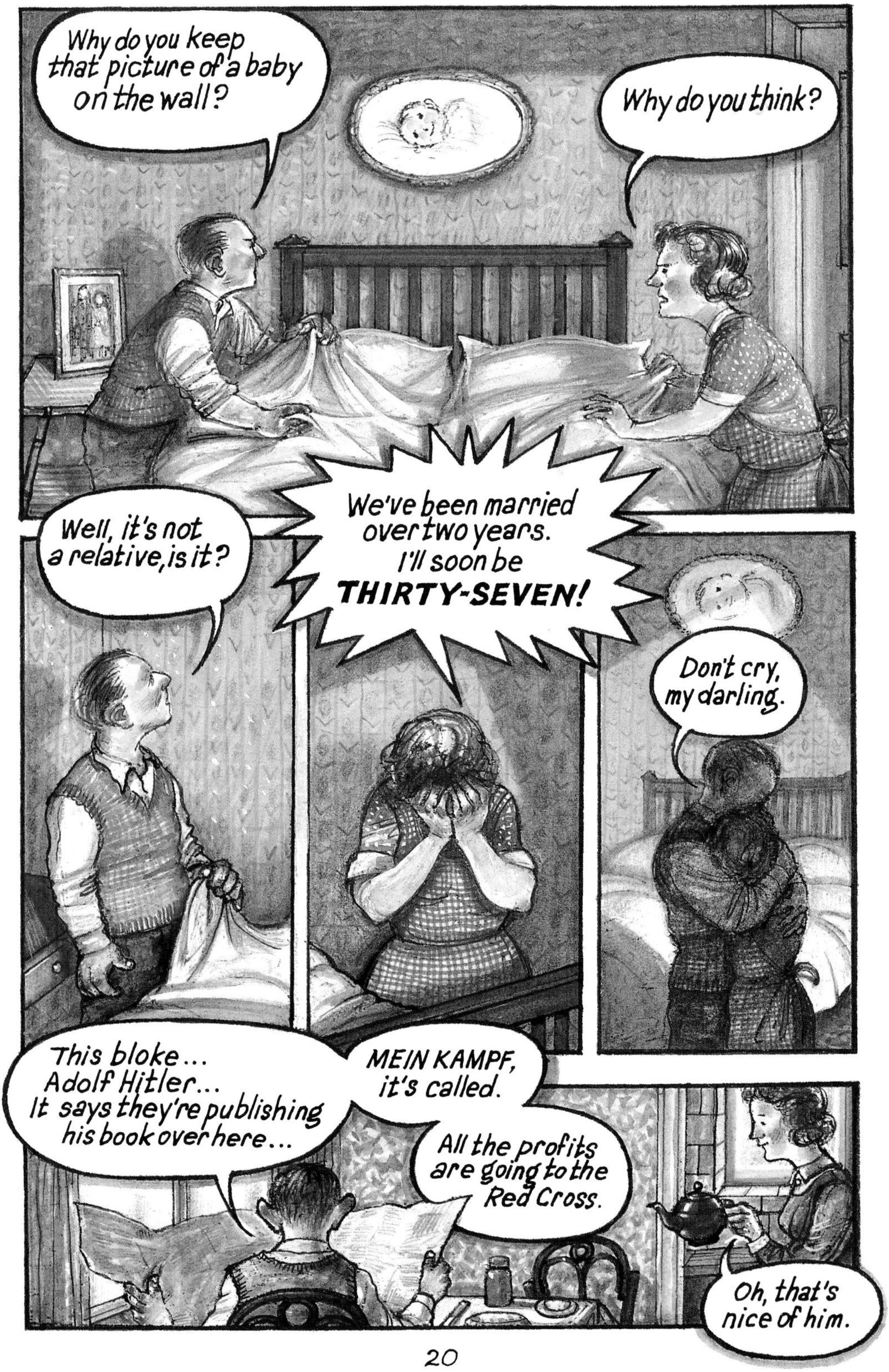
Why do you keep that picture of a baby on the wall?
Why do you think?
Well, it's not a relative, is it?
We've been married over two years. I'll soon be THIRTY-SEVEN!
Don't cry, my darling.
This bloke... Adolf Hitler... It says they're publishing his book over here...
MEIN KAMPF, it's called.
All the profits are going to the Red Cross.
Oh, that's nice of him.

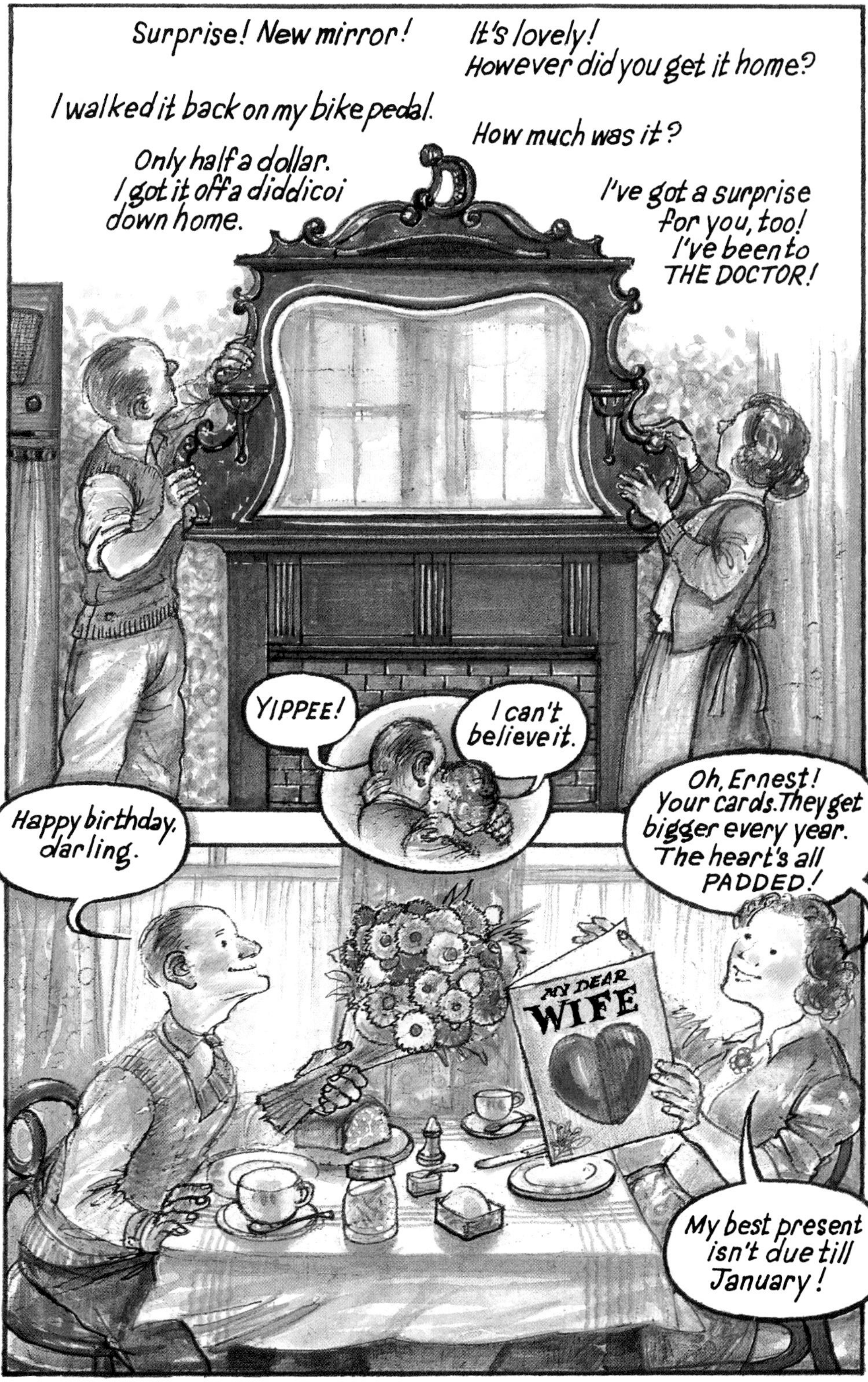
Surprise! New mirror!
It's lovely! However did you get it home?
I walked it back on my bike pedal.
How much was it?
Only half a dollar. I got it offa diddicoi down home.
I've got a surprise for you, too! I've been to THE DOCTOR!
YIPPEE!
I can't believe it.
Happy birthday, darling.
Oh, Ernest! Your cards. They get bigger every year. The heart's all PADDED!
MY DEAR WIFE
My best present isn't due till January!

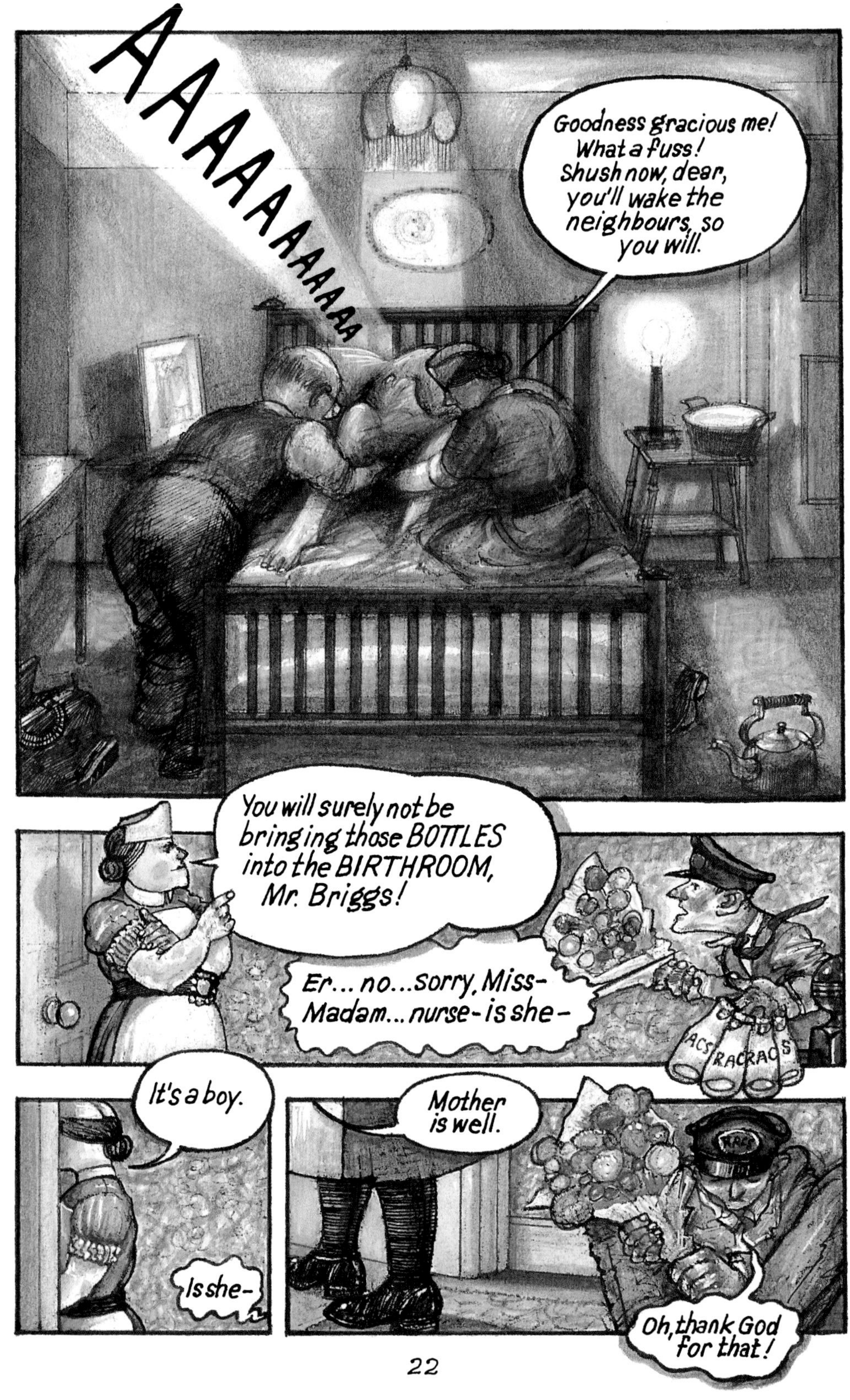
AAAAAAAAAAAAA
Goodness gracious me! What a fuss! Shush now, dear, you'll wake the neighbours, so you will.
You will surely not be bringing those BOTTLES into the BIRTHROOM, Mr. Briggs!
Er... no... sorry, Miss- Madam... nurse- is she-
It's a boy.
Is she-
Mother is well.
Oh, thank God for that!

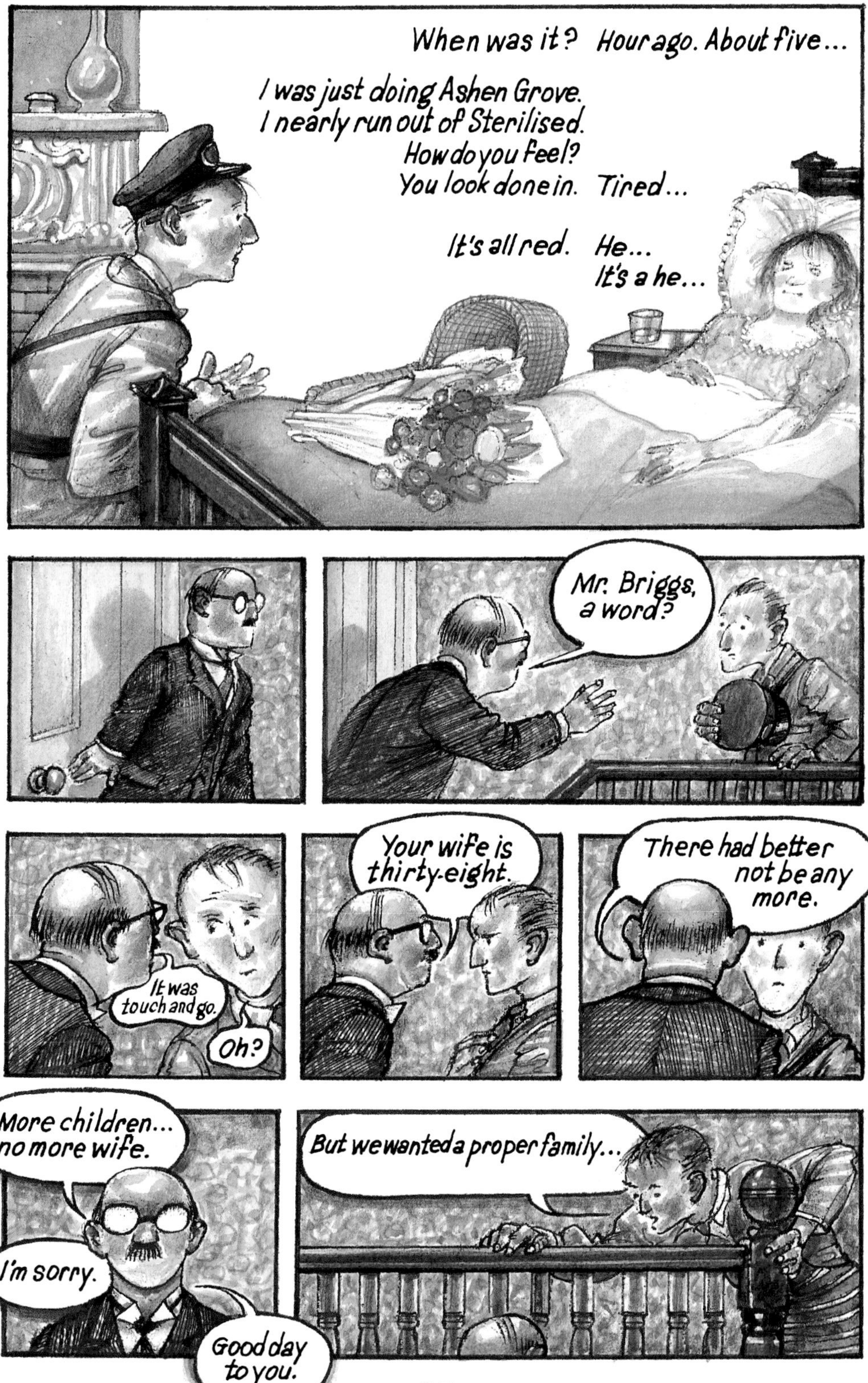
When was it?
Hour ago. About five...
I was just doing Ashen Grove.
I nearly run out of Sterilised.
How do you feel?
You look done in.
Tired...
It's all red.
He...
It's a he...
Mr. Briggs, a word?
It was touch and go.
Oh?
Your wife is thirty-eight.
There had better not be any more.
More children... no more wife.
I'm sorry.
Good day to you.
But we wanted a proper family...

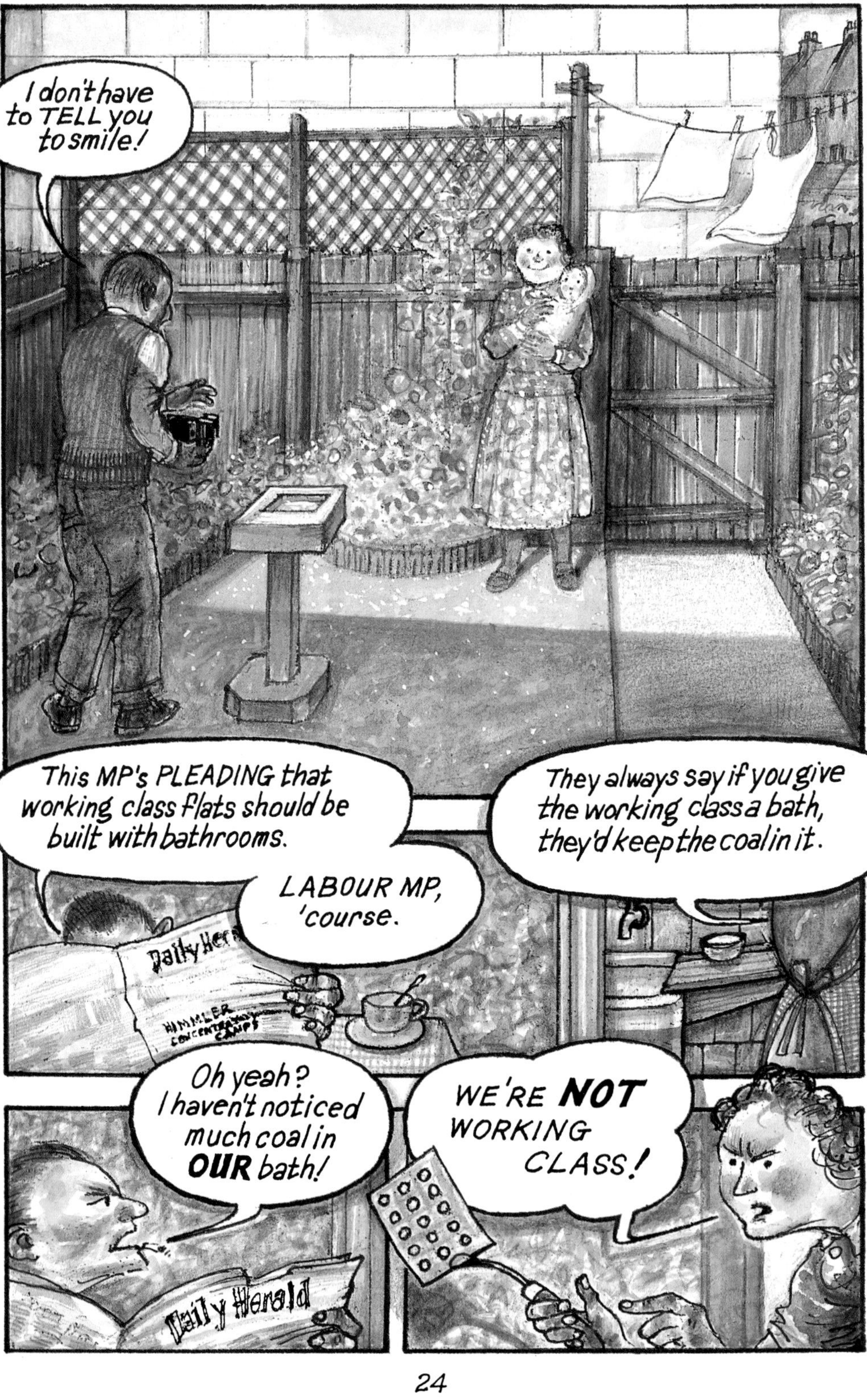
I don't have to TELL you to smile!
This MP's PLEADING that working class flats should be built with bathrooms.
LABOUR MP, 'course.
They always say if you give the working class a bath, they'd keep the coal in it.
Oh yeah? I haven't noticed much coal in **OUR** bath!
WE'RE **NOT** WORKING CLASS!
Daily Herald

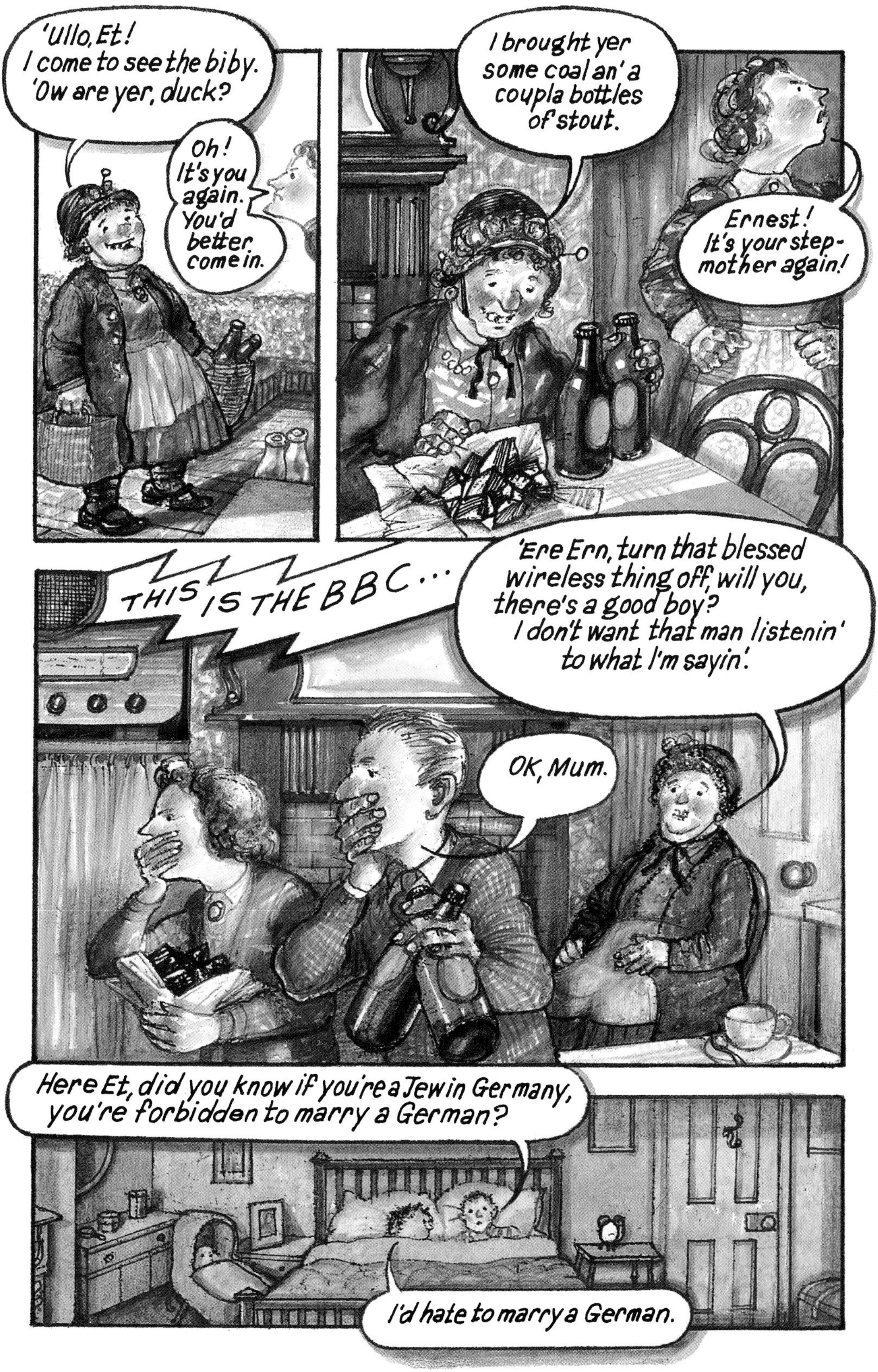
'Ullo, Et! I come to see the biby. 'Ow are yer, duck?
Oh! It's you again. You'd better come in.
I brought yer some coal an' a coupla bottles of stout.
Ernest! It's your step-mother again!
THIS IS THE BBC...
'Ere Ern, turn that blessed wireless thing off, will you, there's a good boy? I don't want that man listenin' to what I'm sayin'.
OK, Mum.
Here Et, did you know if you're a Jew in Germany, you're forbidden to marry a German?
I'd hate to marry a German.

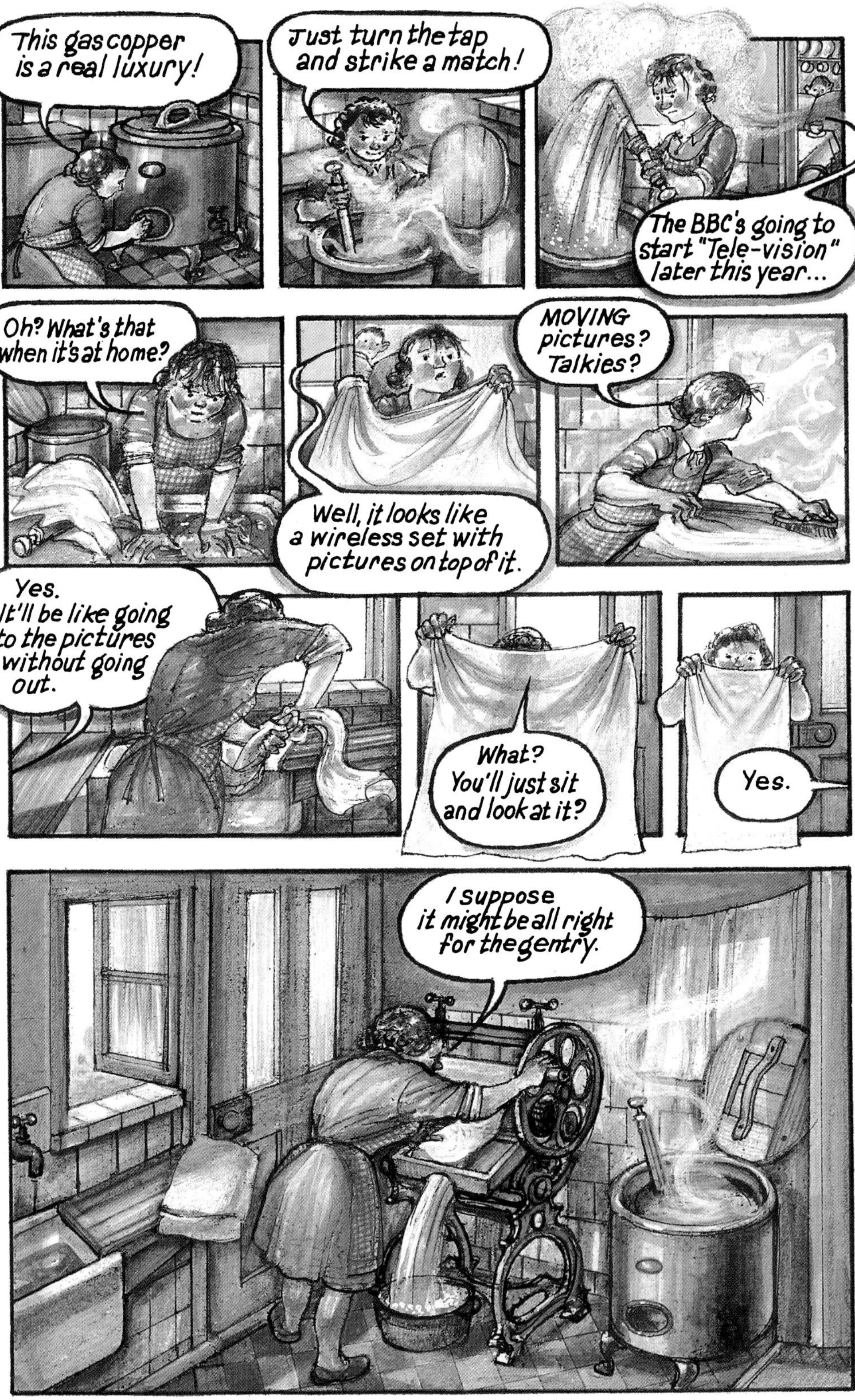
This gas copper is a real luxury!
Just turn the tap and strike a match!
The BBC's going to start "Tele-vision" later this year...
Oh? What's that when it's at home?
MOVING pictures? Talkies?
Well, it looks like a wireless set with pictures on top of it.
Yes. It'll be like going to the pictures without going out.
What? You'll just sit and look at it?
Yes.
I suppose it might be all right for the gentry.

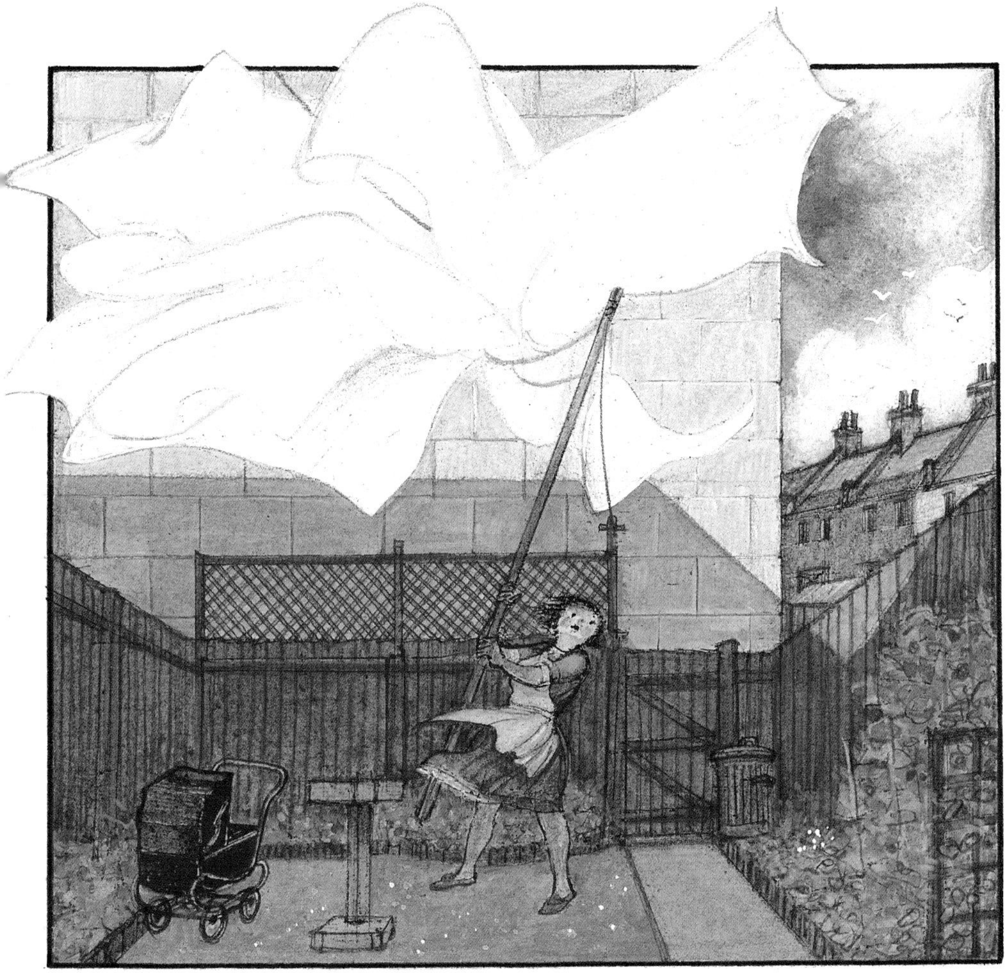

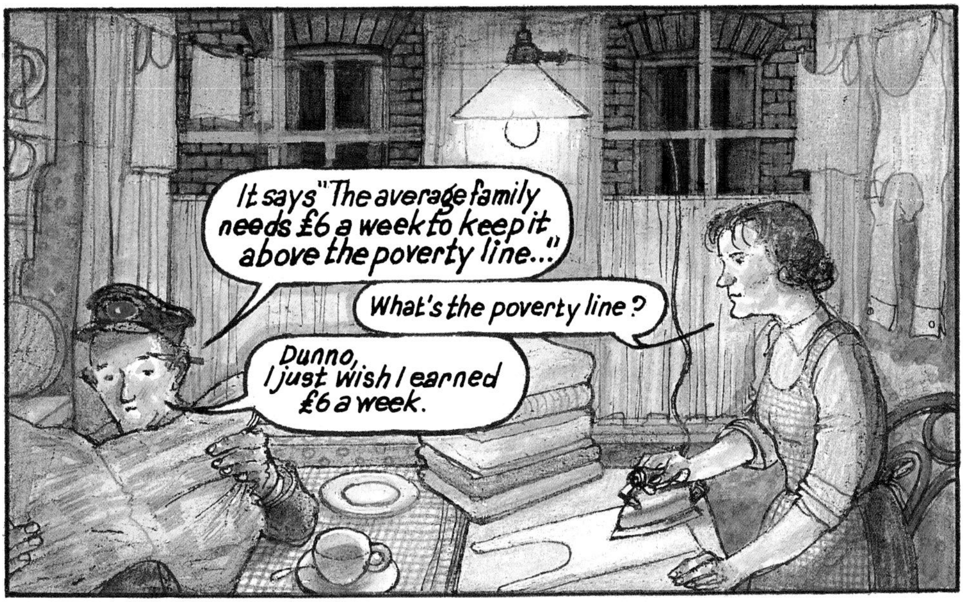
It says "The average family needs £6 a week to keep it above the poverty line..."
What's the poverty line?
Dunno, I just wish I earned £6 a week.

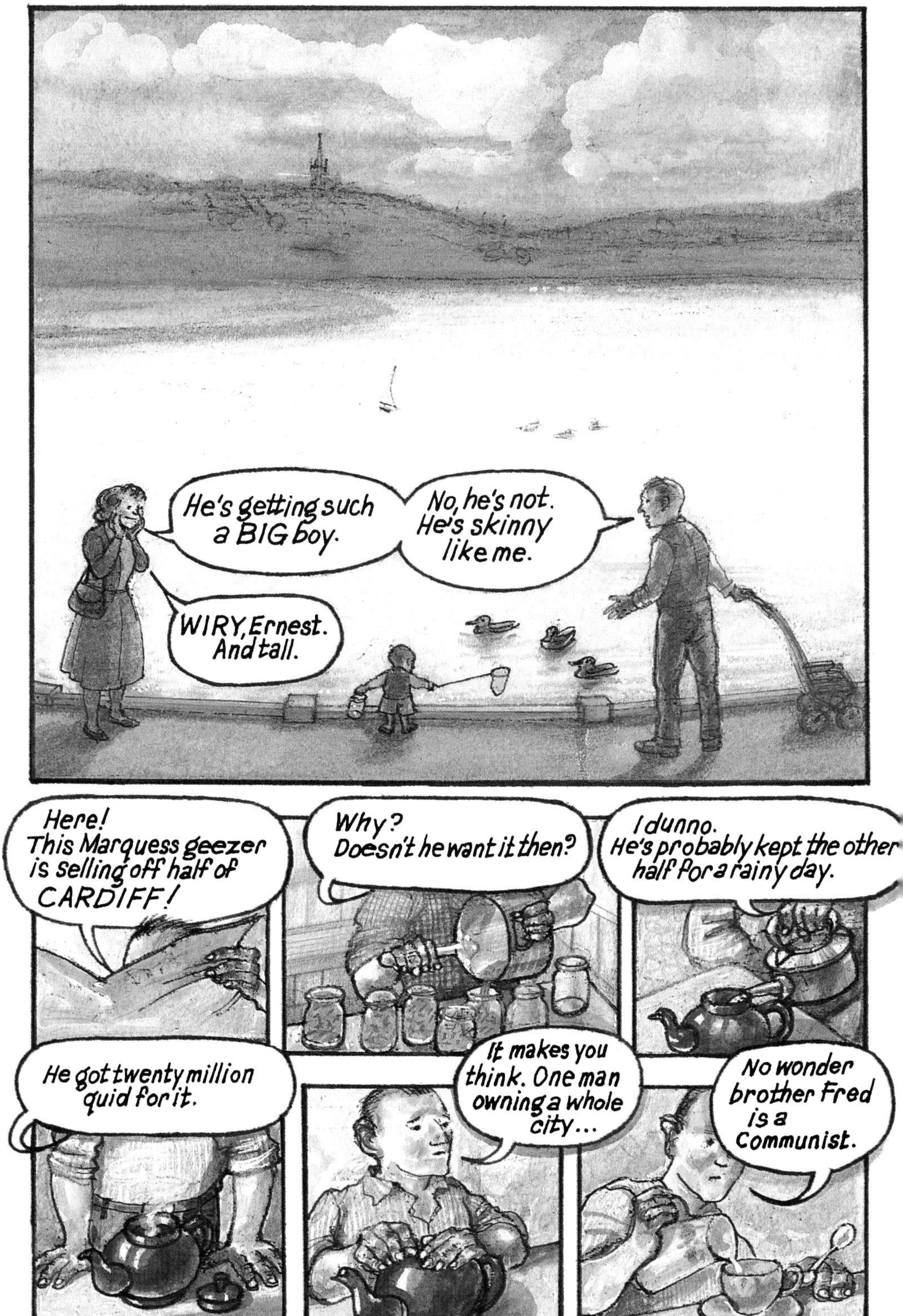
He's getting such a BIG boy.
No, he's not. He's skinny like me.
WIRY, Ernest. And tall.
Here! This Marquess geezer is selling off half of CARDIFF!
Why? Doesn't he want it then?
I dunno. He's probably kept the other half for a rainy day.
He got twenty million quid for it.
It makes you think. One man owning a whole city...
No wonder brother Fred is a Communist.

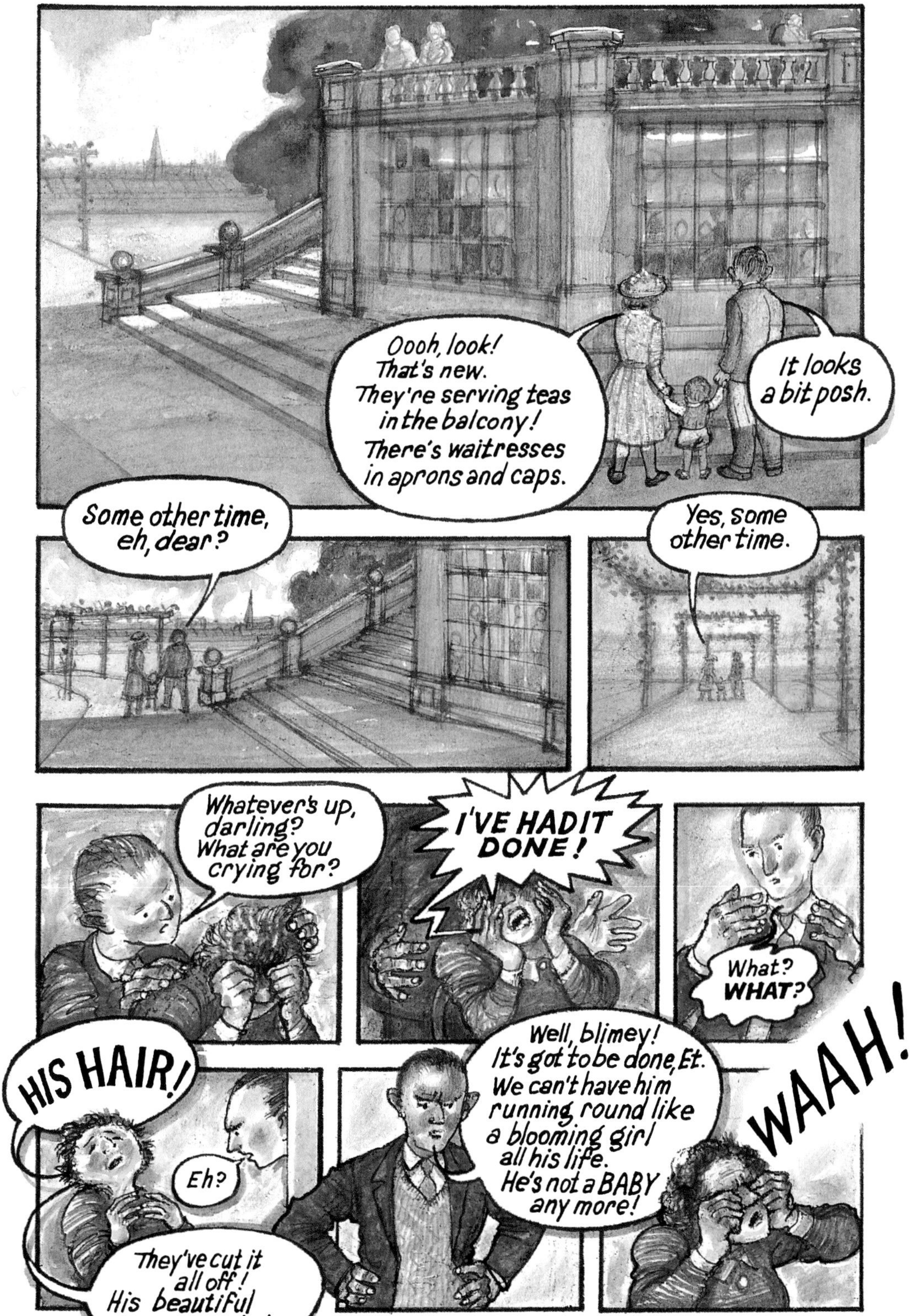
Oooh, look! That's new. They're serving teas in the balcony! There's waitresses in aprons and caps.
It looks a bit posh.
Some other time, eh, dear?
Yes, some other time.
Whatever's up, darling? What are you crying for?
I'VE HAD IT DONE!
What? WHAT?
HIS HAIR!
Eh?
They've cut it all off! His beautiful curls!
Well, blimey! It's got to be done, Et. We can't have him running round like a blooming girl all his life. He's not a BABY any more!
WAAH!

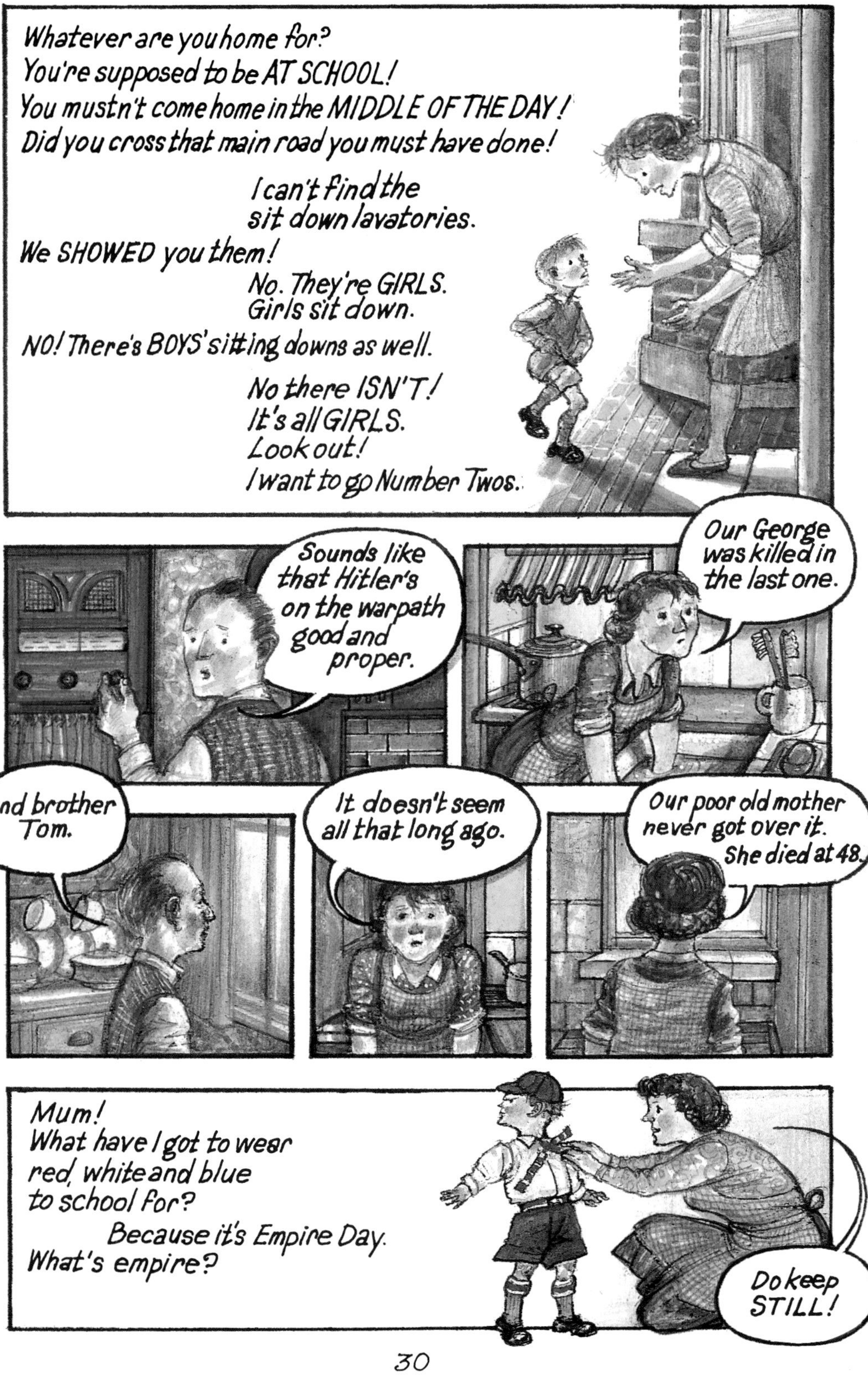
Whatever are you home for?
You're supposed to be AT SCHOOL!
You mustn't come home in the MIDDLE OF THE DAY!
Did you cross that main road you must have done!
I can't find the sit down lavatories.
We SHOWED you them!
No. They're GIRLS. Girls sit down.
NO! There's BOYS' sitting downs as well.
No there ISN'T! It's all GIRLS. Look out! I want to go Number Twos.
Sounds like that Hitler's on the warpath good and proper.
Our George was killed in the last one.
And brother Tom.
It doesn't seem all that long ago.
Our poor old mother never got over it. She died at 48.
Mum! What have I got to wear red, white and blue to school for?
Because it's Empire Day.
What's empire?
Do keep STILL!

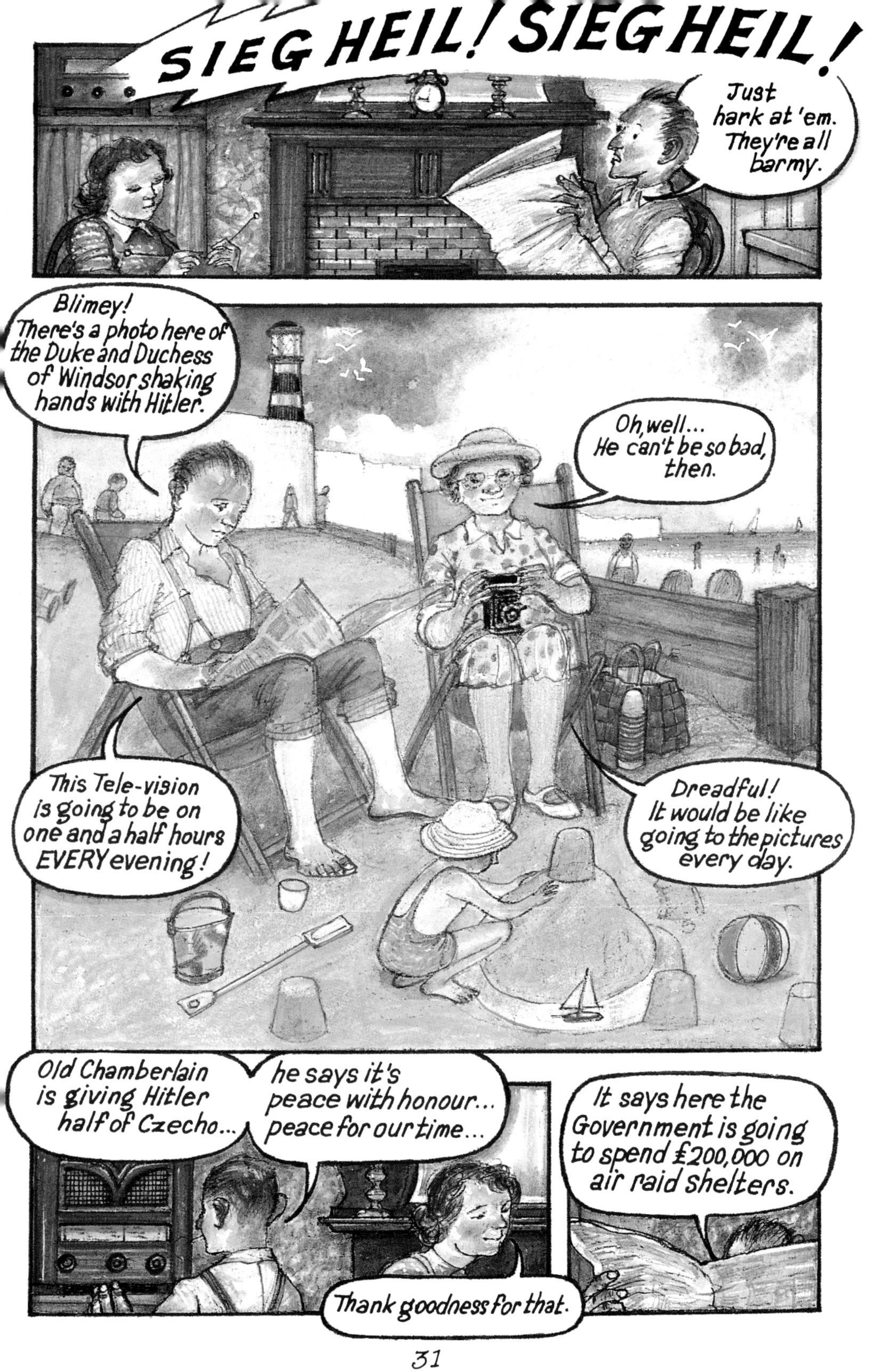
SIEG HEIL! SIEG HEIL!
Just hark at 'em. They're all barmy.
Blimey! There's a photo here of the Duke and Duchess of Windsor shaking hands with Hitler.
Oh, well... He can't be so bad, then.
This Tele-vision is going to be on one and a half hours EVERY evening!
Dreadful! It would be like going to the pictures every day.
Old Chamberlain is giving Hitler half of Czecho...
he says it's peace with honour... peace for our time...
It says here the Government is going to spend £200,000 on air raid shelters.
Thank goodness for that.

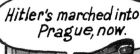 Hitler's marched into Prague, now.

He'll be coming down our road soon.

Adolf Hitler in Wimbledon Park!

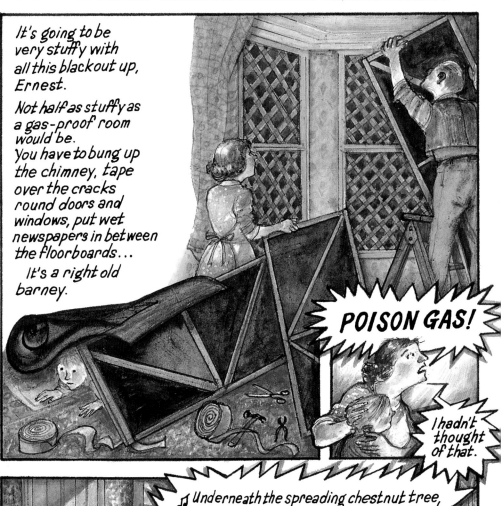

It's going to be very stuffy with all this blackout up, Ernest.

Not half as stuffy as a gas-proof room would be.
You have to bung up the chimney, tape over the cracks round doors and windows, put wet newspapers in between the floorboards...
It's a right old barney.

POISON GAS!

I hadn't thought of that.

♪ Underneath the spreading chestnut tree, Mr. Chamberlain said to me, ♫ if you want your gas mask fitted free - Join the blinking A.R.P. ♪

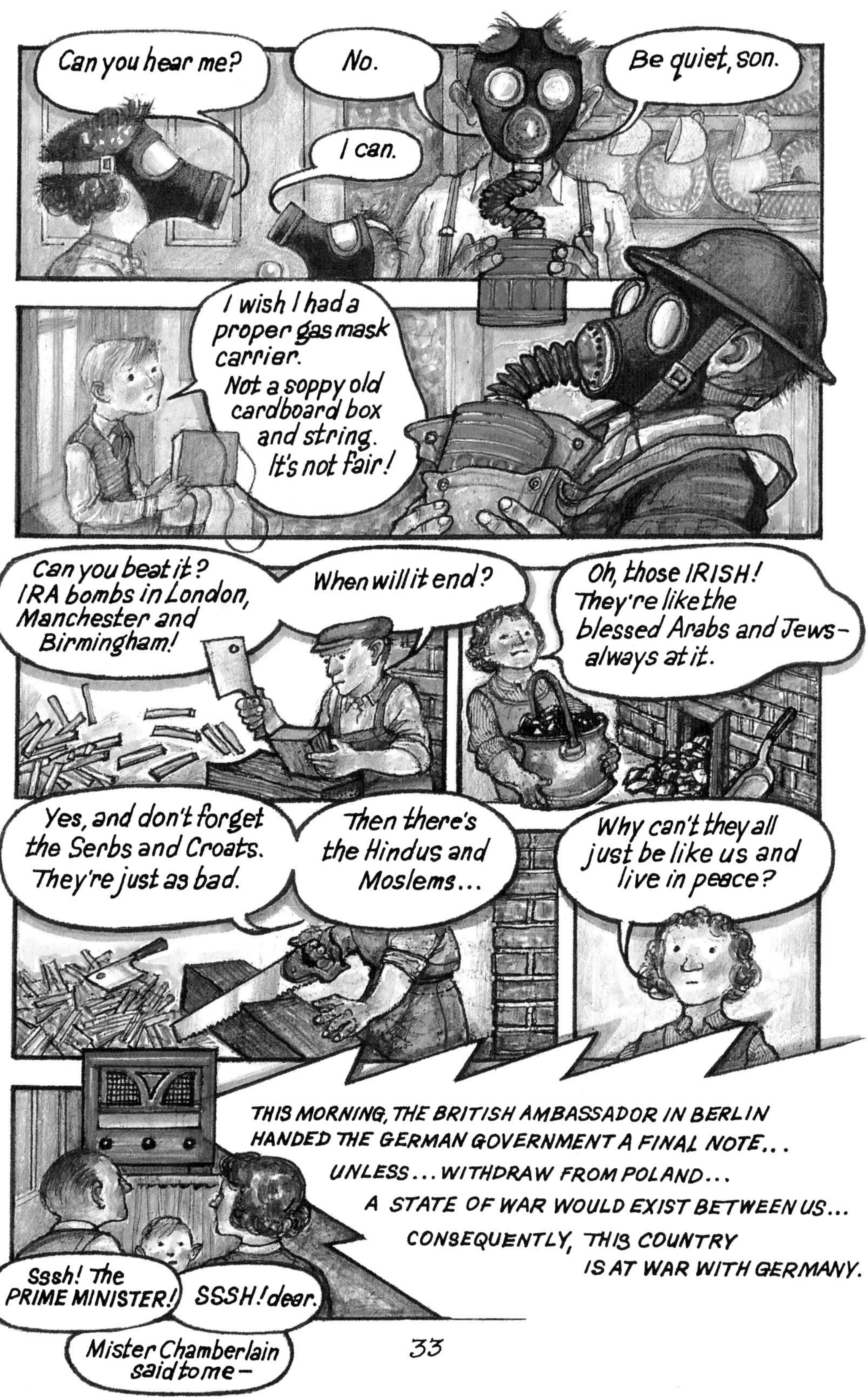
Can you hear me?
No.
Be quiet, son.
I can.
I wish I had a proper gas mask carrier. Not a soppy old cardboard box and string. It's not fair!
Can you beat it? IRA bombs in London, Manchester and Birmingham!
When will it end?
Oh, those IRISH! They're like the blessed Arabs and Jews - always at it.
Yes, and don't forget the Serbs and Croats. They're just as bad.
Then there's the Hindus and Moslems...
Why can't they all just be like us and live in peace?
THIS MORNING, THE BRITISH AMBASSADOR IN BERLIN HANDED THE GERMAN GOVERNMENT A FINAL NOTE... UNLESS... WITHDRAW FROM POLAND... A STATE OF WAR WOULD EXIST BETWEEN US... CONSEQUENTLY, THIS COUNTRY IS AT WAR WITH GERMANY.
Sssh! The PRIME MINISTER!
SSSH! dear.
Mister Chamberlain said to me -

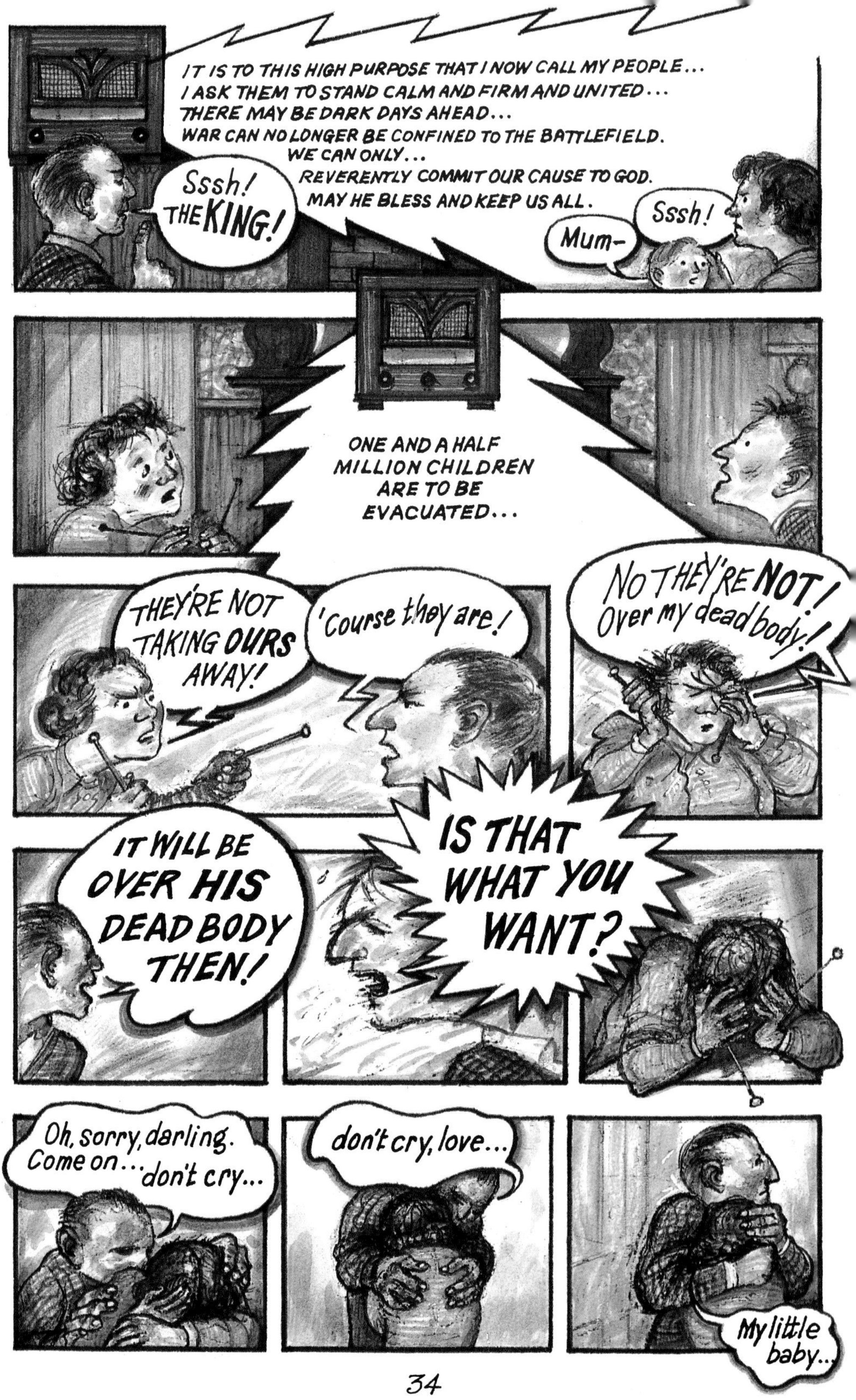
IT IS TO THIS HIGH PURPOSE THAT I NOW CALL MY PEOPLE...
I ASK THEM TO STAND CALM AND FIRM AND UNITED...
THERE MAY BE DARK DAYS AHEAD...
WAR CAN NO LONGER BE CONFINED TO THE BATTLEFIELD.
WE CAN ONLY...
REVERENTLY COMMIT OUR CAUSE TO GOD.
MAY HE BLESS AND KEEP US ALL.
Sssh! THE KING!
Mum-
Sssh!
ONE AND A HALF MILLION CHILDREN ARE TO BE EVACUATED...
THEY'RE NOT TAKING OURS AWAY!
'Course they are!
NO THEY'RE NOT! Over my dead body!
IT WILL BE OVER HIS DEAD BODY THEN!
IS THAT WHAT YOU WANT?
Oh, sorry, darling. Come on... don't cry...
don't cry, love...
My little baby...

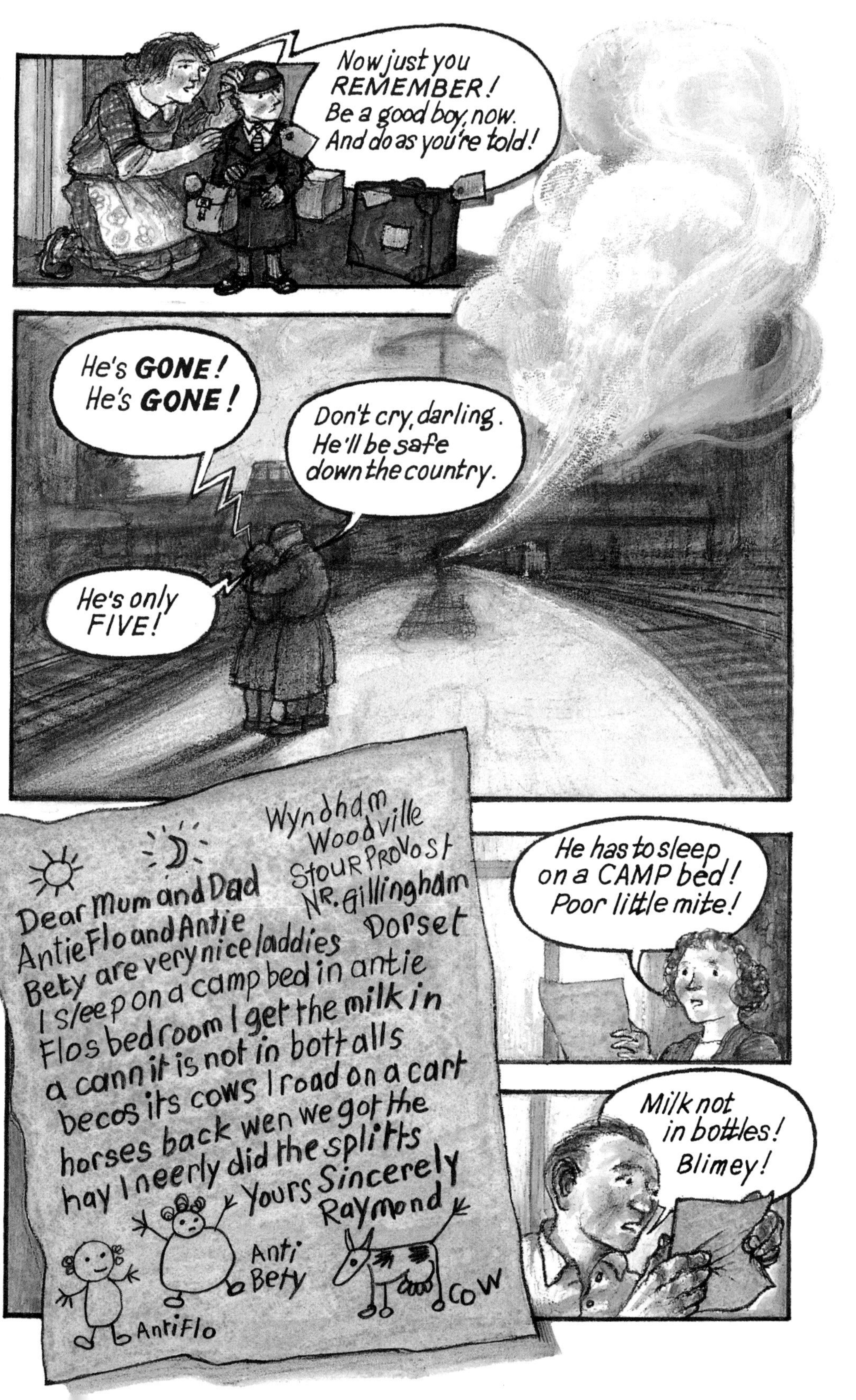
Now just you REMEMBER! Be a good boy, now. And do as you're told!
He's GONE! He's GONE!
Don't cry, darling. He'll be safe down the country.
He's only FIVE!
Wyndham Woodville Stour Provost Nr. Gillingham Dorset
Dear Mum and Dad Antie Flo and Antie Bety are very nice laddies I sleep on a camp bed in antie Flos bedroom I get the milk in a cann it is not in bottalls becos its cows I road on a cart horses back wen we got the hay I neerly did the splitts
Yours Sincerely Raymond
Anti Bety
Anti Flo
cow
He has to sleep on a CAMP bed! Poor little mite!
Milk not in bottles! Blimey!

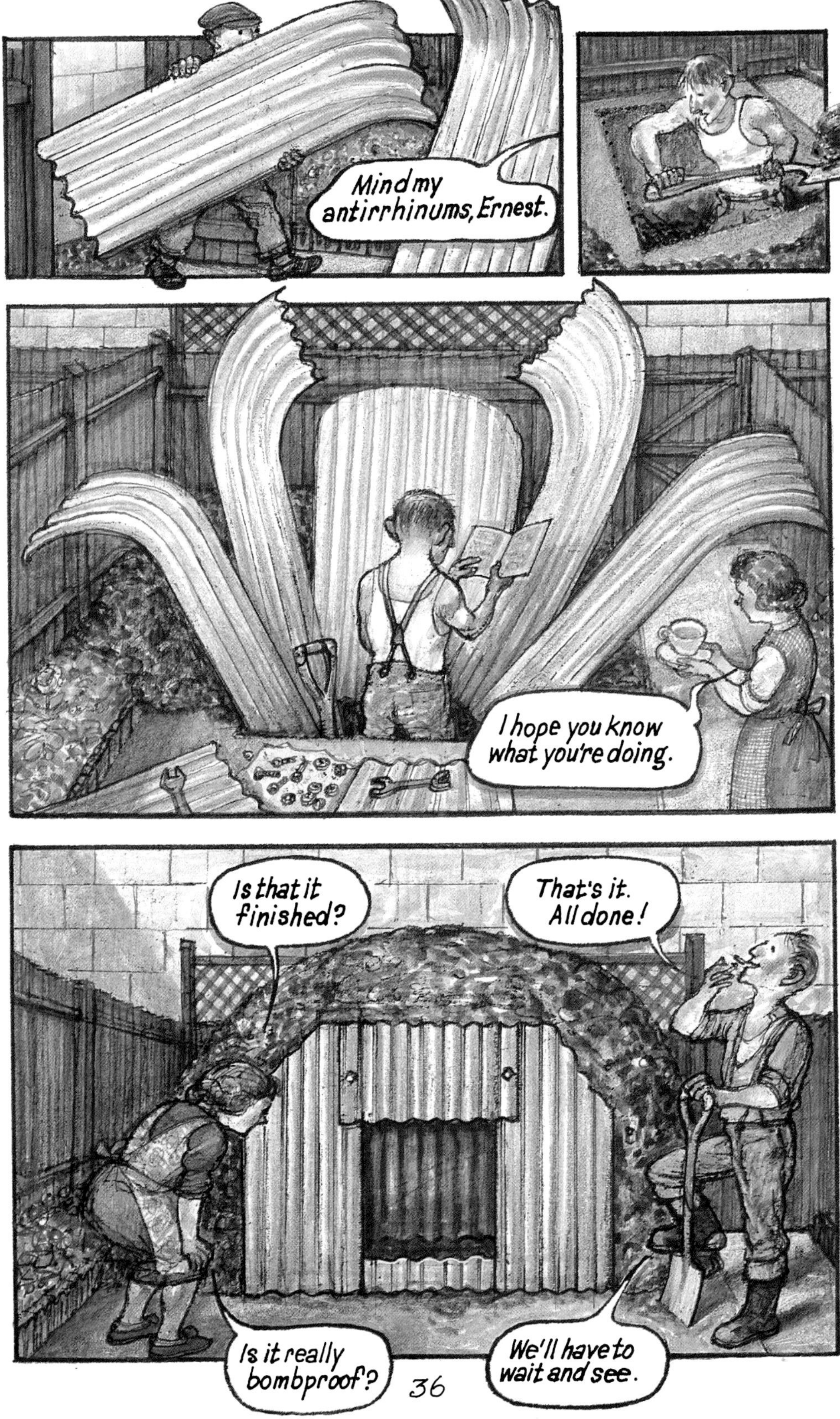
Mind my antirrhinums, Ernest.
I hope you know what you're doing.
Is that it finished?
That's it. All done!
Is it really bombproof?
We'll have to wait and see.

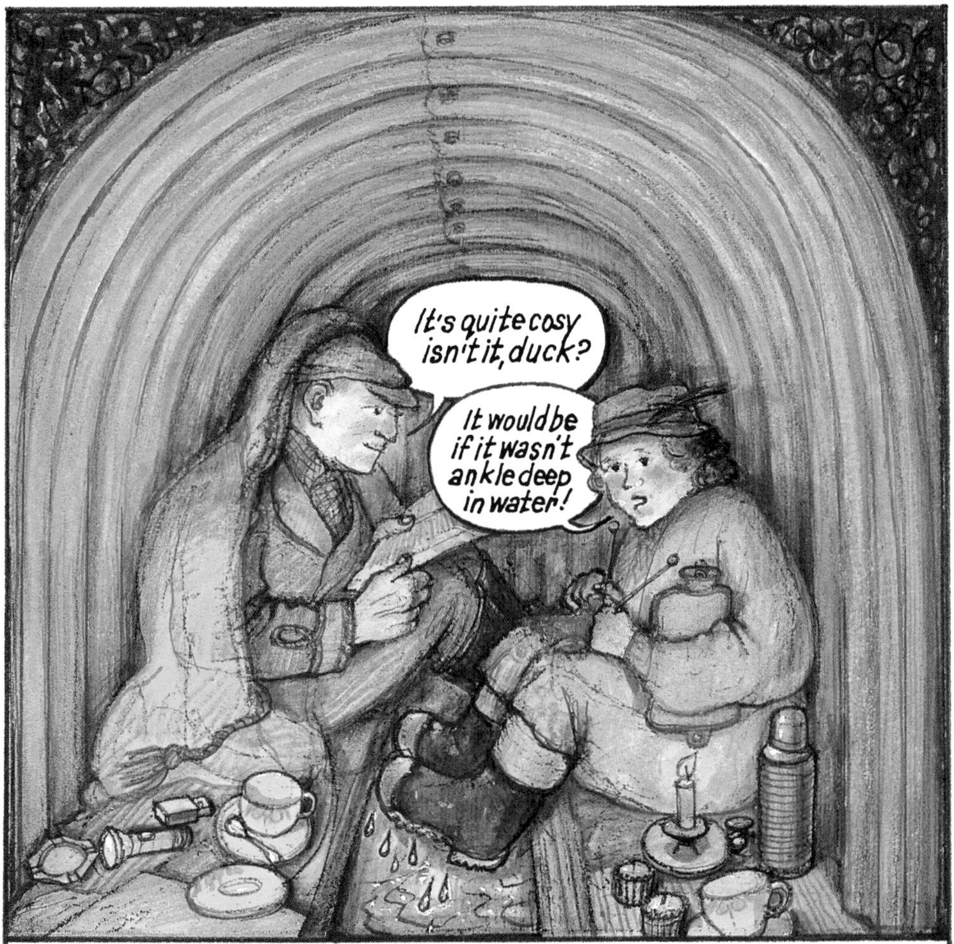
It's quite cosy isn't it, duck?
It would be if it wasn't ankle deep in water!

Russia's invaded Finland now.	I thought they'd invaded POLAND?
Yes, they have.	But you said GERMANY's invaded Poland?
Yes, that's right.	Well, who was it invaded Czechoslovakia?
Germany.	Germany's always invading someone. I expect they'll invade Russia one day –
Cor blimey! Not likely! They're IN LEAGUE!	or Russia will invade Germany.
Oh don't be DAFT!	If they ALL keep invading one another, WE'LL end up invading someone.
Oh Et! You just don't understand politics.	

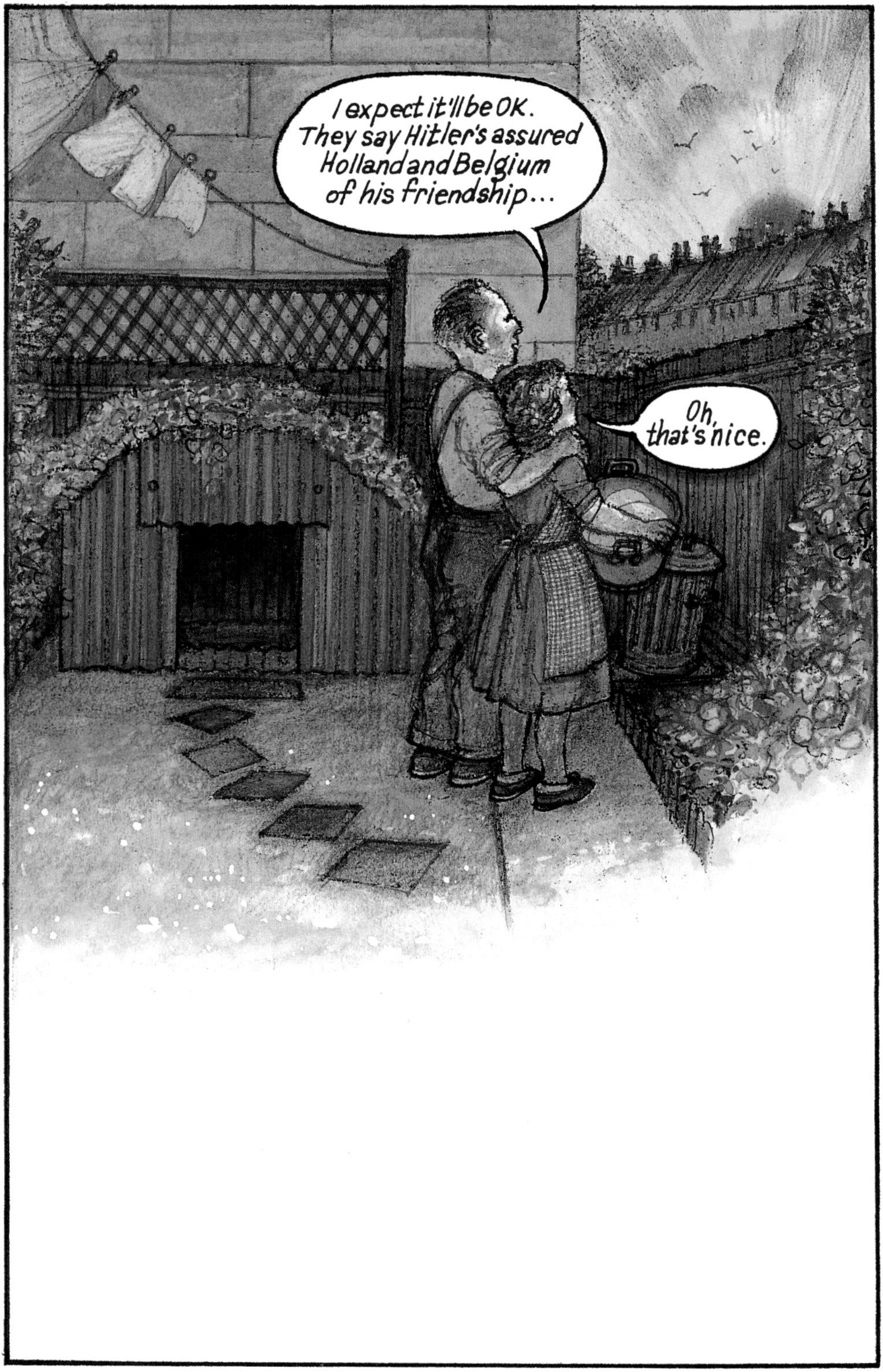
I expect it'll be OK. They say Hitler's assured Holland and Belgium of his friendship...
Oh, that's nice.

1940
~
1950

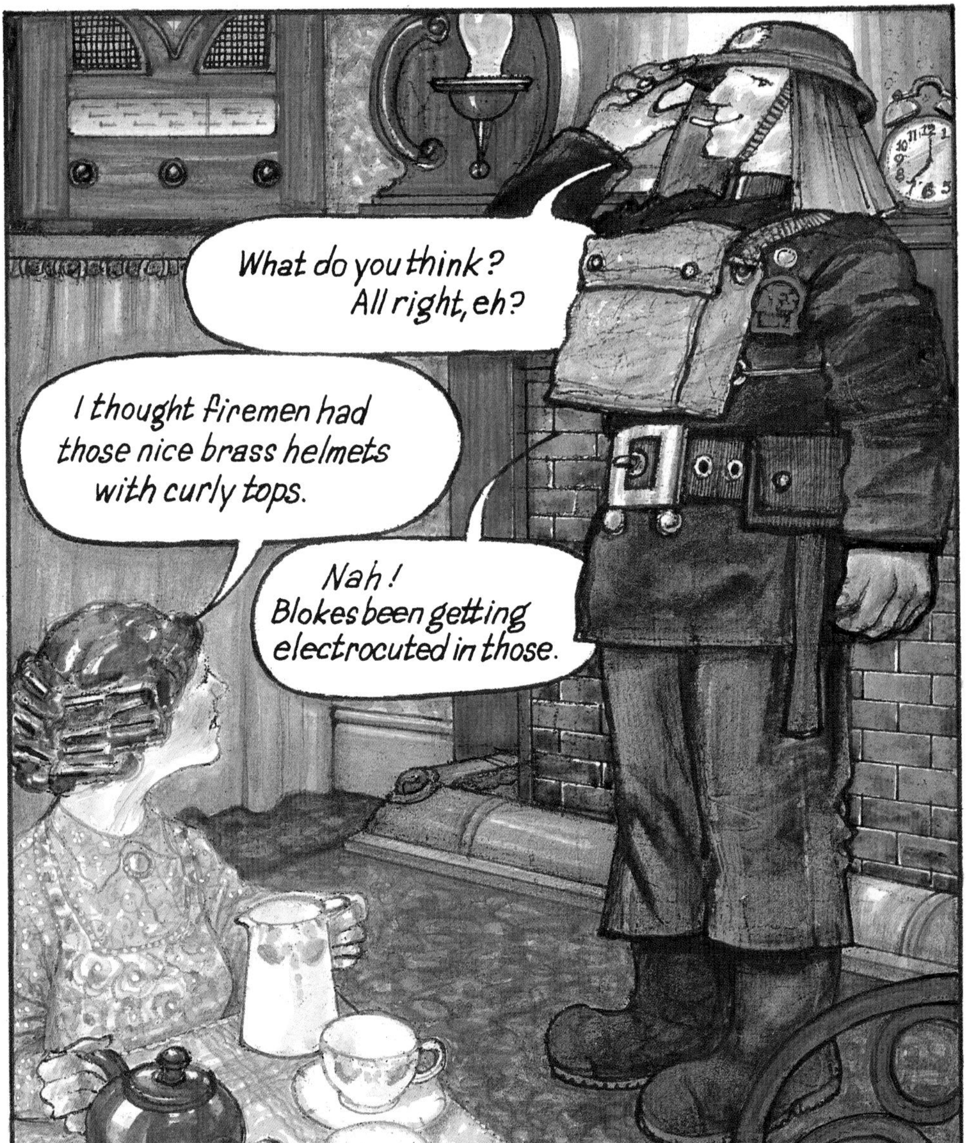
What do you think? All right, eh?
I thought firemen had those nice brass helmets with curly tops.
Nah! Blokes been getting electrocuted in those.

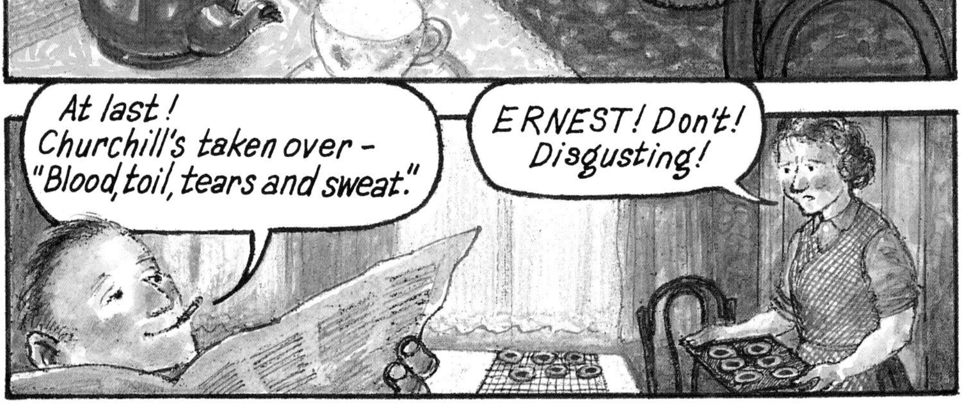
At last! Churchill's taken over - "Blood, toil, tears and sweat."
ERNEST! Don't! Disgusting!

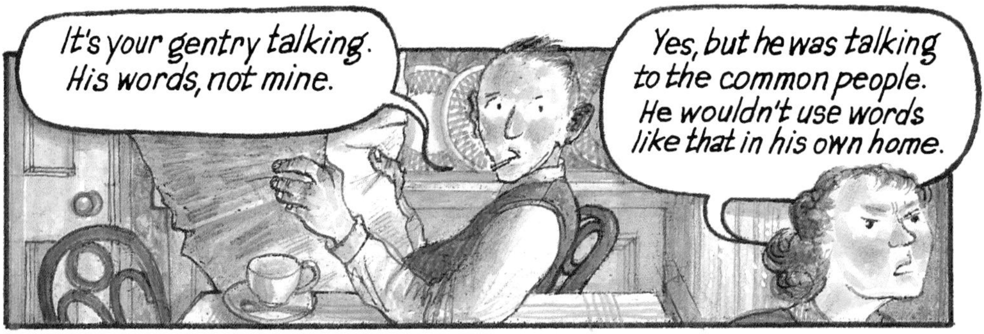
It's your gentry talking. His words, not mine.
Yes, but he was talking to the common people. He wouldn't use words like that in his own home.

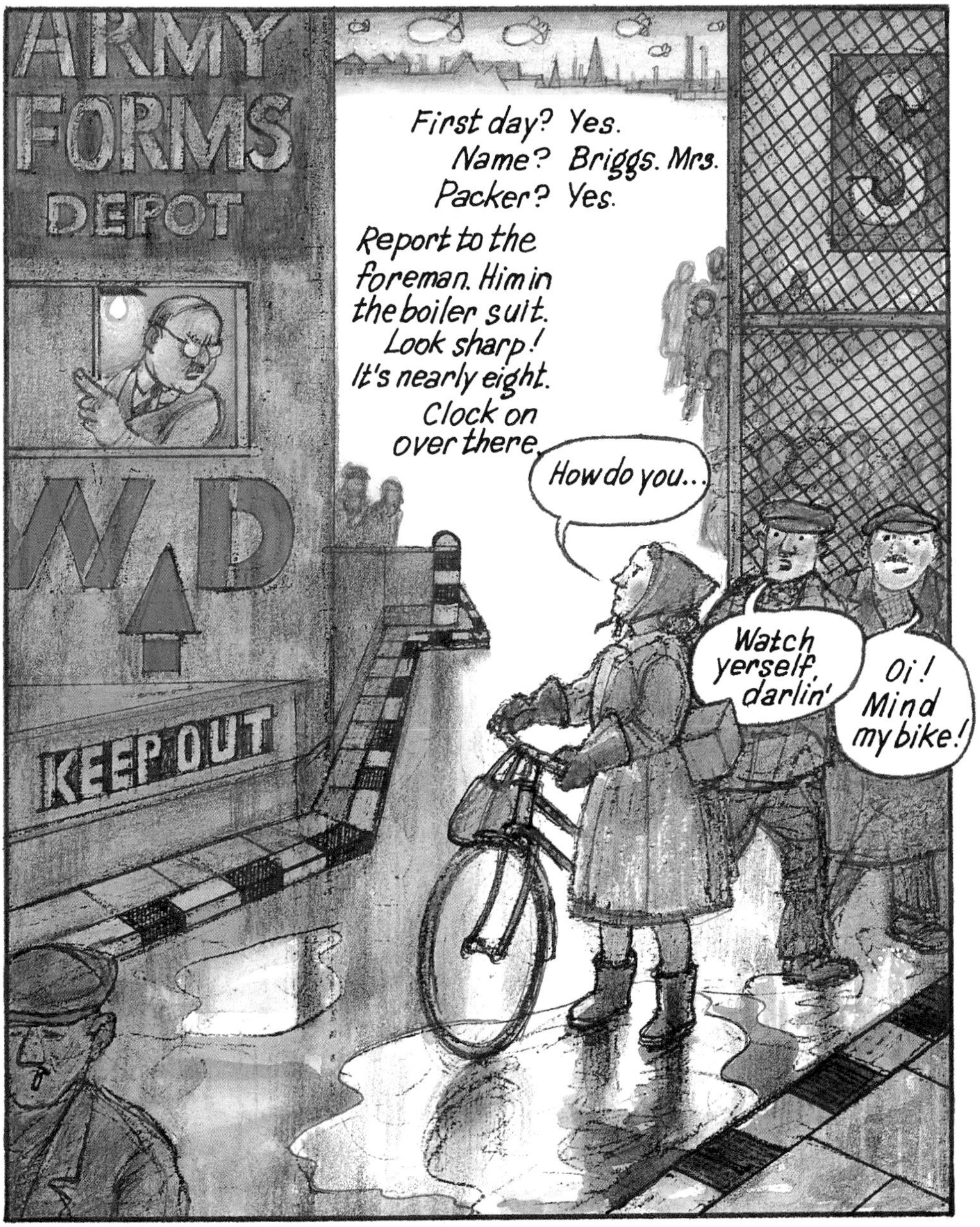
ARMY FORMS DEPOT
W D
KEEP OUT
S
First day? Yes.
Name? Briggs. Mrs.
Packer? Yes.
Report to the foreman. Him in the boiler suit. Look sharp! It's nearly eight. Clock on over there.
How do you...
Watch yerself, darlin'
Oi! Mind my bike!

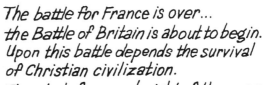

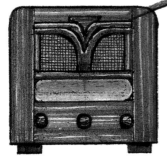

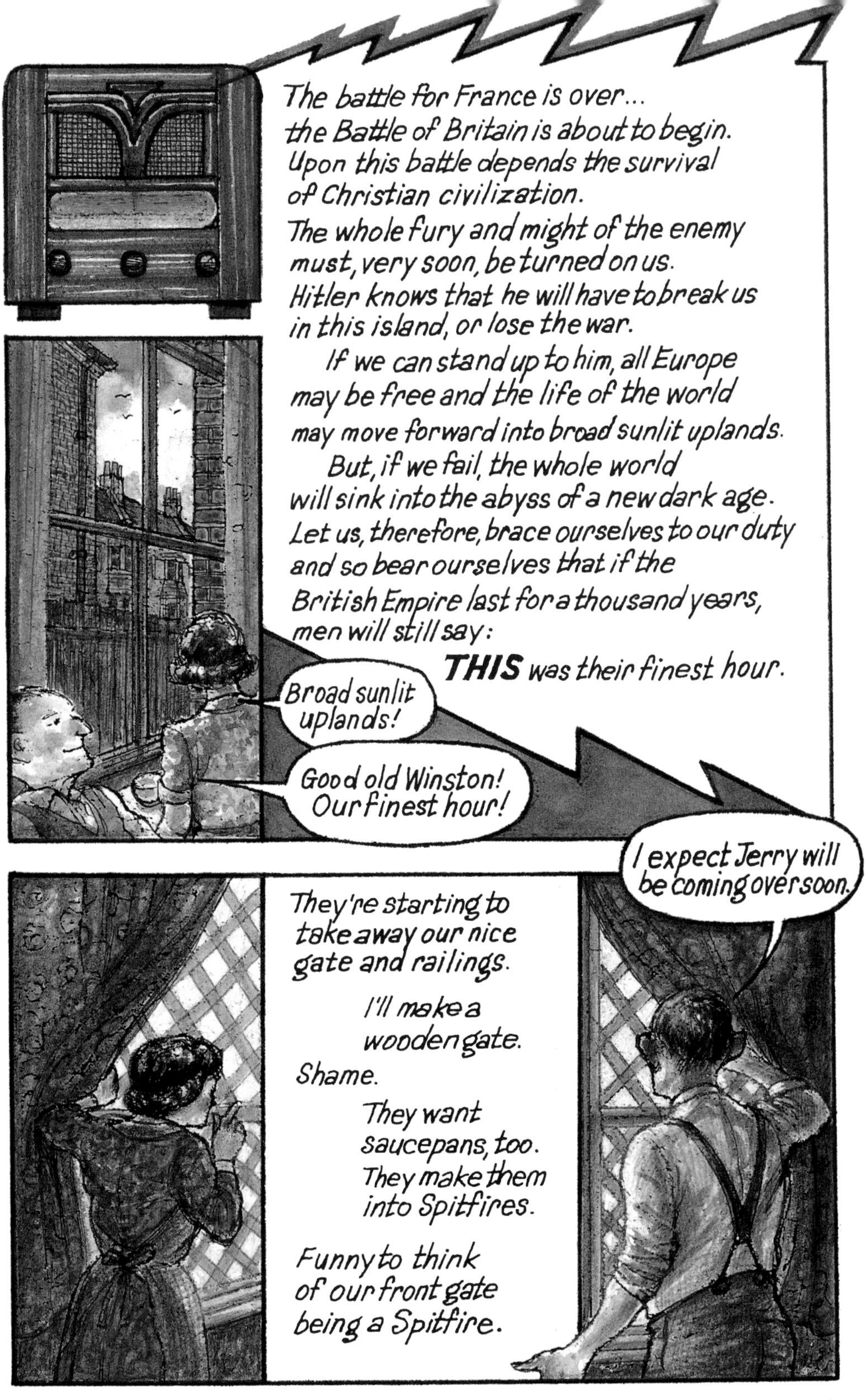

The battle for France is over...
the Battle of Britain is about to begin.
Upon this battle depends the survival
of Christian civilization.
The whole fury and might of the enemy
must, very soon, be turned on us.
Hitler knows that he will have to break us
in this island, or lose the war.

If we can stand up to him, all Europe
may be free and the life of the world
may move forward into broad sunlit uplands.

But, if we fail, the whole world
will sink into the abyss of a new dark age.
Let us, therefore, brace ourselves to our duty
and so bear ourselves that if the
British Empire last for a thousand years,
men will still say:

THIS was their finest hour.

Broad sunlit uplands!

Good old Winston! Our finest hour!

I expect Jerry will be coming over soon.

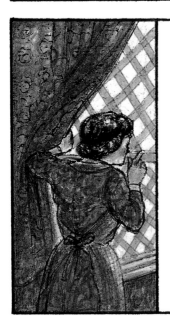

They're starting to take away our nice gate and railings.

I'll make a wooden gate.

Shame.

They want saucepans, too. They make them into Spitfires.

Funny to think of our front gate being a Spitfire.

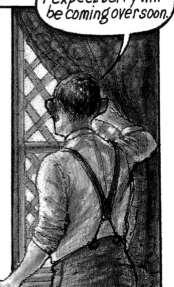

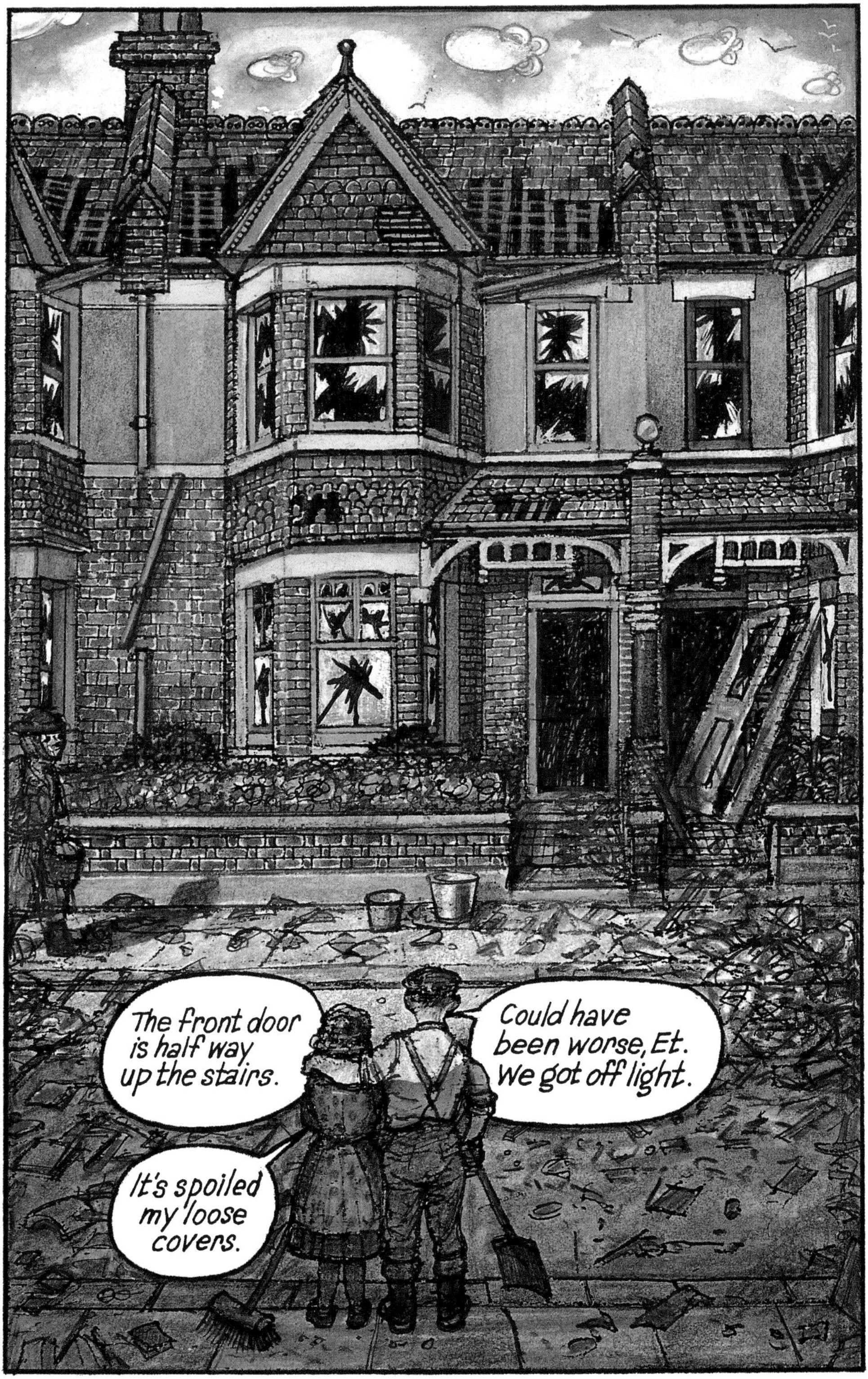
The front door is half way up the stairs.
Could have been worse, Et. We got off light.
It's spoiled my 'loose covers.

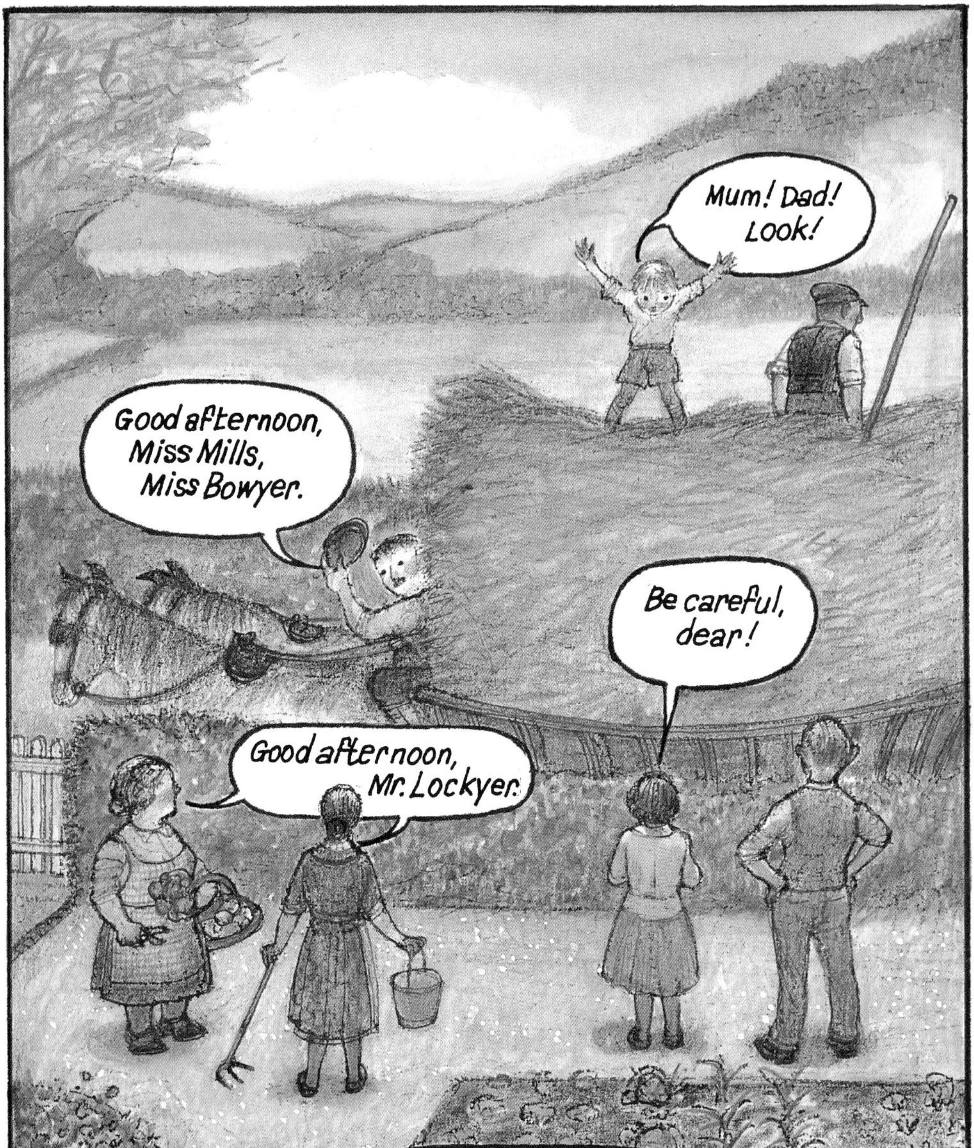
Mum! Dad! Look!
Good afternoon, Miss Mills, Miss Bowyer.
Be careful, dear!
Good afternoon, Mr. Lockyer.

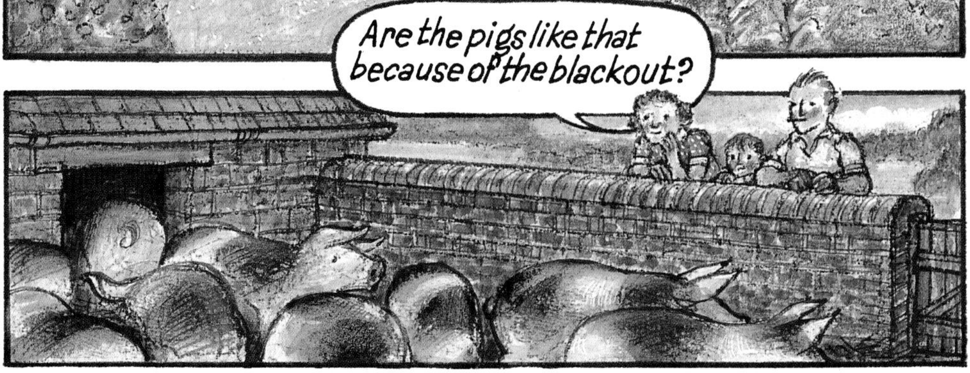
Are the pigs like that because of the blackout?

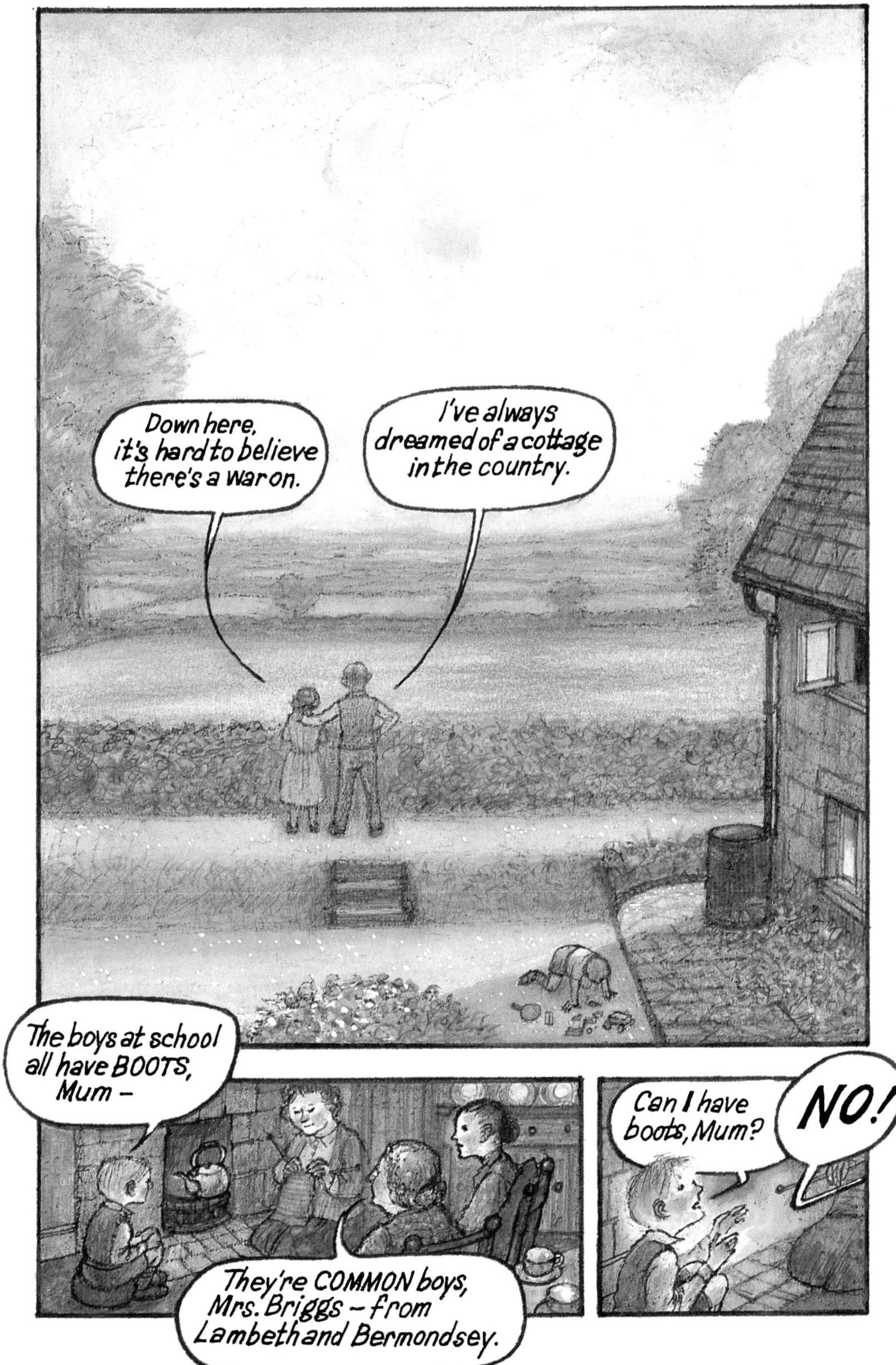
Down here, it's hard to believe there's a war on.
I've always dreamed of a cottage in the country.
The boys at school all have BOOTS, Mum –
They're COMMON boys, Mrs. Briggs – from Lambeth and Bermondsey.
Can I have boots, Mum?
NO!

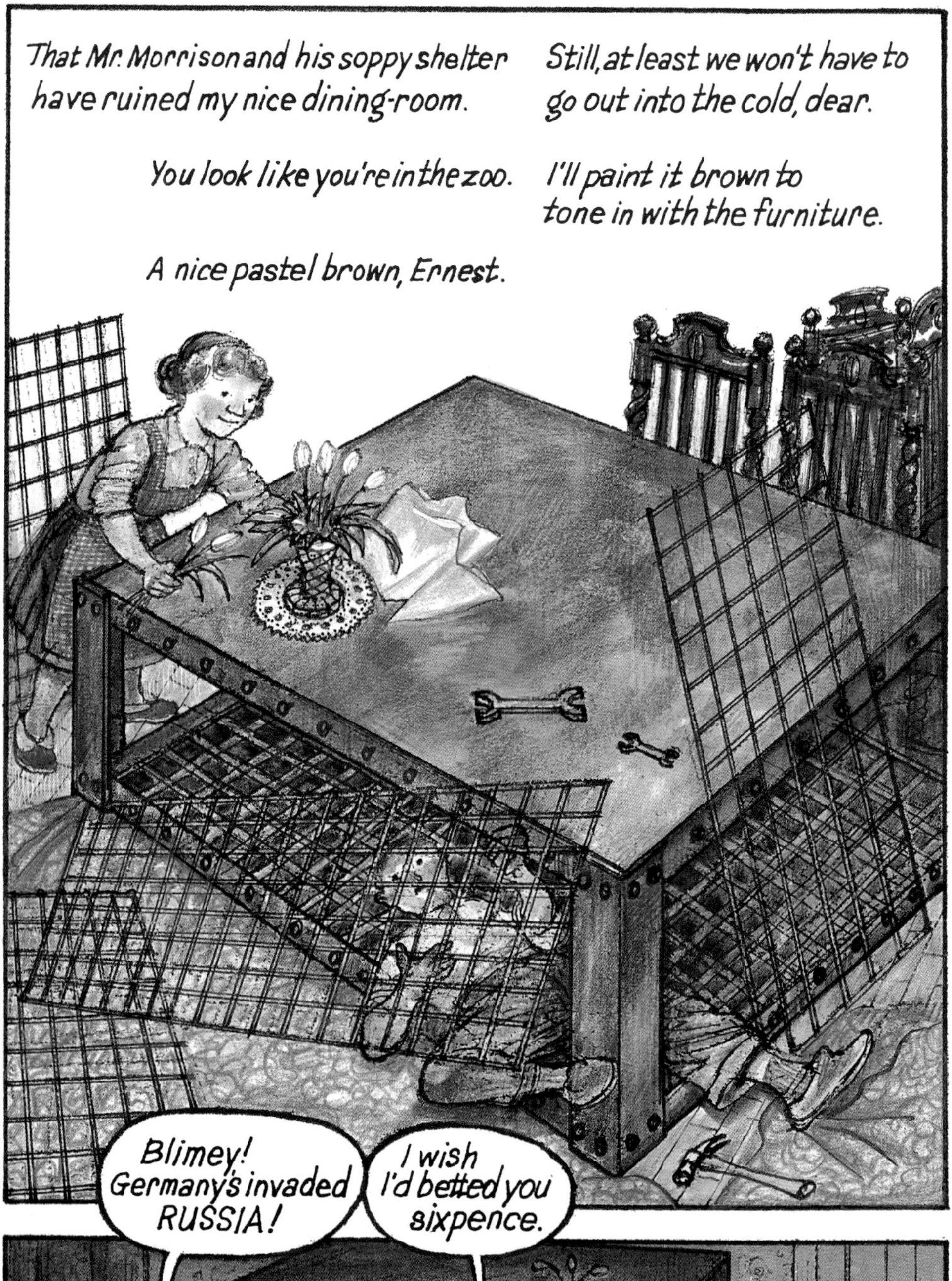
That Mr. Morrison and his soppy shelter have ruined my nice dining-room.
Still, at least we won't have to go out into the cold, dear.
You look like you're in the zoo.
I'll paint it brown to tone in with the furniture.
A nice pastel brown, Ernest.

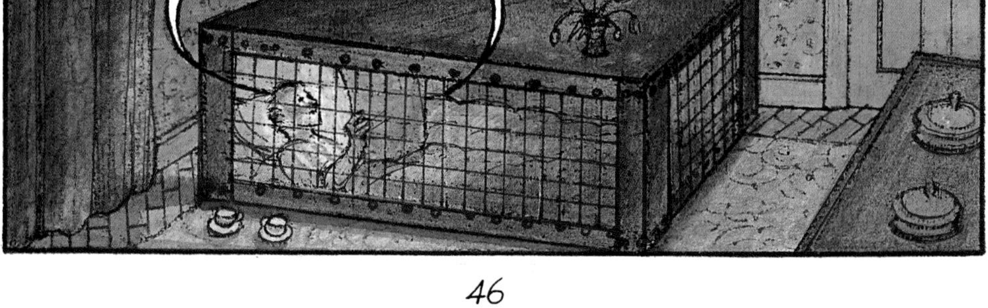
Blimey! Germany's invaded RUSSIA!
I wish I'd betted you sixpence.

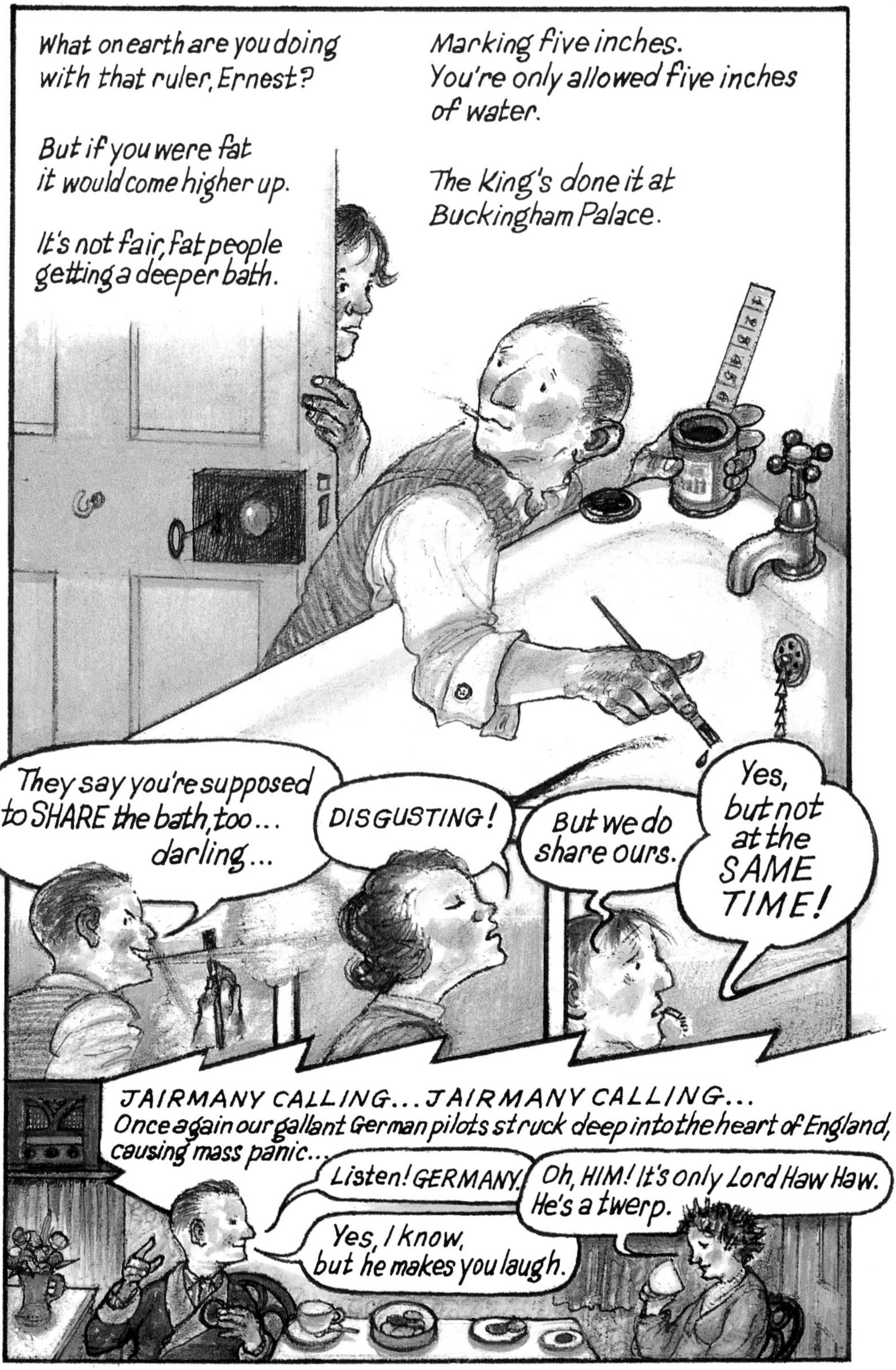
What on earth are you doing with that ruler, Ernest?
Marking five inches. You're only allowed five inches of water.
But if you were fat it would come higher up.
The King's done it at Buckingham Palace.
It's not fair, fat people getting a deeper bath.
They say you're supposed to SHARE the bath, too... darling...
DISGUSTING!
But we do share ours.
Yes, but not at the SAME TIME!
JAIRMANY CALLING... JAIRMANY CALLING...
Once again our gallant German pilots struck deep into the heart of England, causing mass panic...
Listen! GERMANY.
Oh, HIM! It's only Lord Haw Haw. He's a twerp.
Yes, I know, but he makes you laugh.

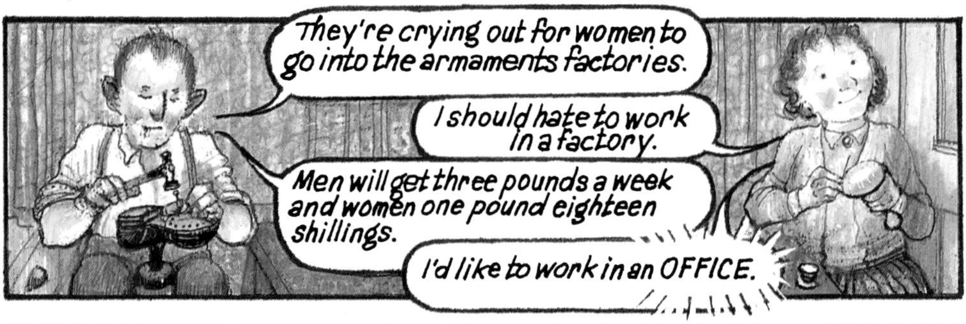
They're crying out for women to go into the armaments factories.
I should hate to work in a factory.
Men will get three pounds a week and women one pound eighteen shillings.
I'd like to work in an OFFICE.

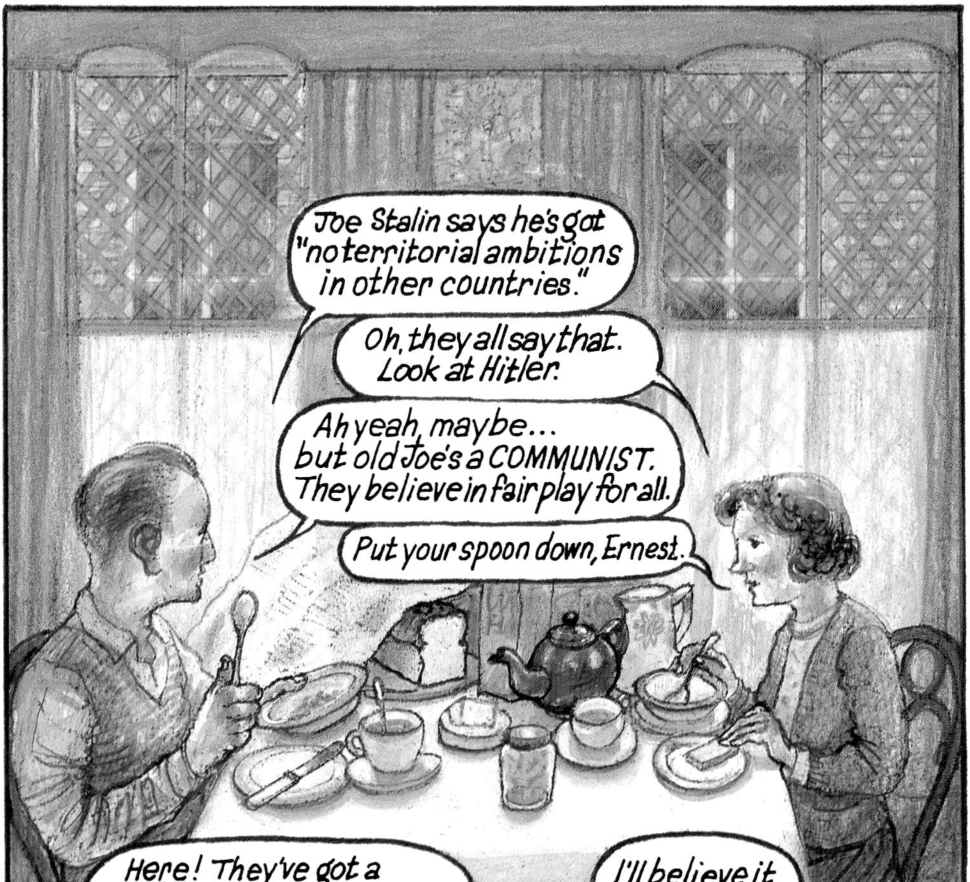
Joe Stalin says he's got "no territorial ambitions in other countries."
Oh, they all say that. Look at Hitler.
Ah yeah, maybe... but old Joe's a COMMUNIST. They believe in fair play for all.
Put your spoon down, Ernest.

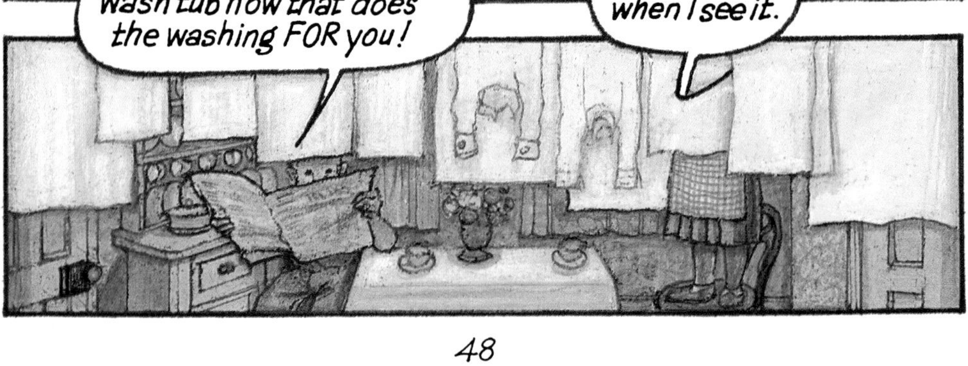
Here! They've got a wash tub now that does the washing FOR you!
I'll believe it when I see it.

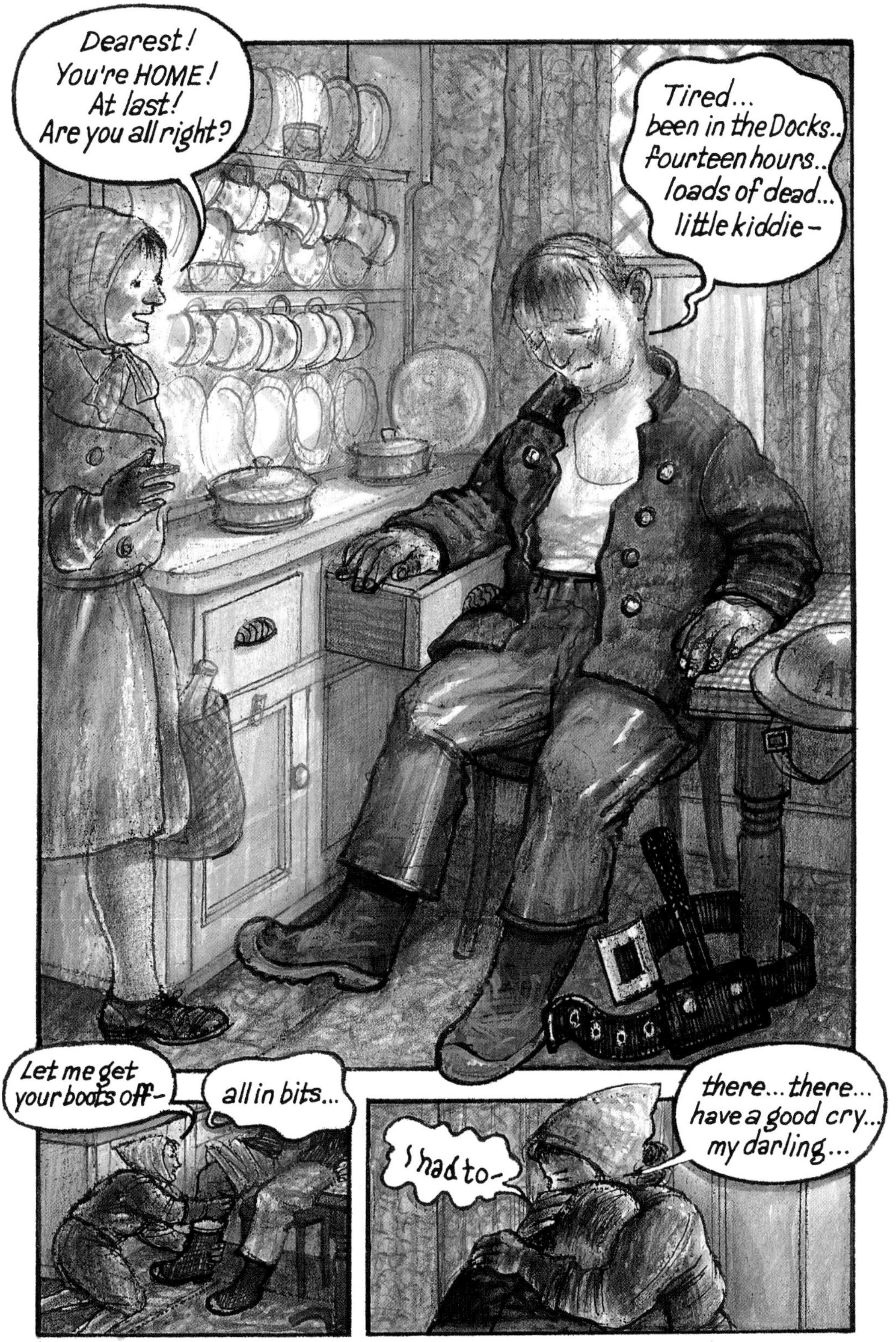
Dearest! You're HOME! At last! Are you all right?
Tired... been in the Docks.. fourteen hours.. loads of dead... little kiddie -
Let me get your boots off-
all in bits...
I had to-
there... there... have a good cry... my darling...

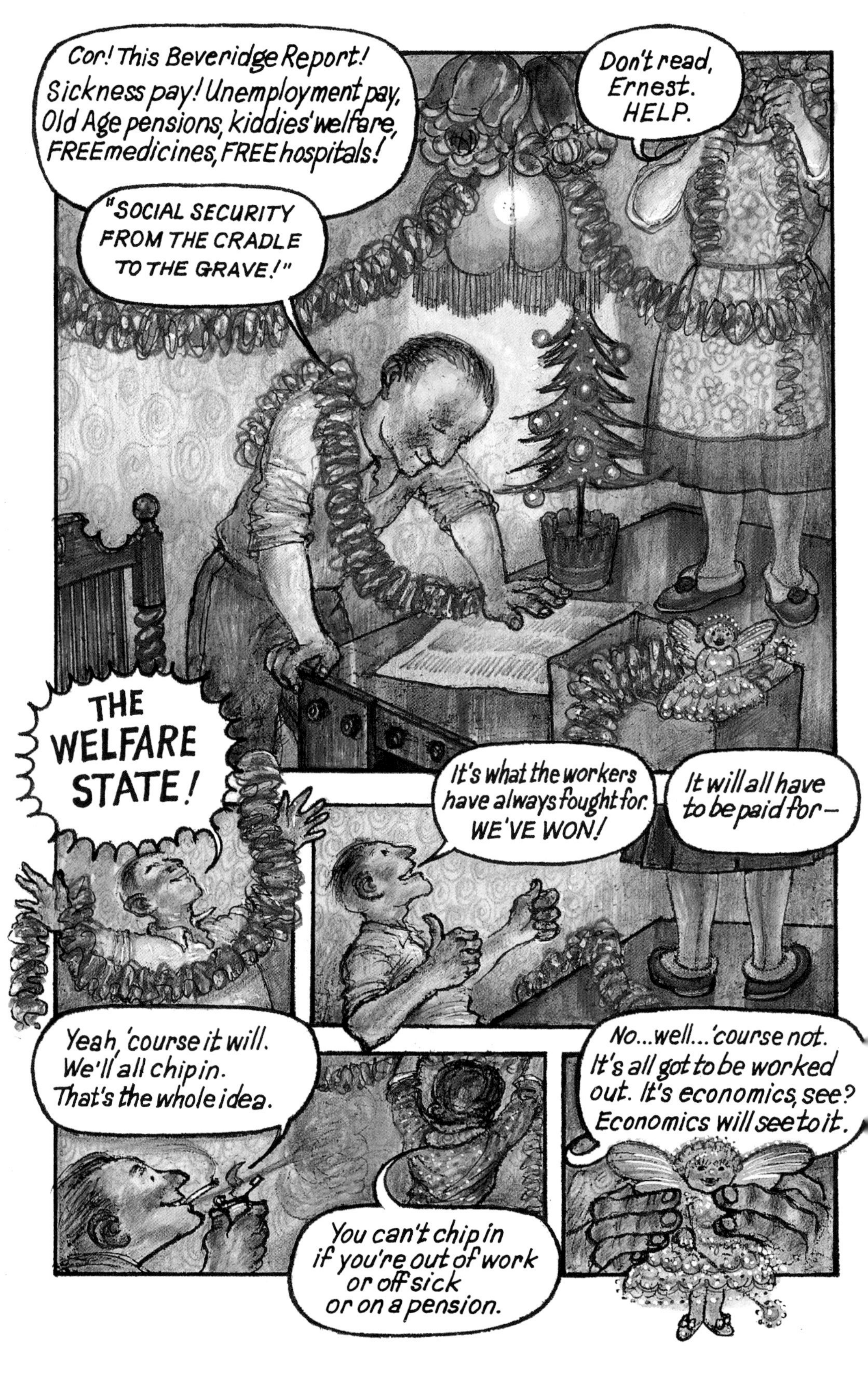
Cor! This Beveridge Report! Sickness pay! Unemployment pay, Old Age pensions, kiddies' welfare, FREE medicines, FREE hospitals!
"SOCIAL SECURITY FROM THE CRADLE TO THE GRAVE!"
Don't read, Ernest. HELP.
THE WELFARE STATE!
It's what the workers have always fought for. WE'VE WON!
It will all have to be paid for—
Yeah, 'course it will. We'll all chip in. That's the whole idea.
You can't chip in if you're out of work or off sick or on a pension.
No...well...'course not. It's all got to be worked out. It's economics, see? Economics will see to it.

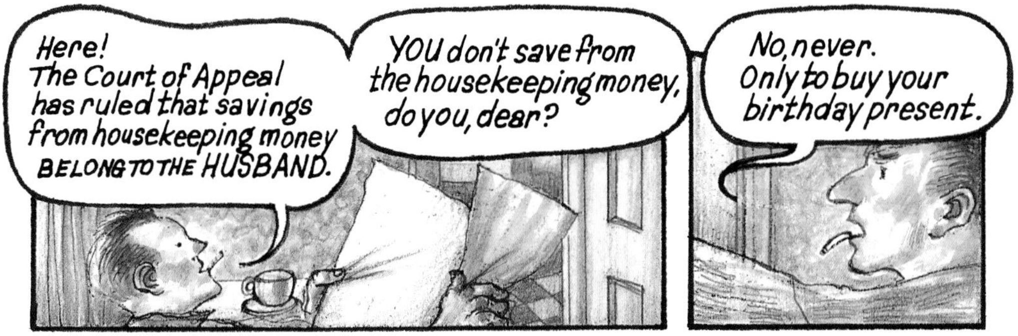
Here! The Court of Appeal has ruled that savings from housekeeping money BELONG TO THE HUSBAND.
YOU don't save from the housekeeping money, do you, dear?
No, never. Only to buy your birthday present.

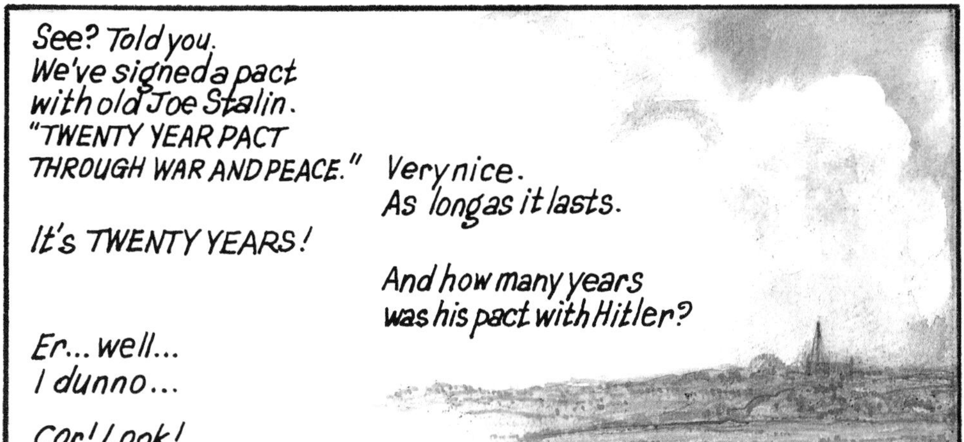
See? Told you. We've signed a pact with old Joe Stalin. "TWENTY YEAR PACT THROUGH WAR AND PEACE."
Very nice. As long as it lasts.
It's TWENTY YEARS!
And how many years was his pact with Hitler?
Er... well... I dunno...
Cor! Look! "Women's Fashions-" "SHORTER SKIRTS-" "Bare legs for Patriotism," it says-
ERNEST!

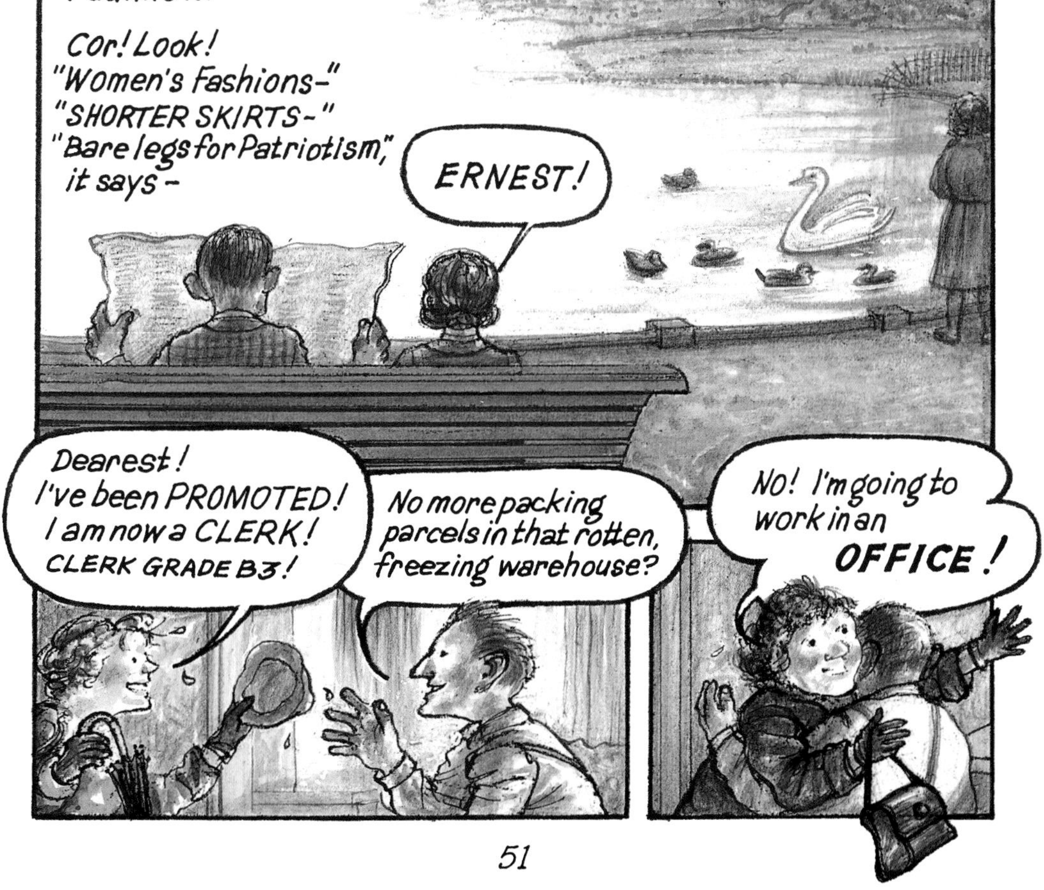
Dearest! I've been PROMOTED! I am now a CLERK! CLERK GRADE B3!
No more packing parcels in that rotten, freezing warehouse?
No! I'm going to work in an OFFICE!

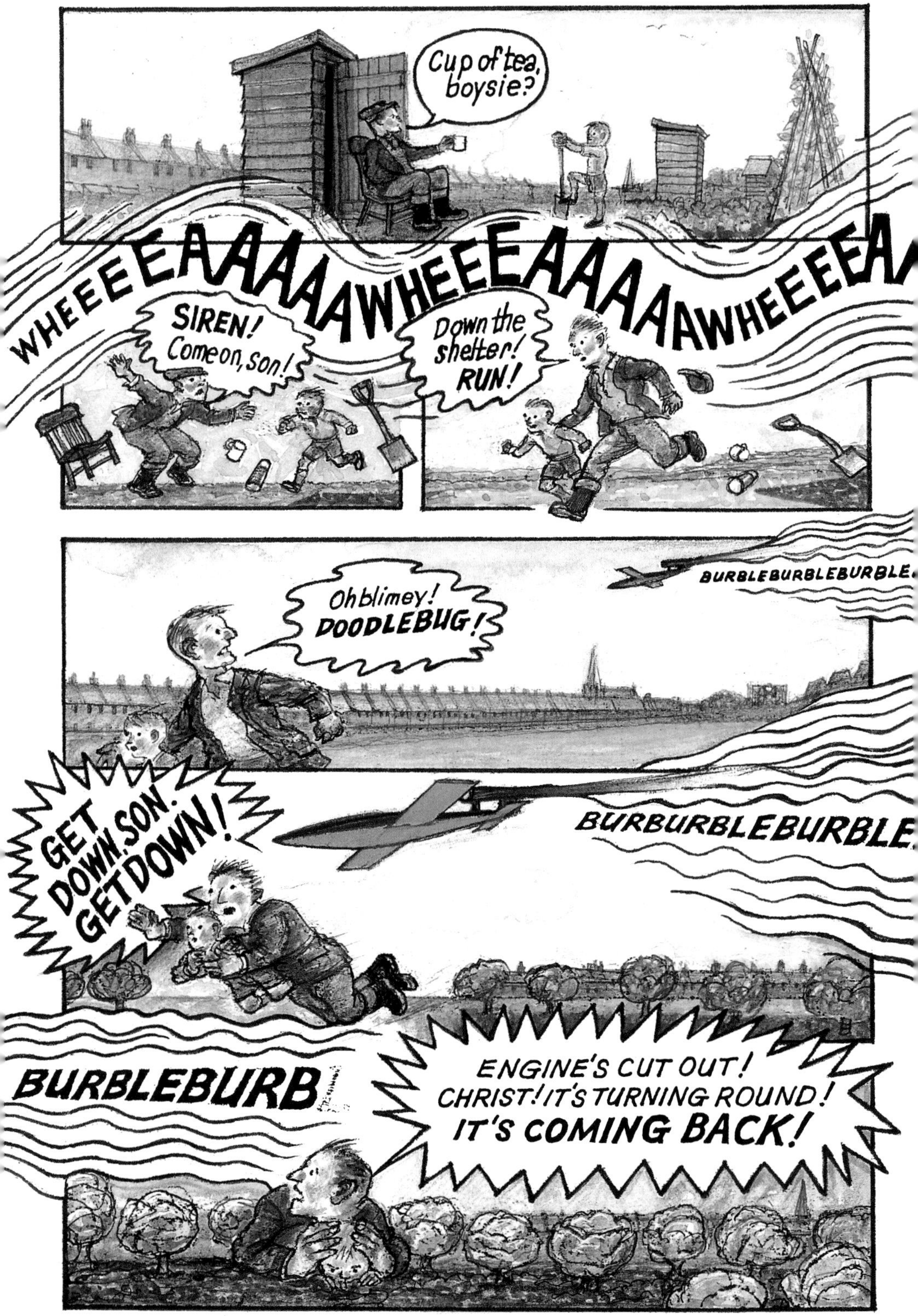
Cup of tea, boysie?
WHEEEEAAAAAWHEEEAAAAAAWHEEEEEA
SIREN! Come on, son!
Down the shelter! RUN!
BURBLEBURBLEBURBLE
Oh blimey! DOODLEBUG!
GET DOWN, SON. GET DOWN!
BURBURBLEBURBLE
BURBLEBURB
ENGINE'S CUT OUT!
CHRIST! IT'S TURNING ROUND!
IT'S COMING BACK!

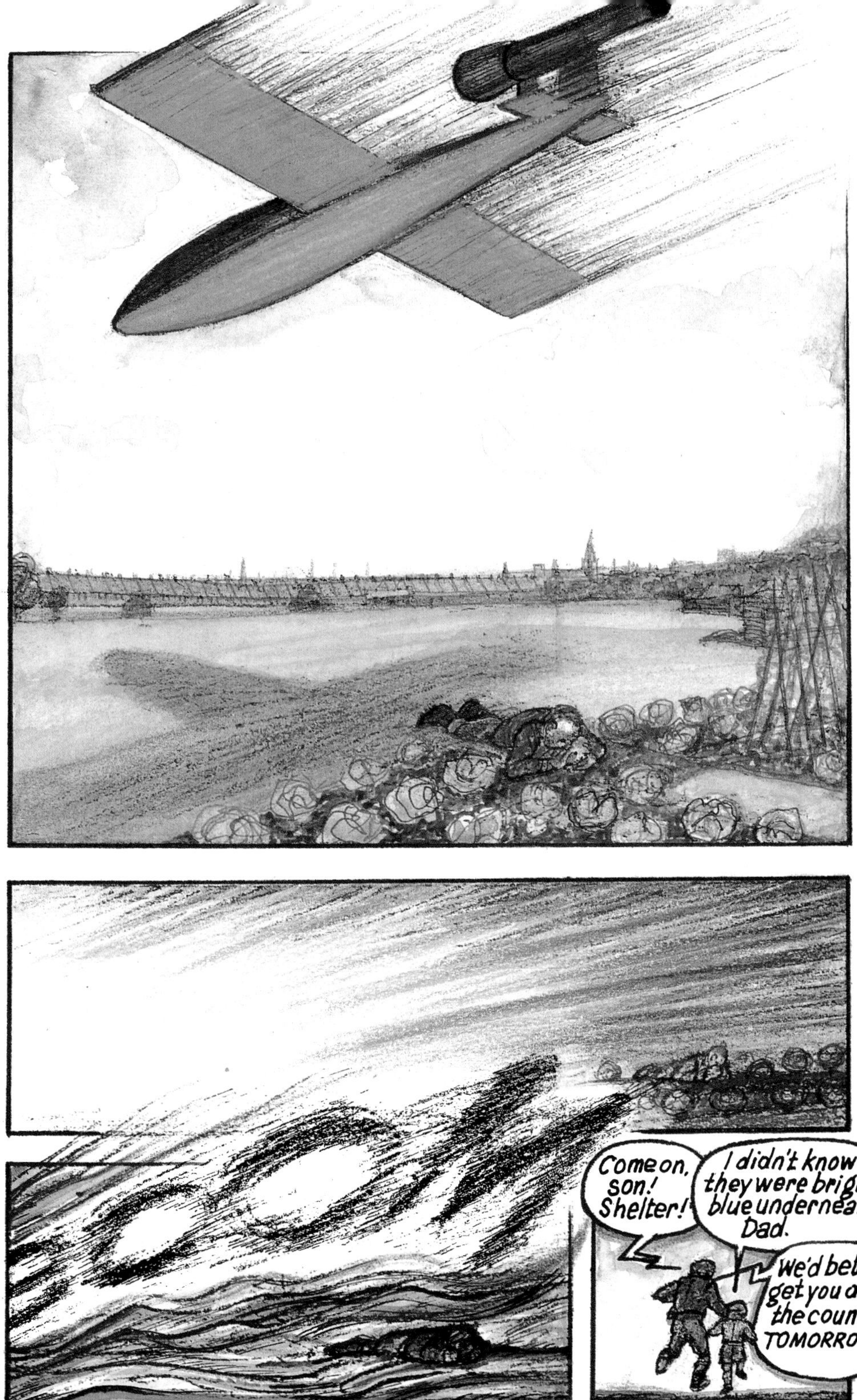
Come on, son! Shelter!
I didn't know they were bright blue underneath, Dad.
We'd better get you down the country - TOMORROW!

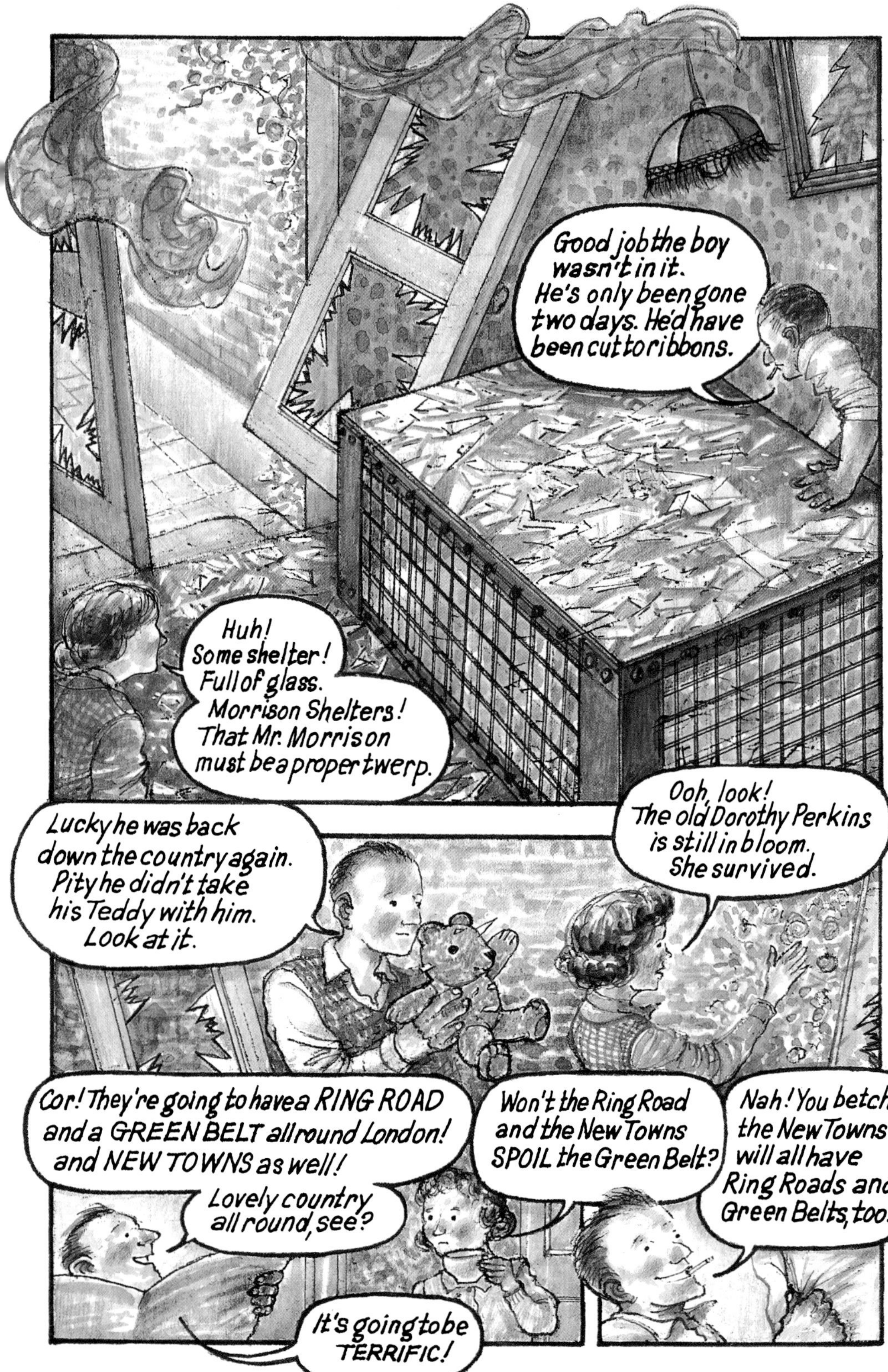
Good job the boy wasn't in it. He's only been gone two days. He'd have been cut to ribbons.
Huh! Some shelter! Full of glass. Morrison Shelters! That Mr. Morrison must be a proper twerp.
Lucky he was back down the country again. Pity he didn't take his Teddy with him. Look at it.
Ooh, look! The old Dorothy Perkins is still in bloom. She survived.
Cor! They're going to have a RING ROAD and a GREEN BELT all round London! and NEW TOWNS as well!
Lovely country all round, see?
It's going to be TERRIFIC!
Won't the Ring Road and the New Towns SPOIL the Green Belt?
Nah! You betcha the New Towns will all have Ring Roads and Green Belts, too!

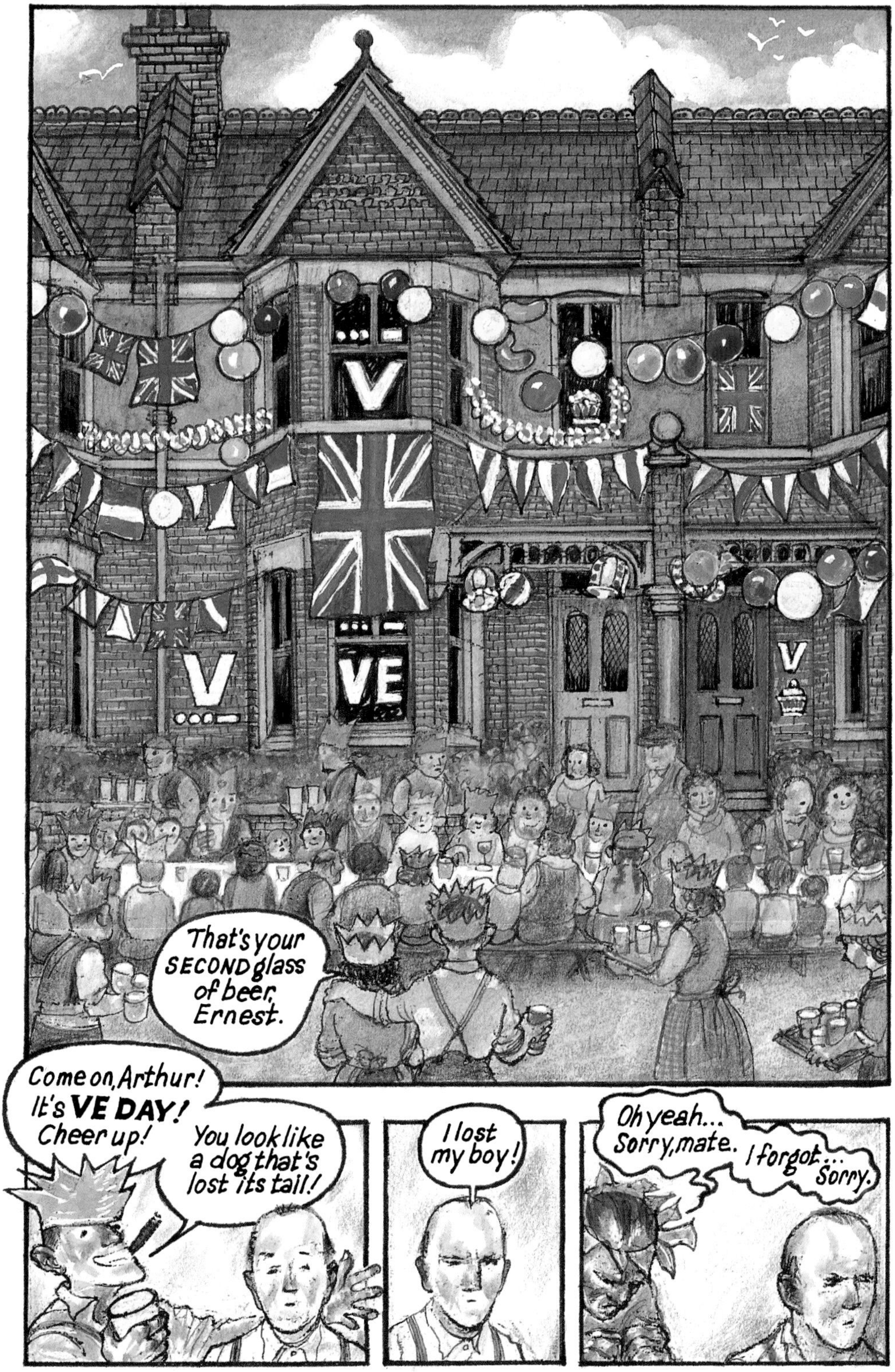
That's your SECOND glass of beer, Ernest.
Come on, Arthur! It's VE DAY! Cheer up!
You look like a dog that's lost its tail!
I lost my boy!
Oh yeah... Sorry, mate.
I forgot... Sorry.

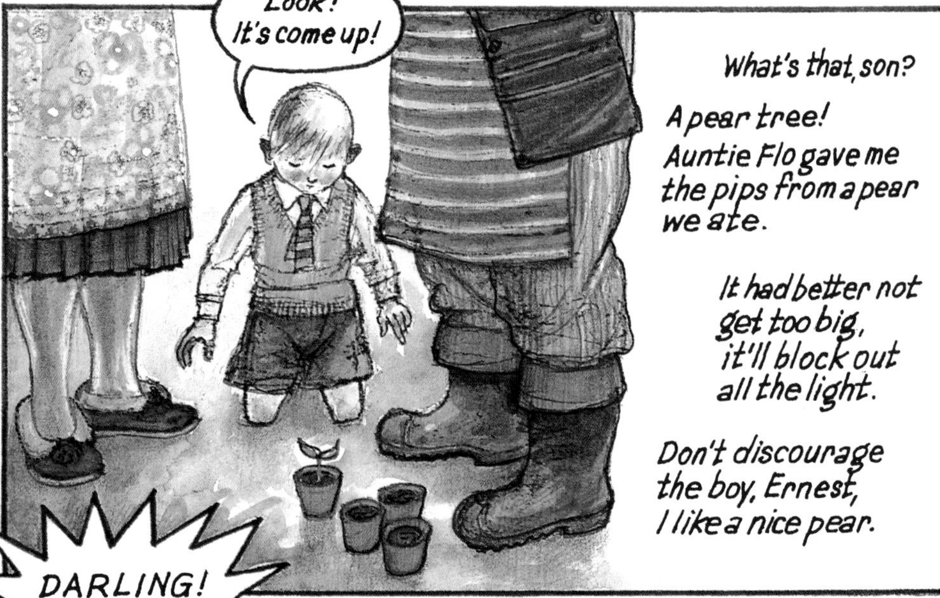
Look! It's come up!
What's that, son?
A pear tree! Auntie Flo gave me the pips from a pear we ate.
It had better not get too big, it'll block out all the light.
Don't discourage the boy, Ernest, I like a nice pear.

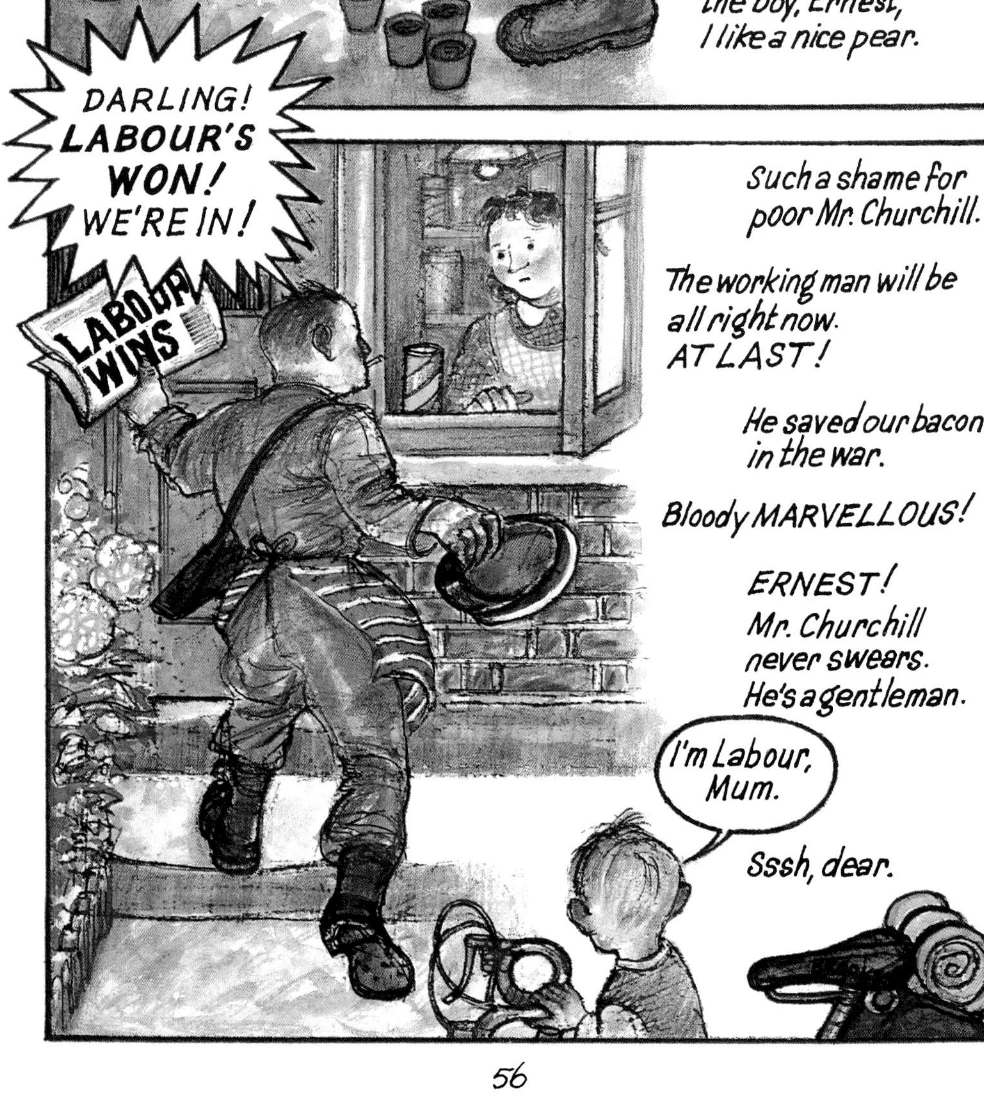
DARLING! LABOUR'S WON! WE'RE IN!
LABOUR WINS
Such a shame for poor Mr. Churchill.
The working man will be all right now. AT LAST!
He saved our bacon in the war.
Bloody MARVELLOUS!
ERNEST! Mr. Churchill never swears. He's a gentleman.
I'm Labour, Mum.
Sssh, dear.

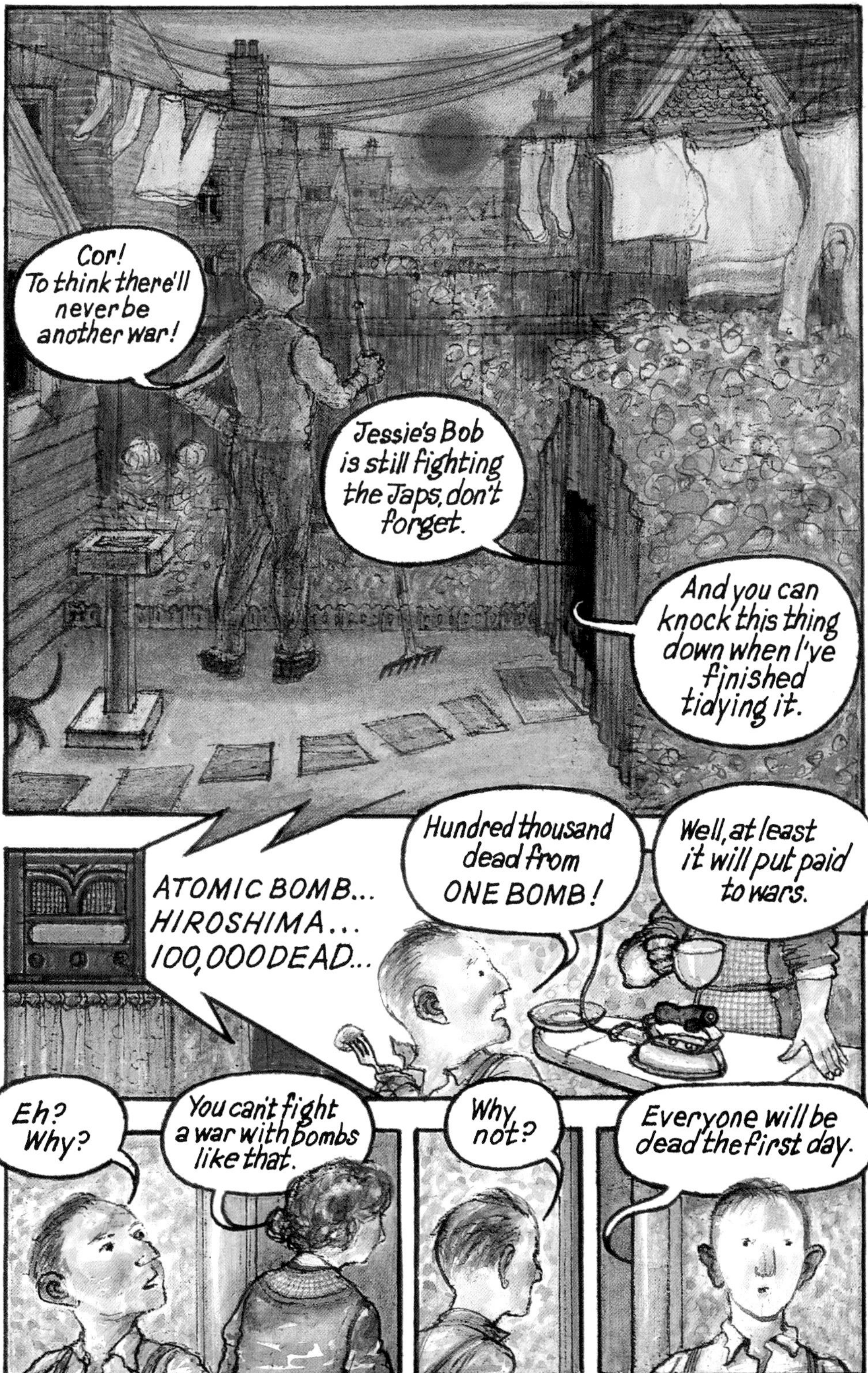
Cor! To think there'll never be another war!
Jessie's Bob is still fighting the Japs, don't forget.
And you can knock this thing down when I've finished tidying it.
ATOMIC BOMB... HIROSHIMA... 100,000 DEAD...
Hundred thousand dead from ONE BOMB!
Well, at least it will put paid to wars.
Eh? Why?
You can't fight a war with bombs like that.
Why not?
Everyone will be dead the first day.

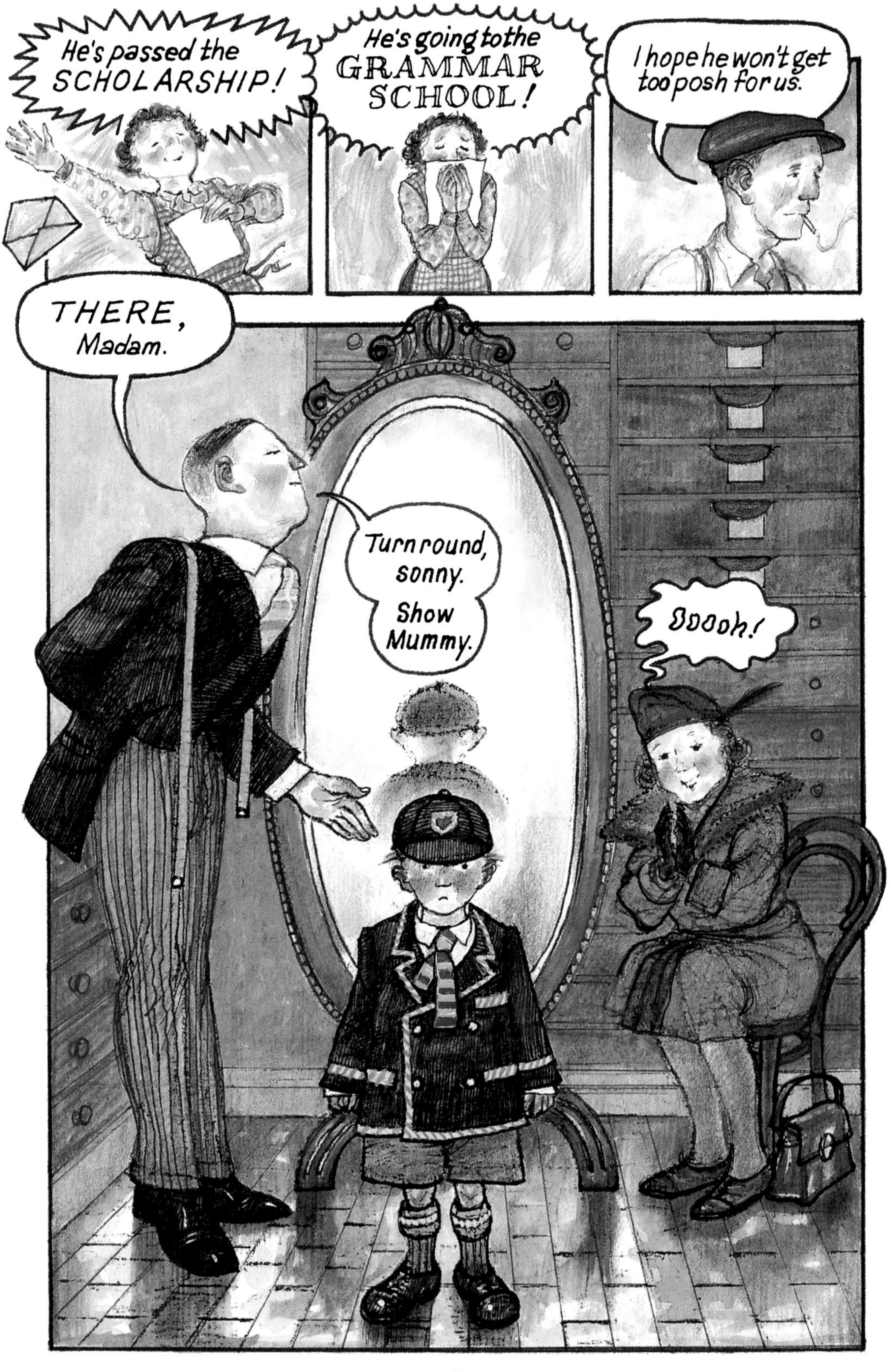
He's passed the SCHOLARSHIP!
He's going to the GRAMMAR SCHOOL!
I hope he won't get too posh for us.
THERE, Madam.
Turn round, sonny.
Show Mummy.
Ooooh!

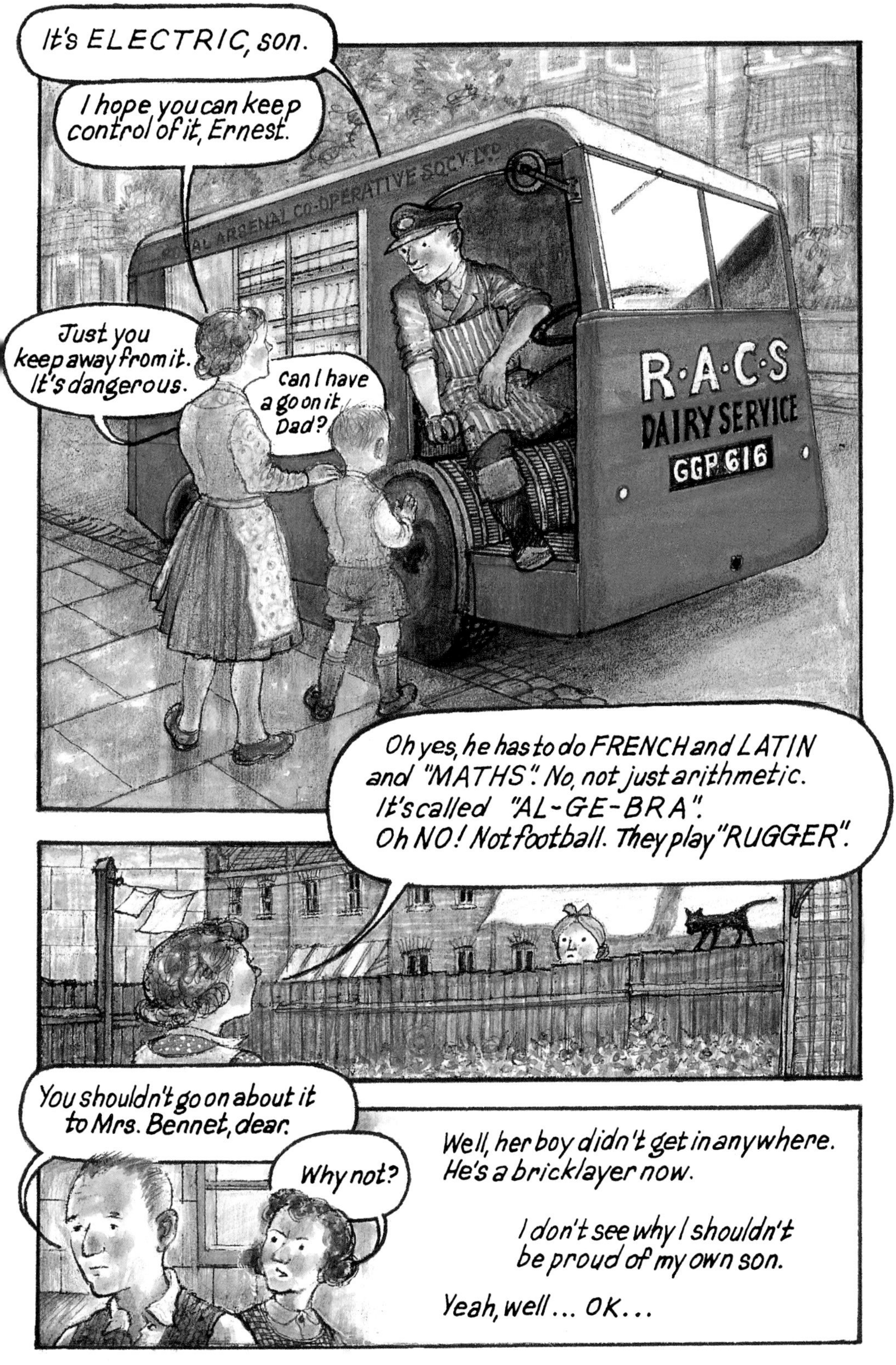
It's ELECTRIC, son.
I hope you can keep control of it, Ernest.
CO-OPERATIVE SOC'Y LTD
R·A·C·S
DAIRY SERVICE
GGP 616
Just you keep away from it. It's dangerous.
Can I have a go on it, Dad?
Oh yes, he has to do FRENCH and LATIN and "MATHS". No, not just arithmetic. It's called "AL-GE-BRA". Oh NO! Not football. They play "RUGGER".
You shouldn't go on about it to Mrs. Bennet, dear.
Why not?
Well, her boy didn't get in anywhere. He's a bricklayer now.
I don't see why I shouldn't be proud of my own son.
Yeah, well ... OK ...

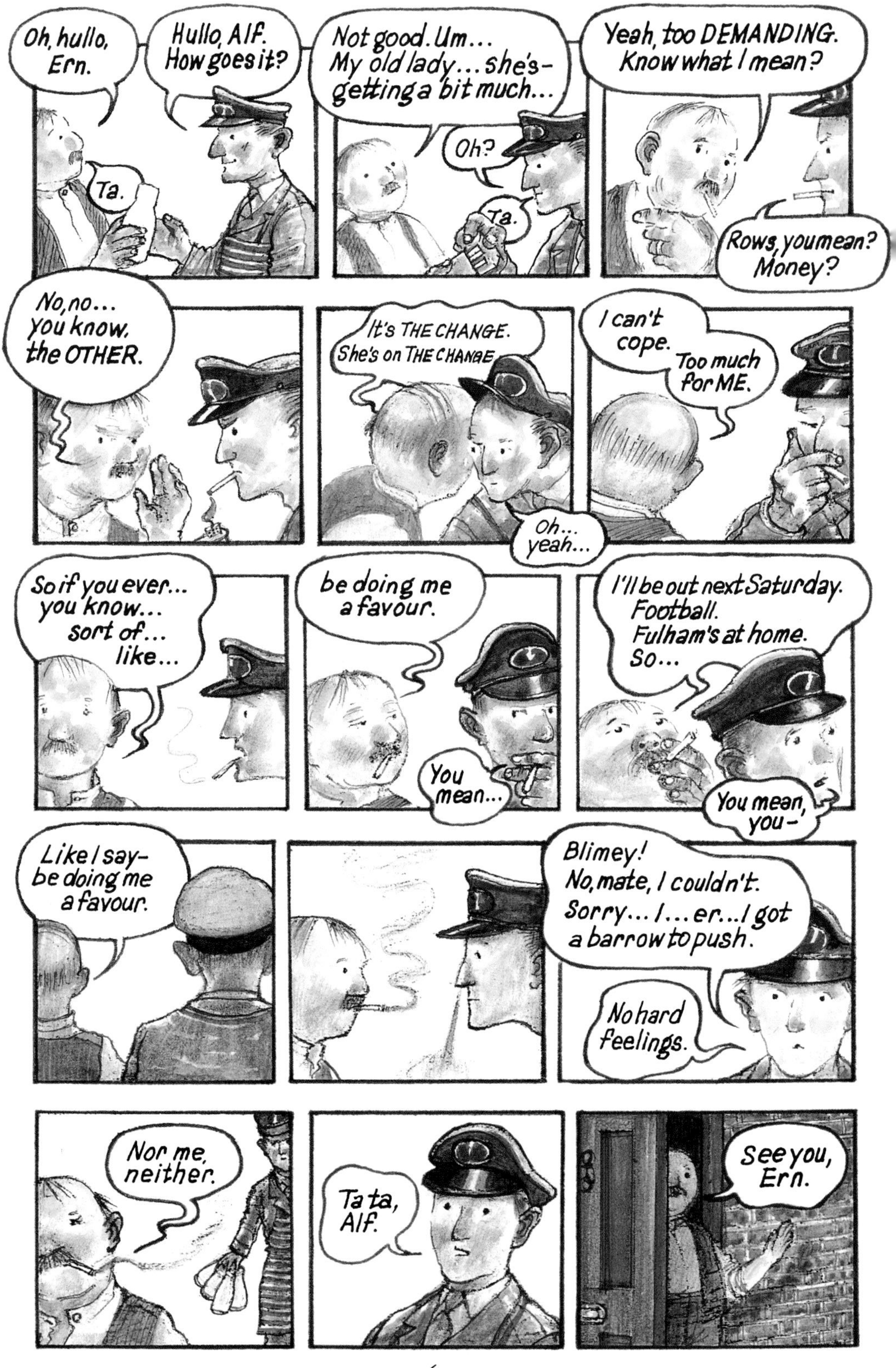
Oh, hullo, Ern.
Hullo, Alf. How goes it?
Ta.
Not good. Um... My old lady... she's-getting a bit much...
Oh?
Ta.
Yeah, too DEMANDING. Know what I mean?
Rows, you mean? Money?
No, no... you know, the OTHER.
It's THE CHANGE. She's on THE CHANGE.
Oh... yeah...
I can't cope.
Too much for ME.
So if you ever... you know... sort of... like...
be doing me a favour.
You mean...
I'll be out next Saturday. Football. Fulham's at home. So...
You mean, you-
Like I say-be doing me a favour.
Blimey! No, mate, I couldn't. Sorry... I... er... I got a barrow to push.
No hard feelings.
Nor me, neither.
Ta ta, Alf.
See you, Ern.

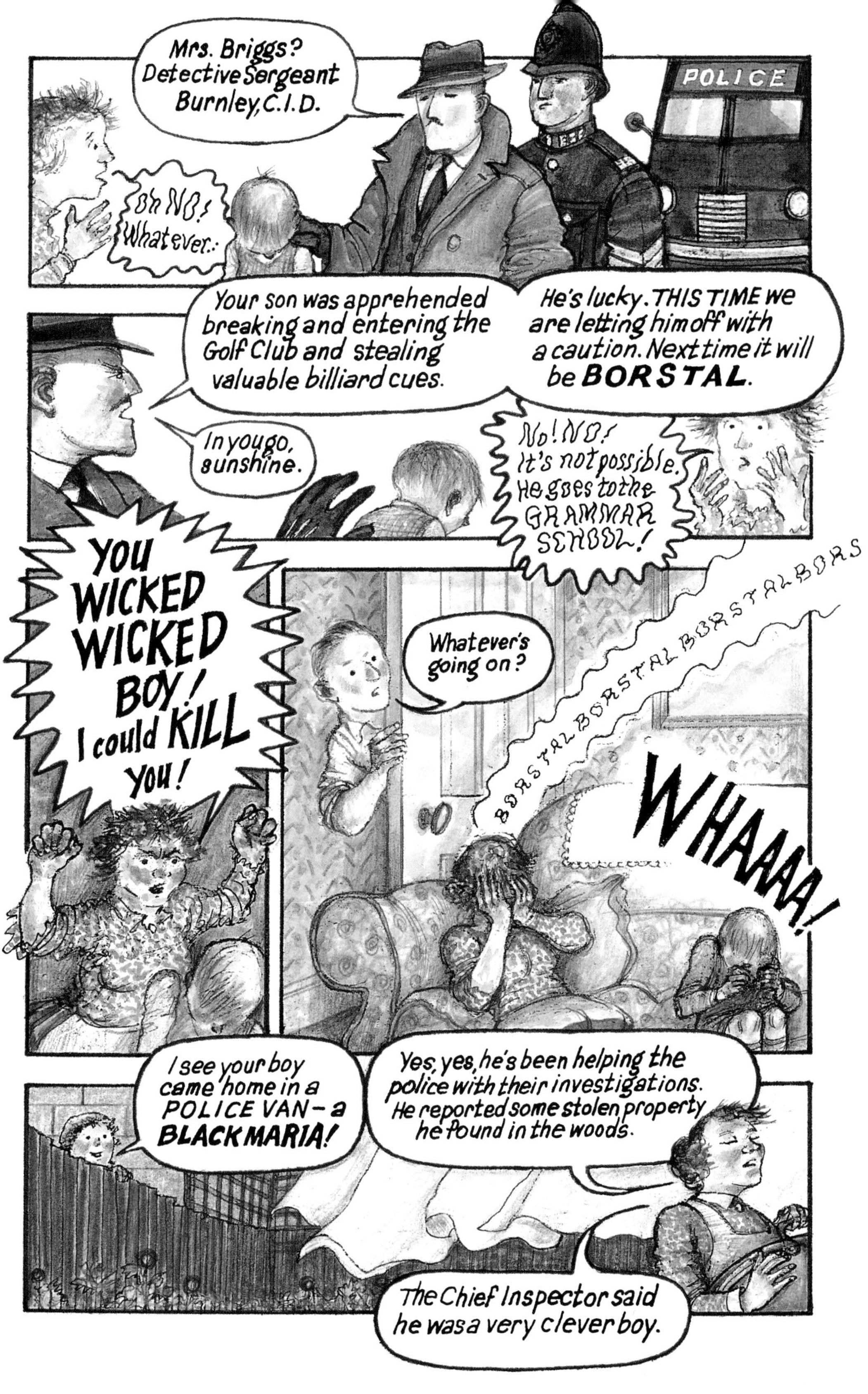
Mrs. Briggs? Detective Sergeant Burnley, C.I.D.
POLICE
Oh NO! Whatever.:
Your son was apprehended breaking and entering the Golf Club and stealing valuable billiard cues.
He's lucky. THIS TIME we are letting him off with a caution. Next time it will be BORSTAL.
In you go, sunshine.
No! NO! It's not possible. He goes to the GRAMMAR SCHOOL!
YOU WICKED WICKED BOY! I could KILL you!
Whatever's going on?
BORSTALBORSTALBORSTALBORSTALBORS
WHAAAA!
I see your boy came home in a POLICE VAN – a BLACK MARIA!
Yes, yes, he's been helping the police with their investigations. He reported some stolen property he found in the woods.
The Chief Inspector said he was a very clever boy.

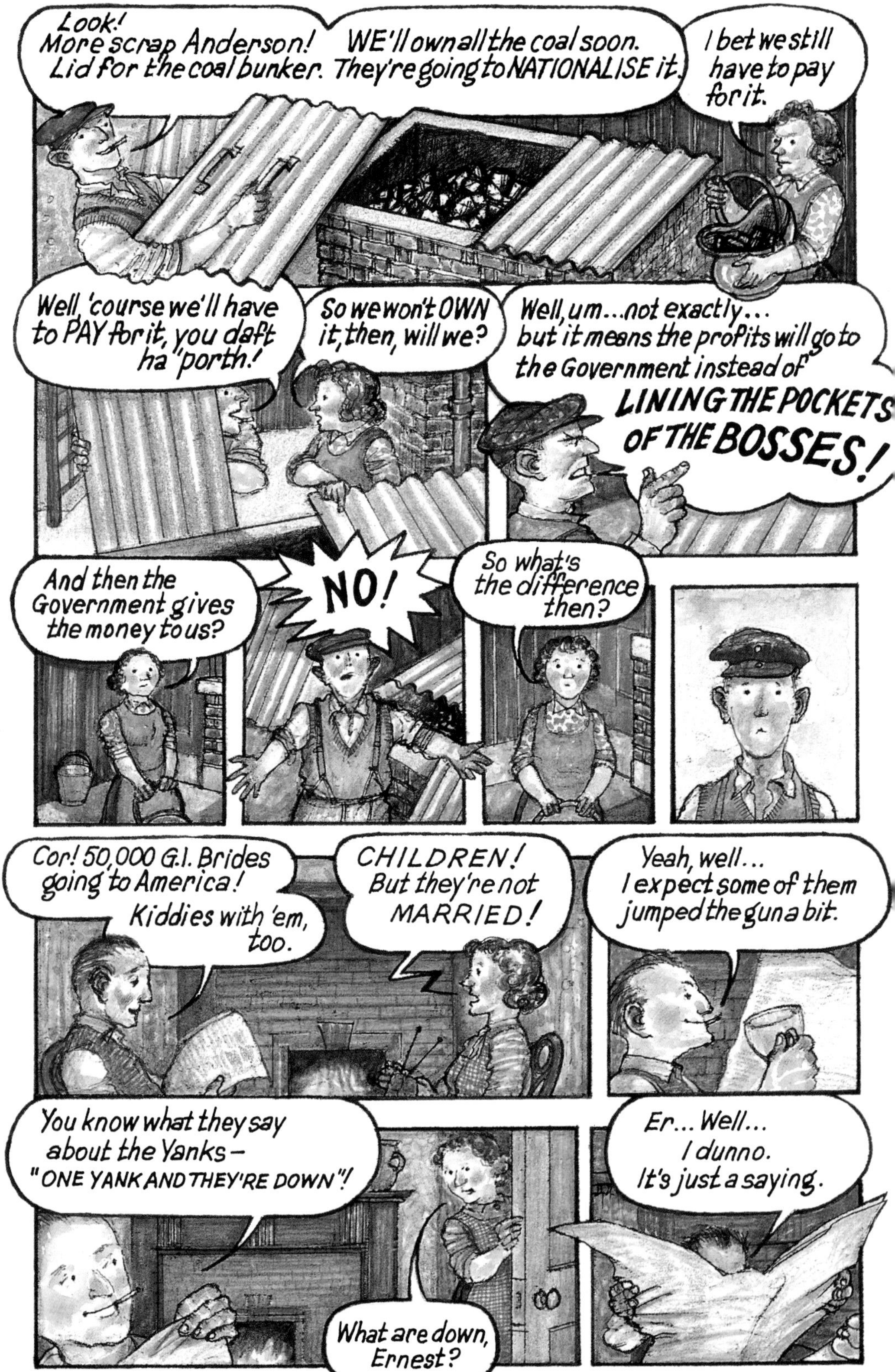
Look! More scrap Anderson! Lid for the coal bunker.
WE'll own all the coal soon. They're going to NATIONALISE it.
I bet we still have to pay for it.
Well, 'course we'll have to PAY for it, you daft ha'porth!
So we won't OWN it, then, will we?
Well, um... not exactly... but it means the profits will go to the Government instead of LINING THE POCKETS OF THE BOSSES!
And then the Government gives the money to us?
NO!
So what's the difference then?
Cor! 50,000 G.I. Brides going to America! Kiddies with 'em, too.
CHILDREN! But they're not MARRIED!
Yeah, well... I expect some of them jumped the gun a bit.
You know what they say about the Yanks – "ONE YANK AND THEY'RE DOWN"!
What are down, Ernest?
Er... Well... I dunno. It's just a saying.

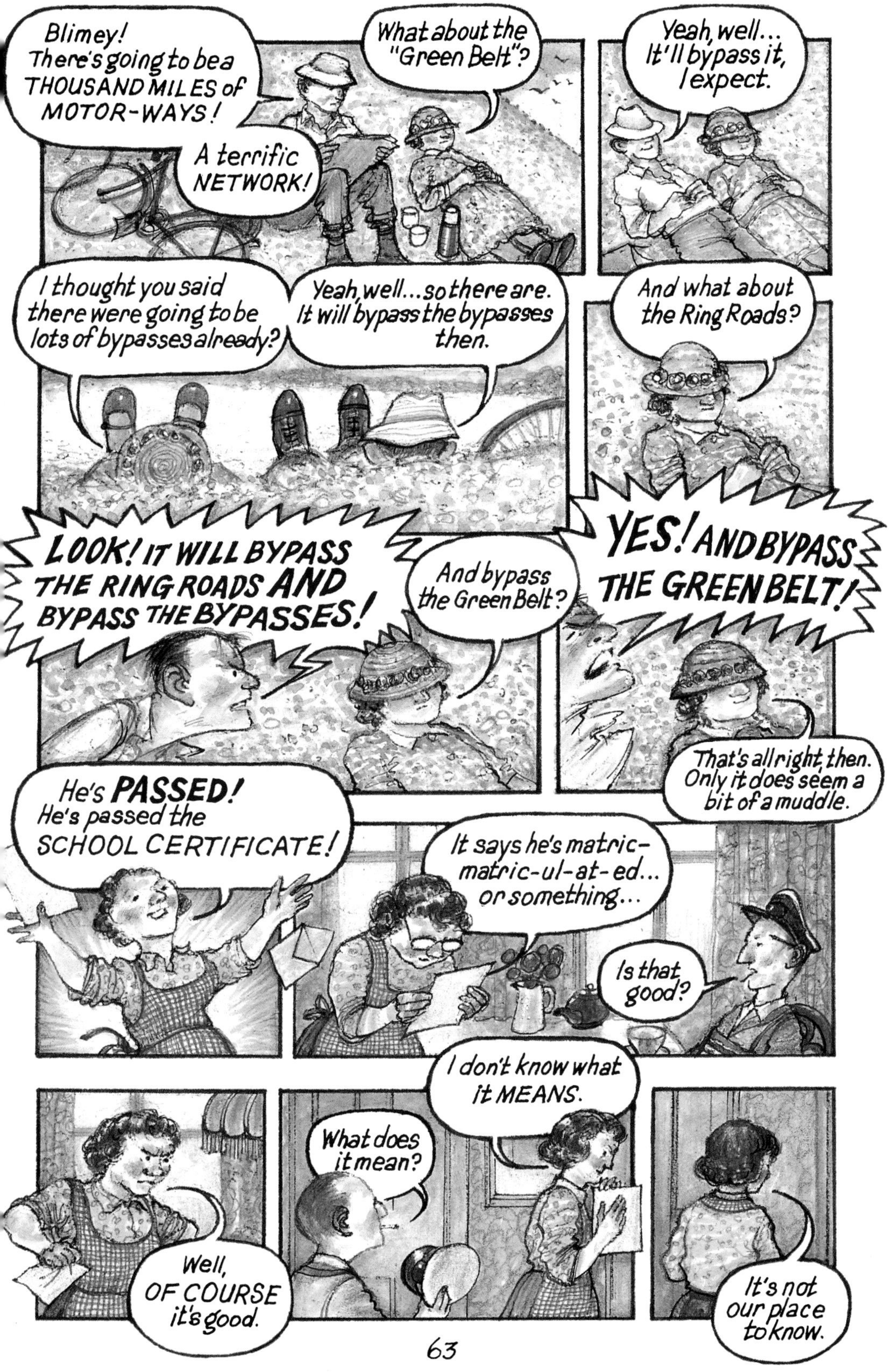
Blimey! There's going to be a THOUSAND MILES of MOTOR-WAYS!
A terrific NETWORK!
What about the "Green Belt"?
Yeah, well... It'll bypass it, I expect.
I thought you said there were going to be lots of bypasses already?
Yeah, well... so there are. It will bypass the bypasses then.
And what about the Ring Roads?
LOOK! IT WILL BYPASS THE RING ROADS AND BYPASS THE BYPASSES!
And bypass the Green Belt?
YES! AND BYPASS THE GREEN BELT!
That's all right, then. Only it does seem a bit of a muddle.
He's PASSED! He's passed the SCHOOL CERTIFICATE!
It says he's matric-matric-ul-at-ed... or something...
Is that good?
Well, OF COURSE it's good.
What does it mean?
I don't know what it MEANS.
It's not our place to know.

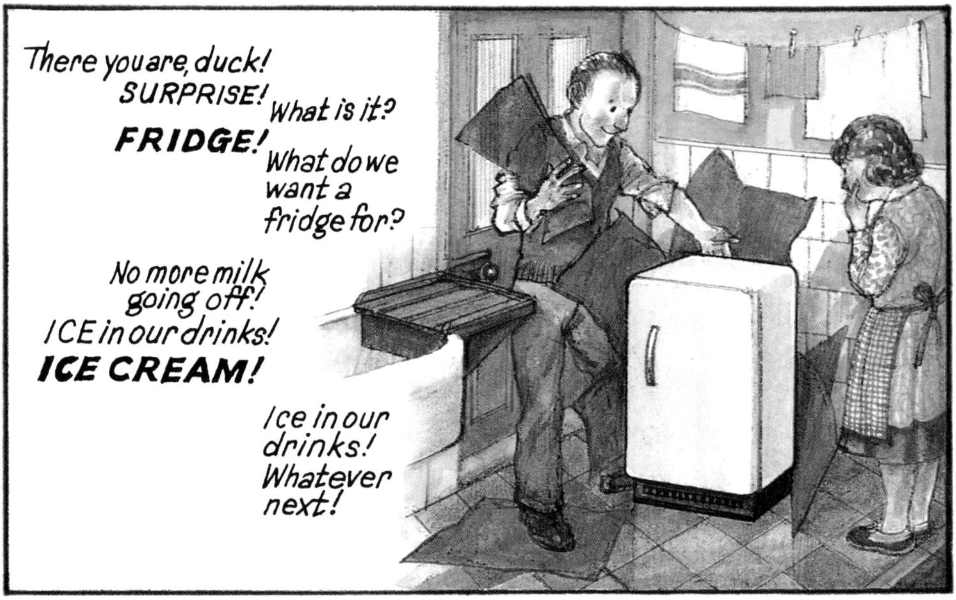
There you are, duck!
SURPRISE!
What is it?
FRIDGE!
What do we want a fridge for?
No more milk going off!
ICE in our drinks!
ICE CREAM!
Ice in our drinks! Whatever next!

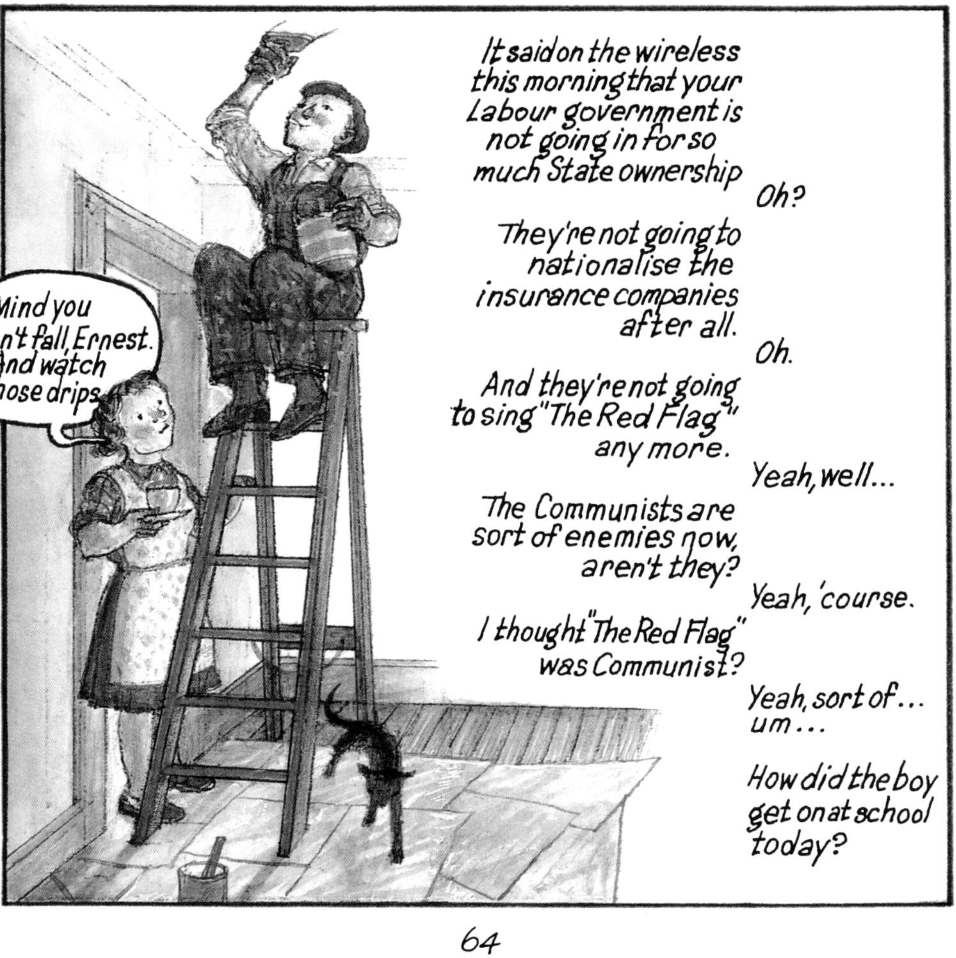
It said on the wireless this morning that your Labour government is not going in for so much State ownership
Oh?
They're not going to nationalise the insurance companies after all.
Oh.
And they're not going to sing "The Red Flag" any more.
Yeah, well...
The Communists are sort of enemies now, aren't they?
Yeah, 'course.
I thought "The Red Flag" was Communist?
Yeah, sort of... um...
How did the boy get on at school today?
Mind you don't fall, Ernest. And watch those drips.

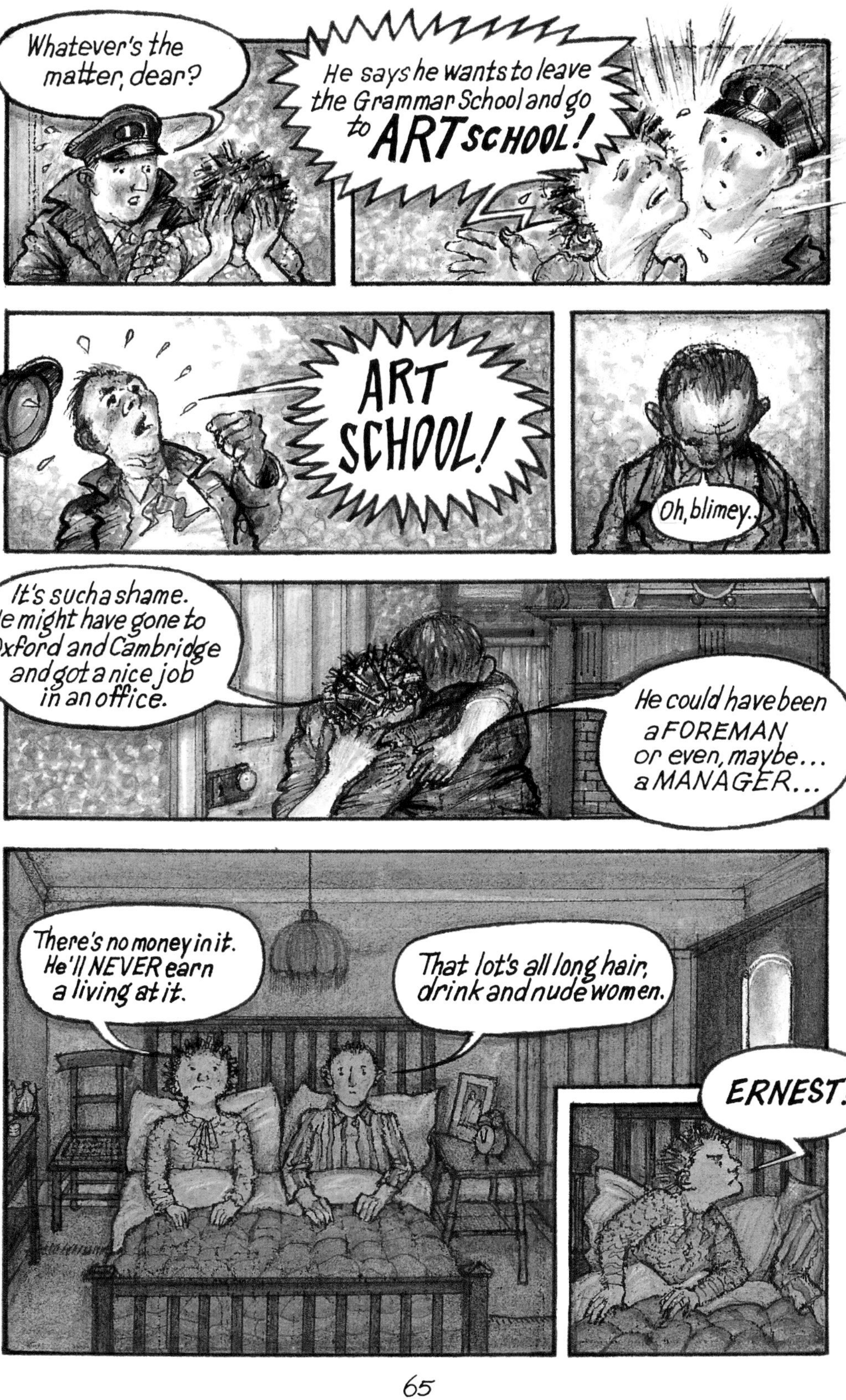
Whatever's the matter, dear?
He says he wants to leave the Grammar School and go to ART SCHOOL!
ART SCHOOL!
Oh, blimey..
It's such a shame. He might have gone to Oxford and Cambridge and got a nice job in an office.
He could have been a FOREMAN or even, maybe... a MANAGER...
There's no money in it. He'll NEVER earn a living at it.
That lot's all long hair, drink and nude women.
ERNEST!

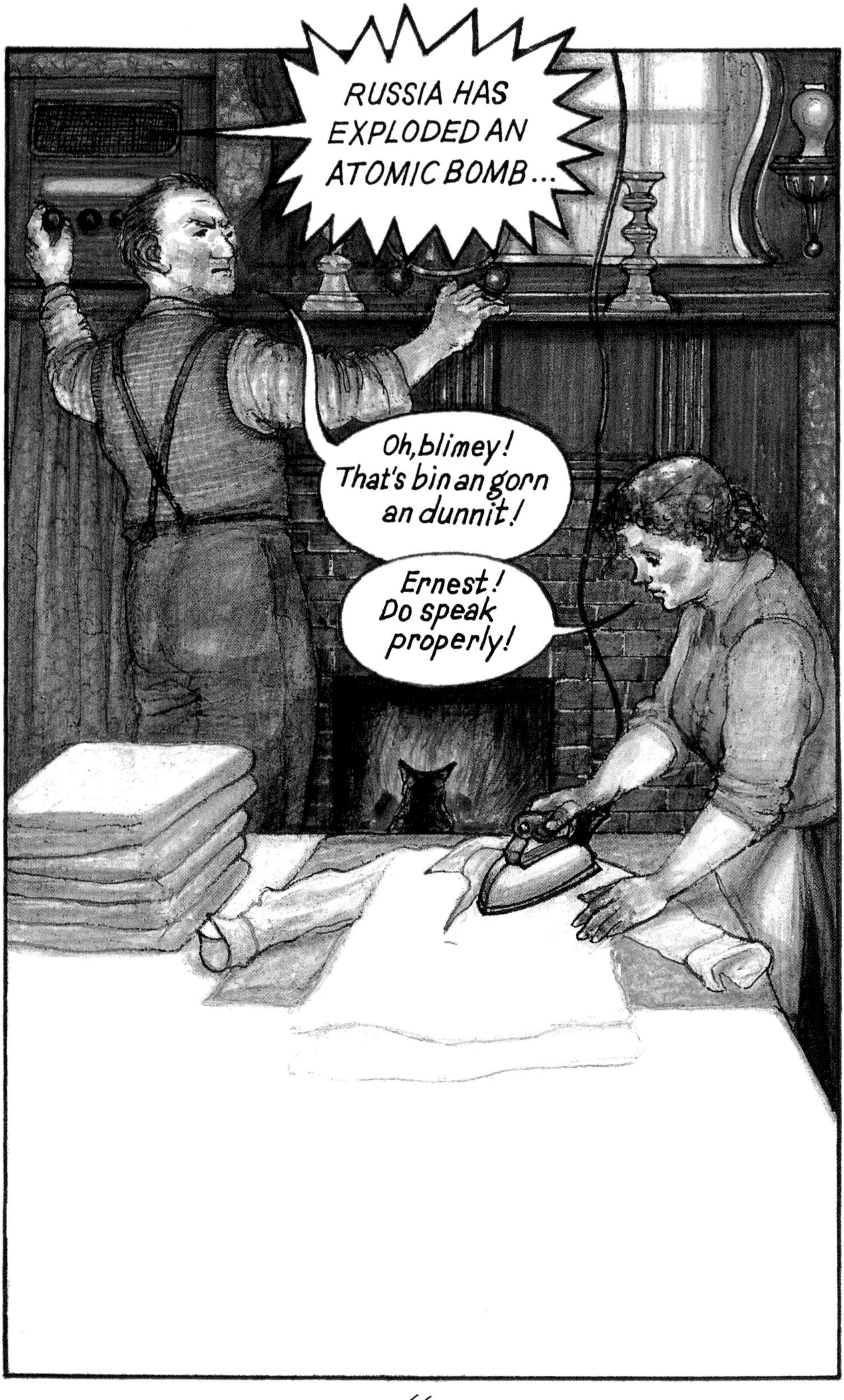
RUSSIA HAS EXPLODED AN ATOMIC BOMB...
Oh, blimey! That's bin an gorn an dunnit!
Ernest! Do speak properly!

1950
~
1960

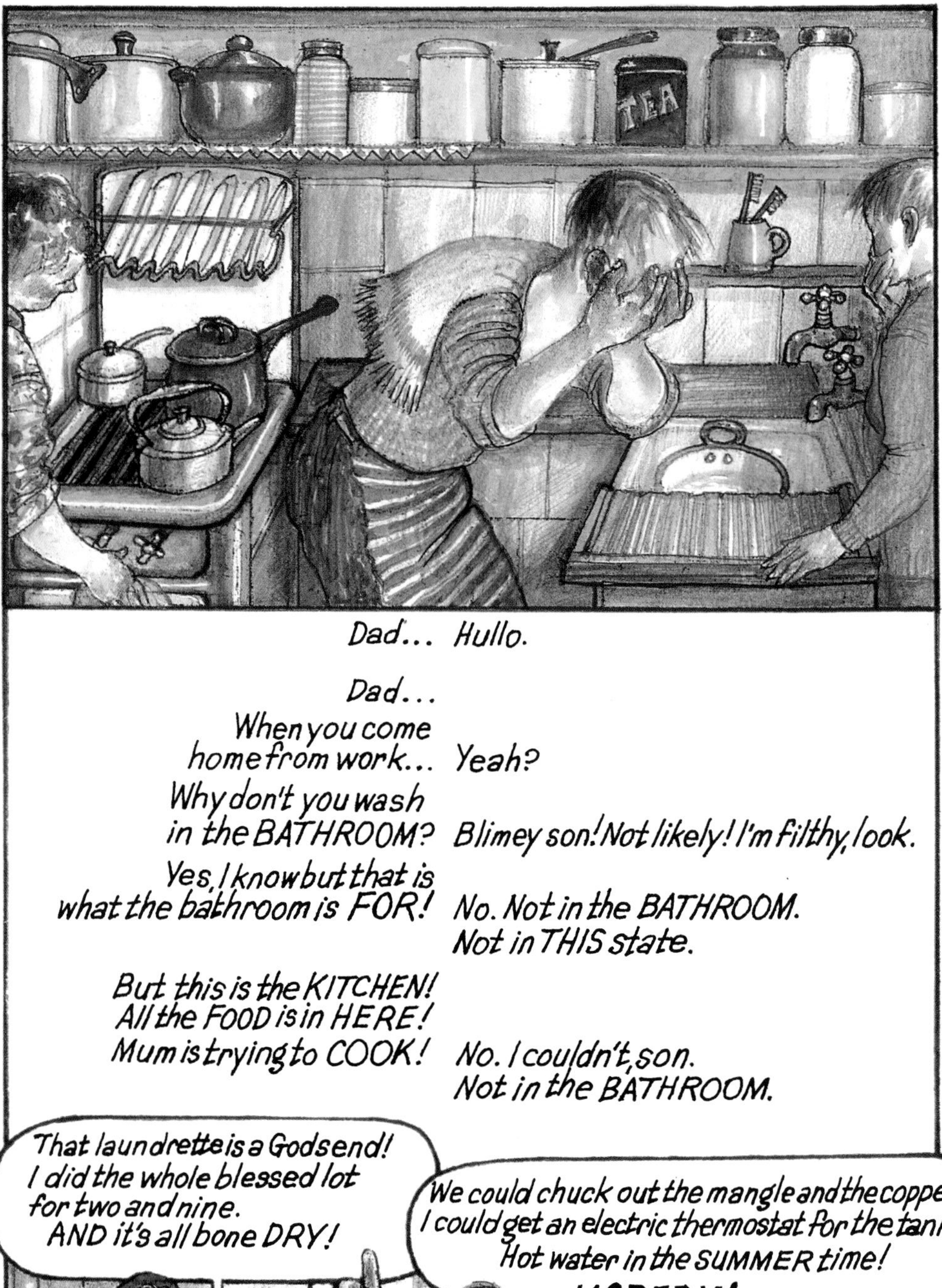
Dad... Hullo.
Dad...
When you come home from work... Yeah?
Why don't you wash in the BATHROOM? Blimey son! Not likely! I'm filthy, look.
Yes, I know but that is what the bathroom is FOR! No. Not in the BATHROOM. Not in THIS state.
But this is the KITCHEN! All the FOOD is in HERE! Mum is trying to COOK! No. I couldn't, son. Not in the BATHROOM.
That laundrette is a Godsend! I did the whole blessed lot for two and nine. AND it's all bone DRY!
We could chuck out the mangle and the copper. I could get an electric thermostat for the tank! Hot water in the SUMMER time!
MODERN!

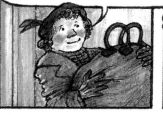

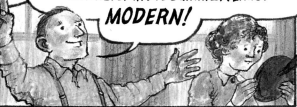

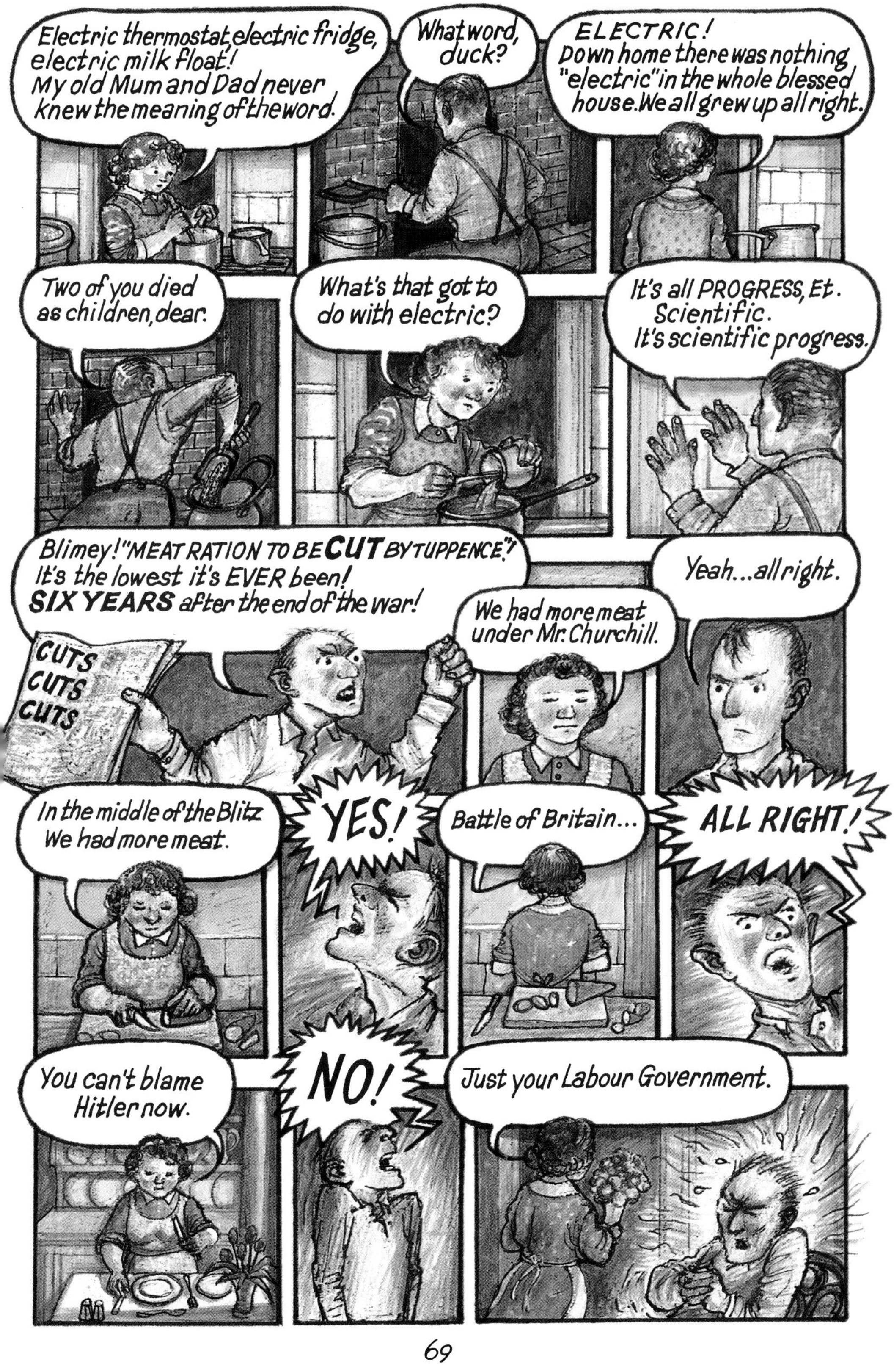
Electric thermostat, electric fridge, electric milk float! My old Mum and Dad never knew the meaning of the word.
What word, duck?
ELECTRIC! Down home there was nothing "electric" in the whole blessed house. We all grew up all right.
Two of you died as children, dear.
What's that got to do with electric?
It's all PROGRESS, Et. Scientific. It's scientific progress.
Blimey! "MEAT RATION TO BE CUT BY TUPPENCE"! It's the lowest it's EVER been! SIX YEARS after the end of the war!
CUTS CUTS CUTS
We had more meat under Mr. Churchill.
Yeah... all right.
In the middle of the Blitz we had more meat.
YES!
Battle of Britain...
ALL RIGHT!
You can't blame Hitler now.
NO!
Just your Labour Government.

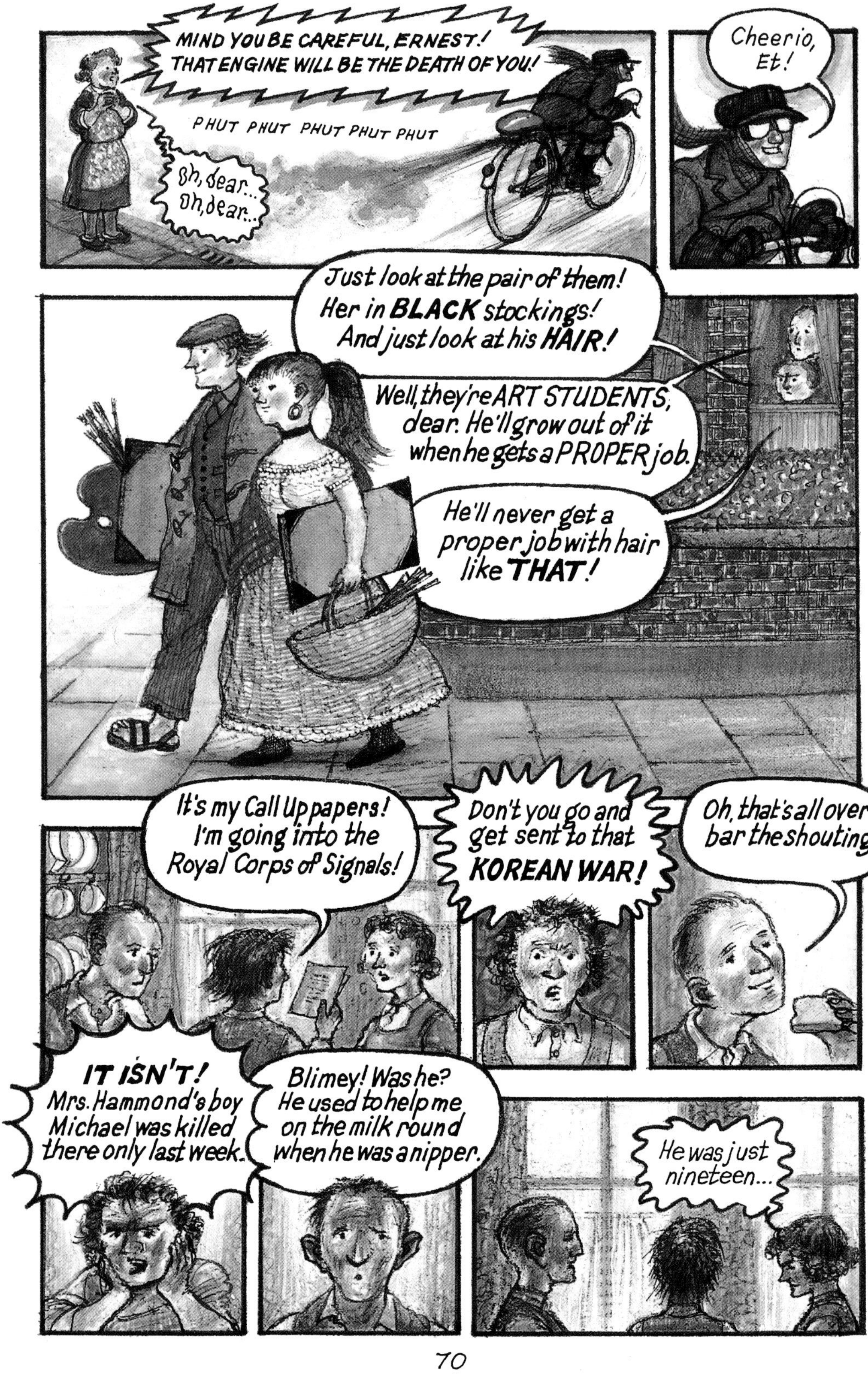
MIND YOU BE CAREFUL, ERNEST! THAT ENGINE WILL BE THE DEATH OF YOU!
PHUT PHUT PHUT PHUT PHUT
Oh, dear... Oh, dear...
Cheerio, Et!
Just look at the pair of them! Her in BLACK stockings! And just look at his HAIR!
Well, they're ART STUDENTS, dear. He'll grow out of it when he gets a PROPER job.
He'll never get a proper job with hair like THAT!
It's my Call Up papers! I'm going into the Royal Corps of Signals!
Don't you go and get sent to that KOREAN WAR!
Oh, that's all over bar the shouting.
IT ISN'T! Mrs. Hammond's boy Michael was killed there only last week.
Blimey! Was he? He used to help me on the milk round when he was a nipper.
He was just nineteen...

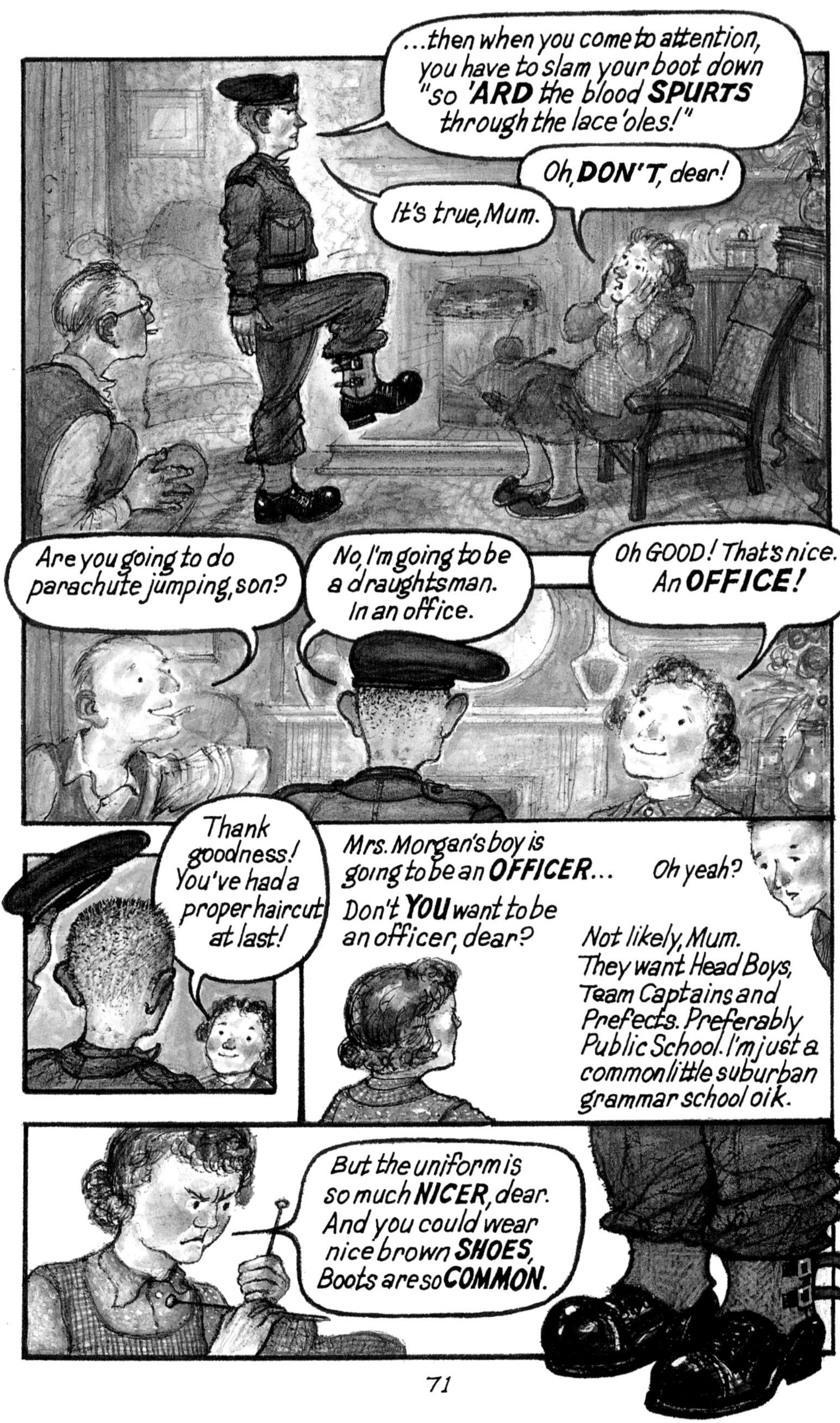
...then when you come to attention, you have to slam your boot down "so 'ARD the blood SPURTS through the lace'oles!"
Oh, DON'T, dear!
It's true, Mum.
Are you going to do parachute jumping, son?
No, I'm going to be a draughtsman. In an office.
Oh GOOD! That's nice. An OFFICE!
Thank goodness! You've had a proper haircut at last!
Mrs. Morgan's boy is going to be an OFFICER...
Oh yeah?
Don't YOU want to be an officer, dear?
Not likely, Mum. They want Head Boys, Team Captains and Prefects. Preferably Public School. I'm just a common little suburban grammar school oik.
But the uniform is so much NICER, dear. And you could wear nice brown SHOES, Boots are so COMMON.

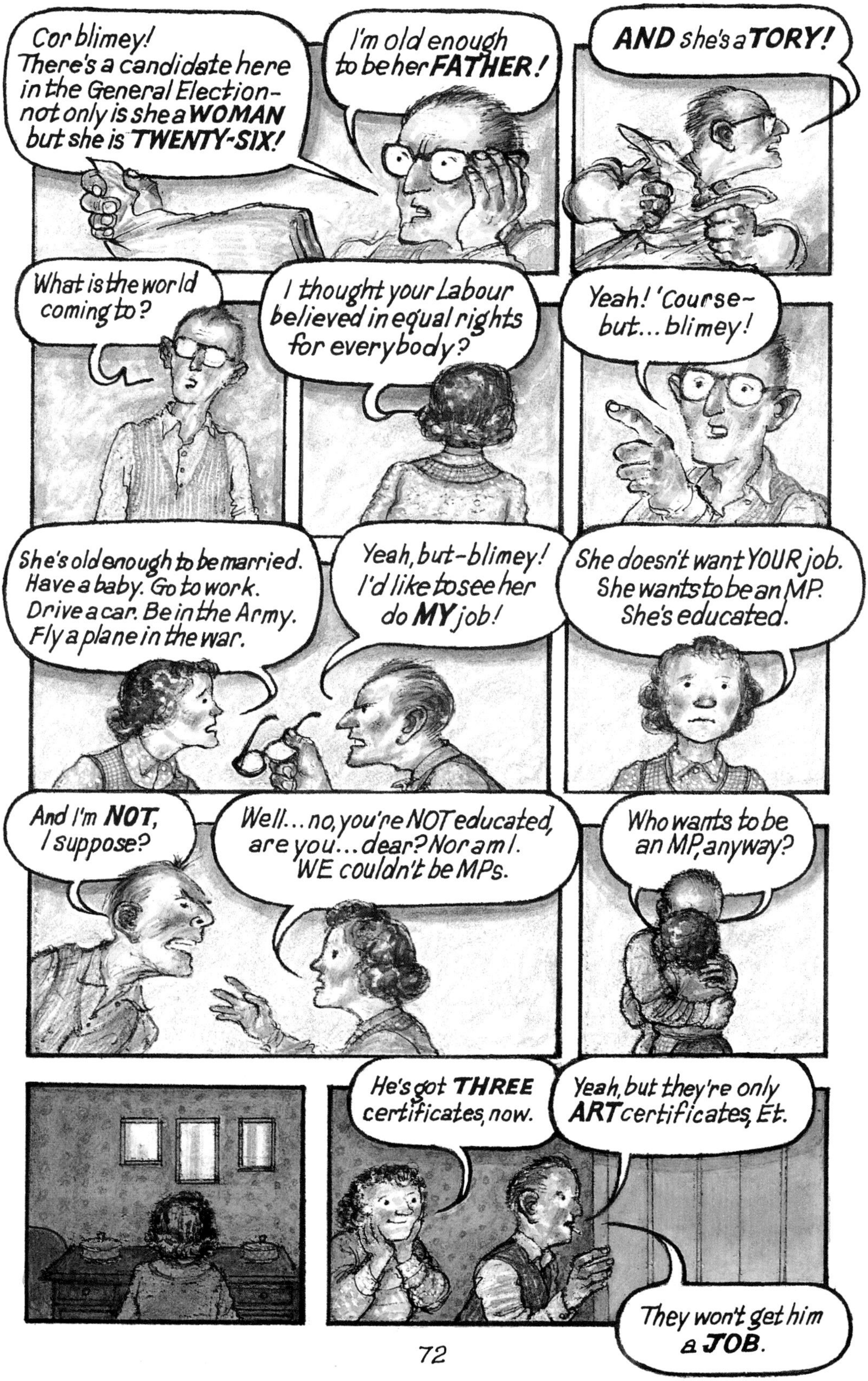
Cor blimey! There's a candidate here in the General Election - not only is she a WOMAN but she is TWENTY-SIX!
I'm old enough to be her FATHER!
AND she's a TORY!
What is the world coming to?
I thought your Labour believed in equal rights for everybody?
Yeah! 'Course - but... blimey!
She's old enough to be married. Have a baby. Go to work. Drive a car. Be in the Army. Fly a plane in the war.
Yeah, but - blimey! I'd like to see her do MY job!
She doesn't want YOUR job. She wants to be an MP. She's educated.
And I'm NOT, I suppose?
Well... no, you're NOT educated, are you... dear? Nor am I. WE couldn't be MPs.
Who wants to be an MP, anyway?
He's got THREE certificates, now.
Yeah, but they're only ART certificates, Et.
They won't get him a JOB.

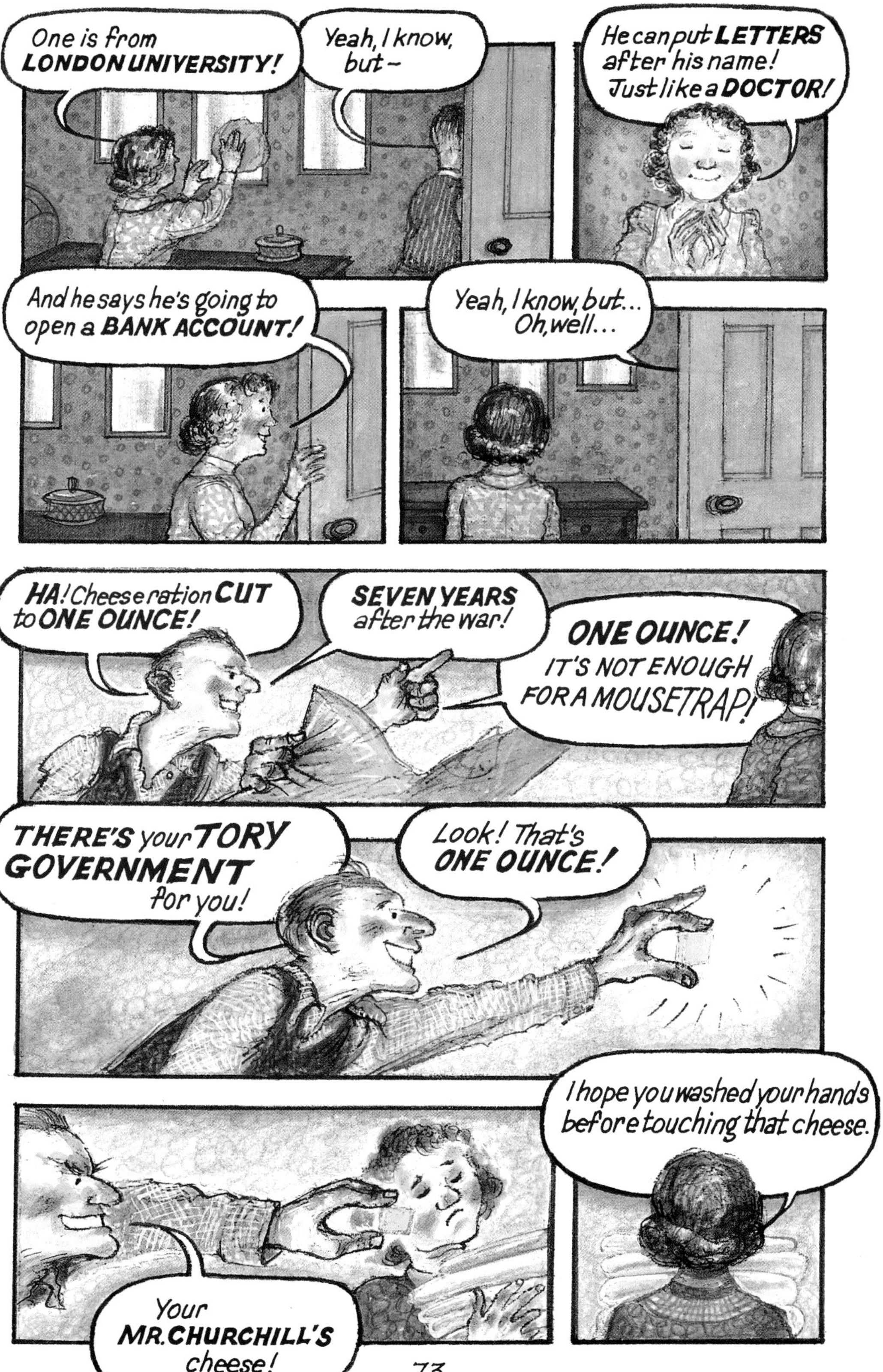
One is from **LONDON UNIVERSITY!**
Yeah, I know, but –
He can put **LETTERS** after his name! Just like a **DOCTOR!**
And he says he's going to open a **BANK ACCOUNT!**
Yeah, I know, but... Oh, well...
HA! Cheese ration **CUT** to **ONE OUNCE!**
SEVEN YEARS after the war!
ONE OUNCE! IT'S NOT ENOUGH FOR A MOUSETRAP!
THERE'S your **TORY GOVERNMENT** for you!
Look! That's **ONE OUNCE!**
Your **MR. CHURCHILL'S** cheese!
I hope you washed your hands before touching that cheese.

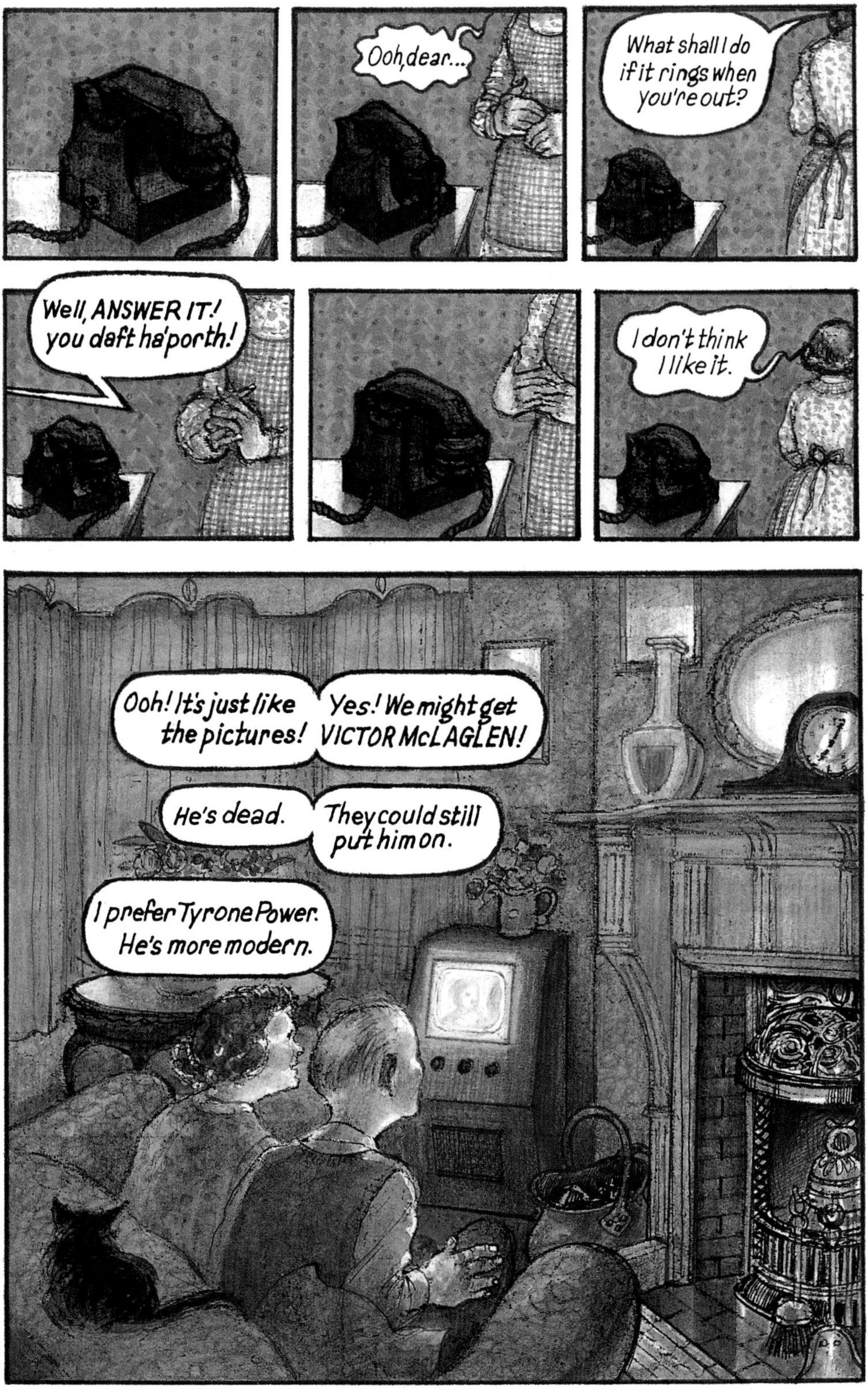
Ooh, dear...
What shall I do if it rings when you're out?
Well, ANSWER IT! you daft ha'porth!
I don't think I like it.
Ooh! It's just like the pictures!
Yes! We might get VICTOR McLAGLEN!
He's dead.
They could still put him on.
I prefer Tyrone Power. He's more modern.

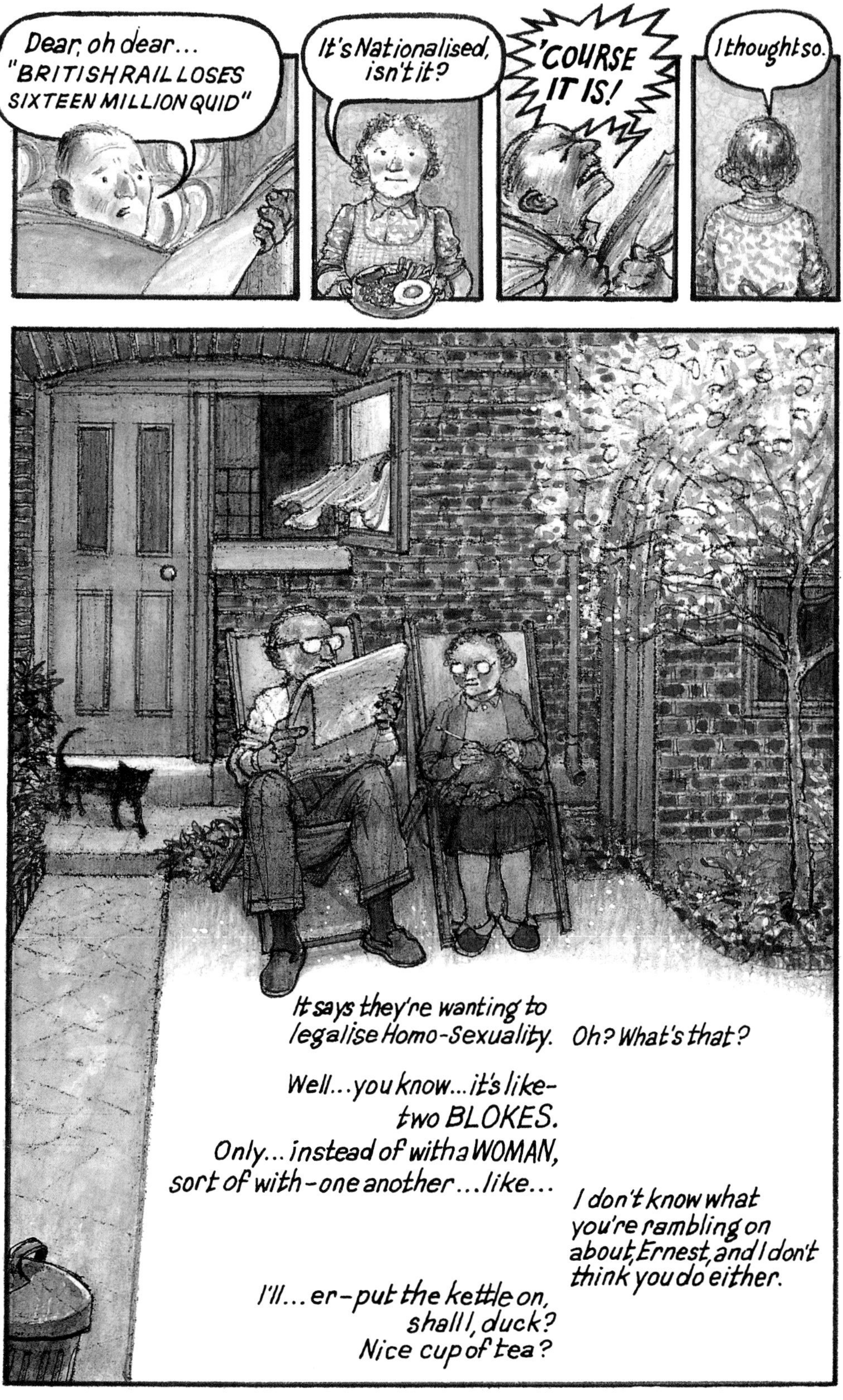
Dear, oh dear... "BRITISH RAIL LOSES SIXTEEN MILLION QUID"
It's Nationalised, isn't it?
'COURSE IT IS!
I thought so.
It says they're wanting to legalise Homo-Sexuality.
Oh? What's that?
Well... you know... it's like- two BLOKES.
Only... instead of with a WOMAN, sort of with - one another... like...
I don't know what you're rambling on about, Ernest, and I don't think you do either.
I'll... er - put the kettle on, shall I, duck? Nice cup of tea?

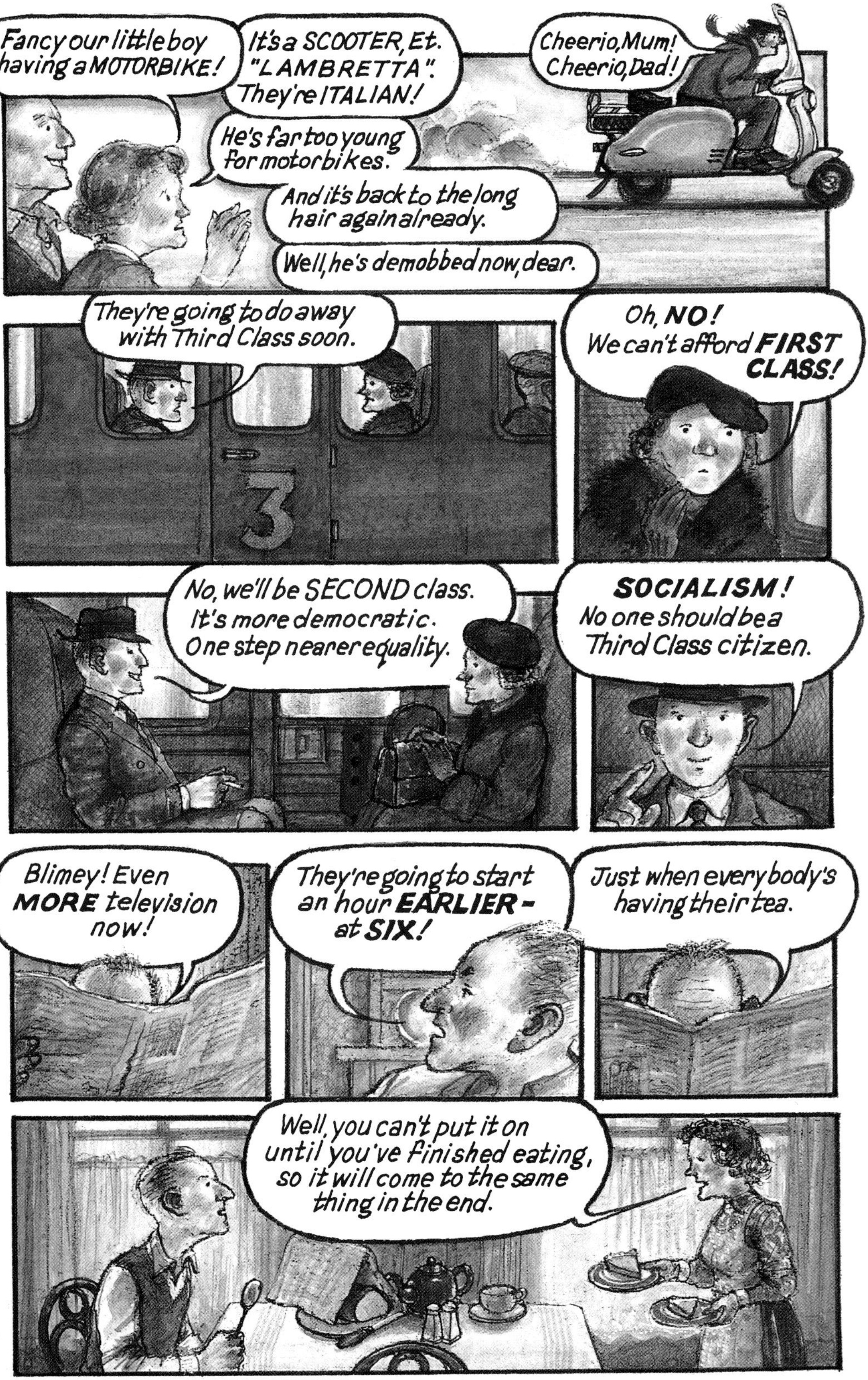
Fancy our little boy having a MOTORBIKE!
It's a SCOOTER, Et. "LAMBRETTA". They're ITALIAN!
Cheerio, Mum! Cheerio, Dad!
He's far too young for motorbikes.
And it's back to the long hair again already.
Well, he's demobbed now, dear.
They're going to do away with Third Class soon.
Oh, NO! We can't afford FIRST CLASS!
3
No, we'll be SECOND class. It's more democratic. One step nearer equality.
SOCIALISM! No one should be a Third Class citizen.
Blimey! Even MORE television now!
They're going to start an hour EARLIER - at SIX!
Just when everybody's having their tea.
Well, you can't put it on until you've finished eating, so it will come to the same thing in the end.

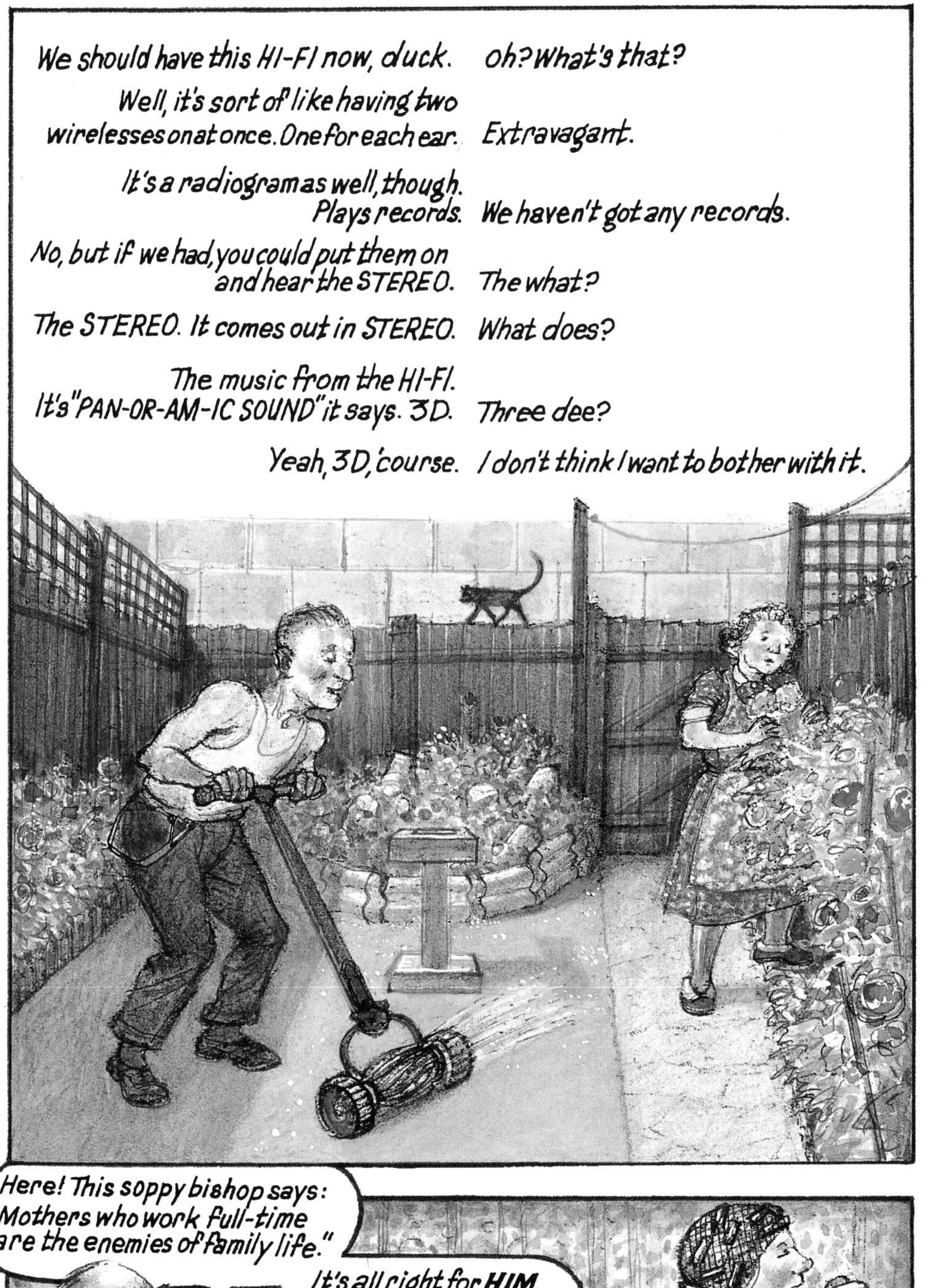
We should have this HI-FI now, duck.
Oh? What's that?
Well, it's sort of like having two wirelesses on at once. One for each ear.
Extravagant.
It's a radiogram as well, though. Plays records.
We haven't got any records.
No, but if we had, you could put them on and hear the STEREO.
The what?
The STEREO. It comes out in STEREO.
What does?
The music from the HI-FI. It's "PAN-OR-AM-IC SOUND" it says. 3D.
Three dee?
Yeah, 3D, 'course.
I don't think I want to bother with it.
Here! This soppy bishop says: "Mothers who work full-time are the enemies of family life."
It's all right for HIM, living in a PALACE with SERVANTS!
He was brought up to different standards, Ernest. He's a GENTLEMAN Christian.

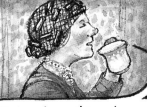

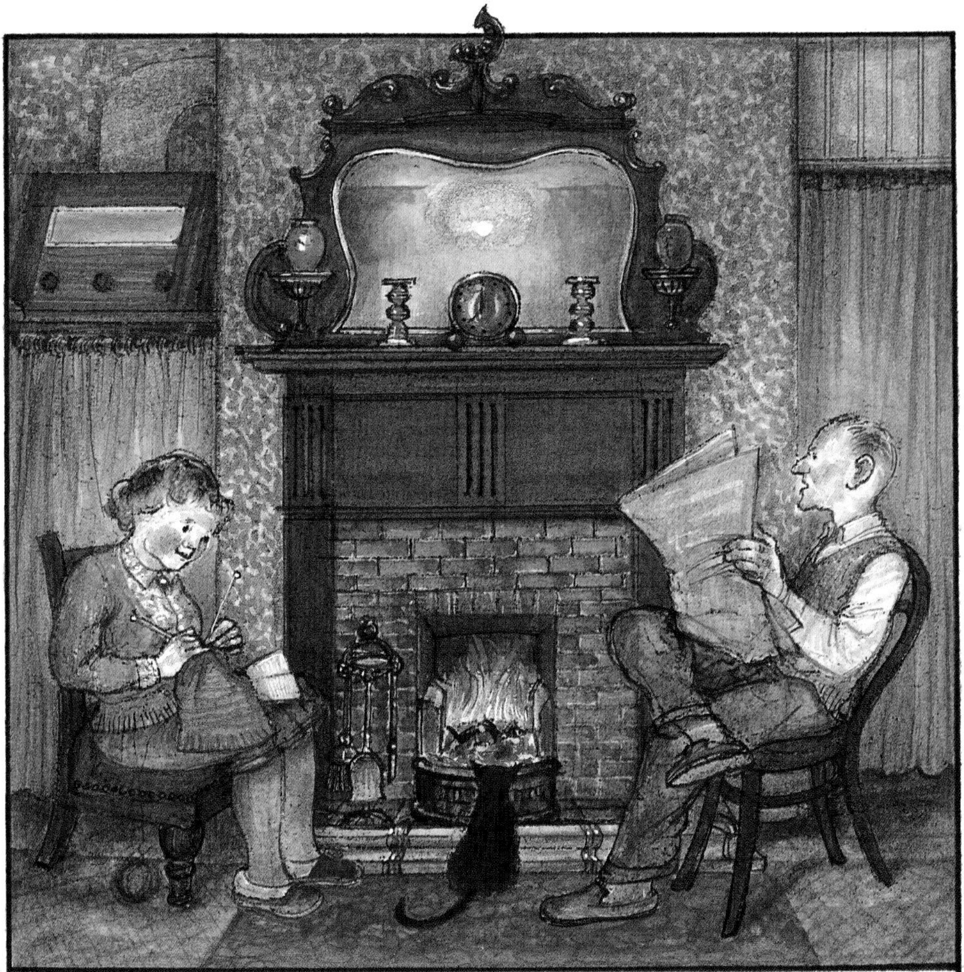

Here Et, listen. It says we've got to be **HIP**.

What?

GROOVY, babe. And **REAL COOL**.

Just talk sense, Ernest.

We've got to **HANG LOOSE** with the **CATS**.

Cats?

YEAH, MAN!

Ernest! Go to bed.
You're overtired.
I'll make the cocoa.

You're a **SQUARE**, baby.

Oh, Ernest...
When will you grow up?

1960
~
1970

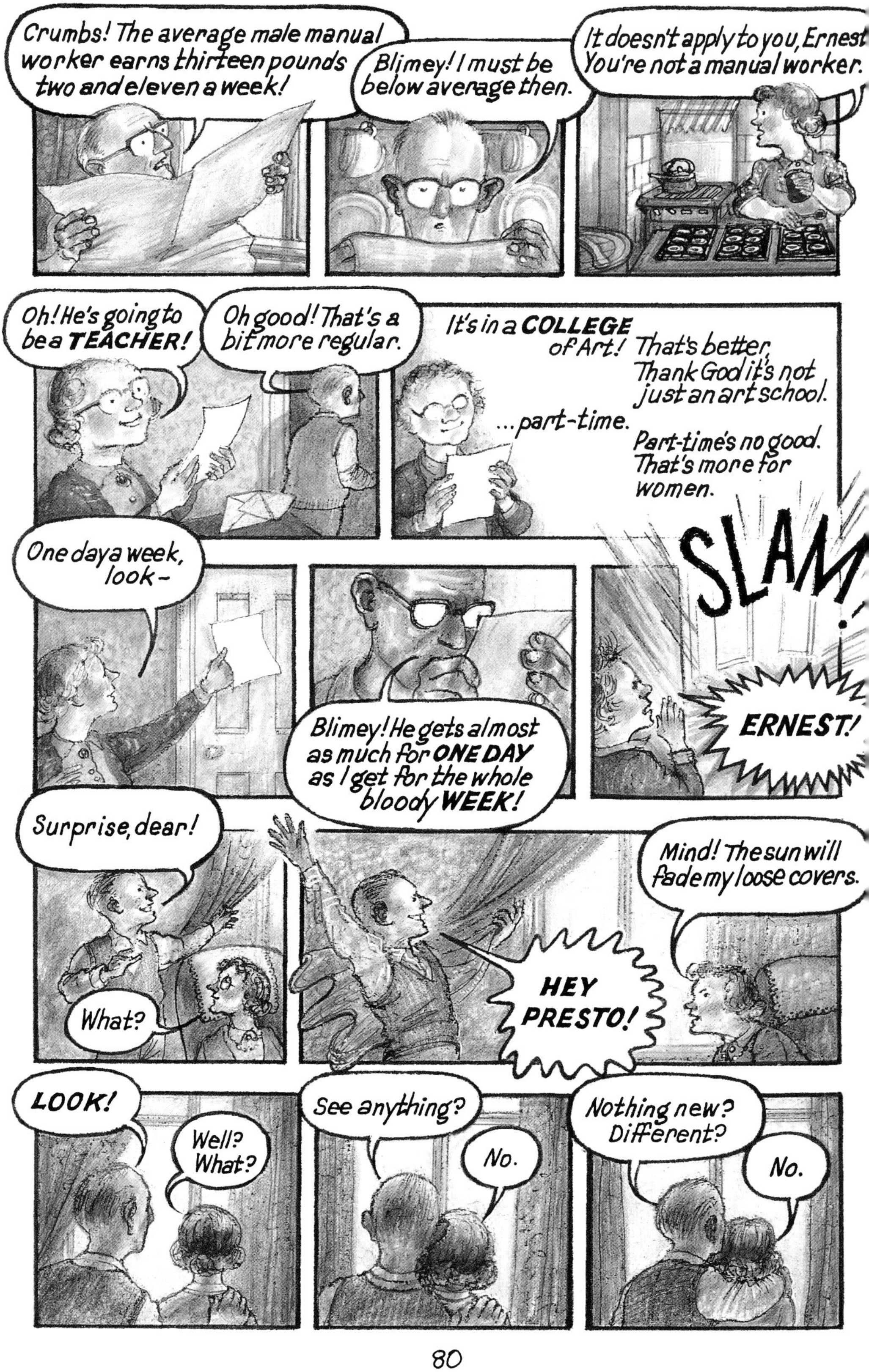

Crumbs! The average male manual worker earns thirteen pounds two and eleven a week!
Blimey! I must be below average then.
It doesn't apply to you, Ernest. You're not a manual worker.
Oh! He's going to be a TEACHER!
Oh good! That's a bit more regular.
It's in a COLLEGE of Art!
That's better. Thank God it's not just an art school.
...part-time.
Part-time's no good. That's more for women.
SLAM!
One day a week, look –
Blimey! He gets almost as much for ONE DAY as I get for the whole bloody WEEK!
ERNEST!
Surprise, dear!
What?
HEY PRESTO!
Mind! The sun will fade my loose covers.
LOOK!
Well? What?
See anything?
No.
Nothing new? Different?
No.

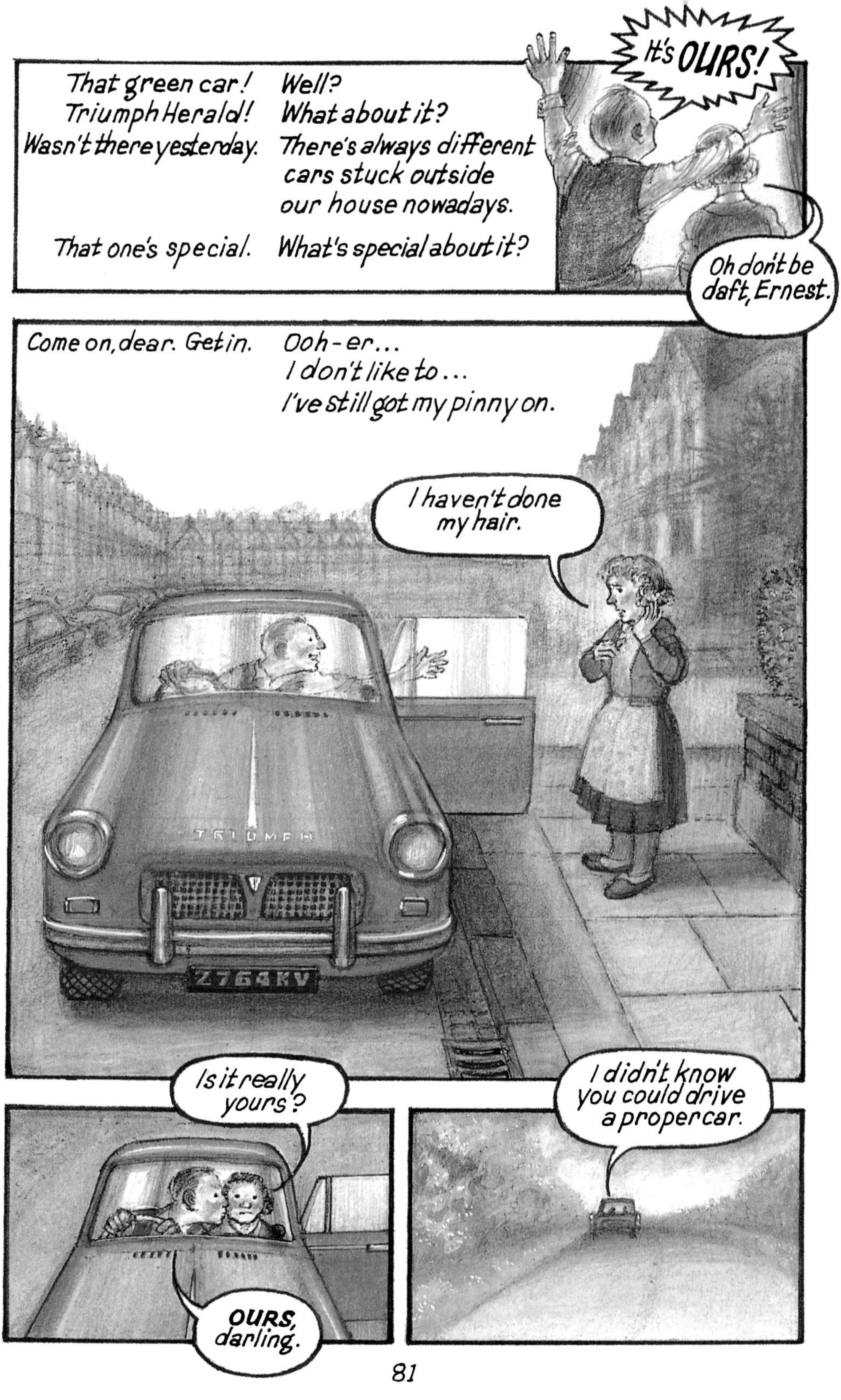

That green car! Triumph Herald! Wasn't there yesterday.
Well? What about it? There's always different cars stuck outside our house nowadays.
That one's special.
What's special about it?
It's OURS!
Oh don't be daft, Ernest.
Come on, dear. Get in.
Ooh-er... I don't like to... I've still got my pinny on.
I haven't done my hair.
TRIUMPH
Z 764 KV
Is it really yours?
OURS, darling.
I didn't know you could drive a proper car.

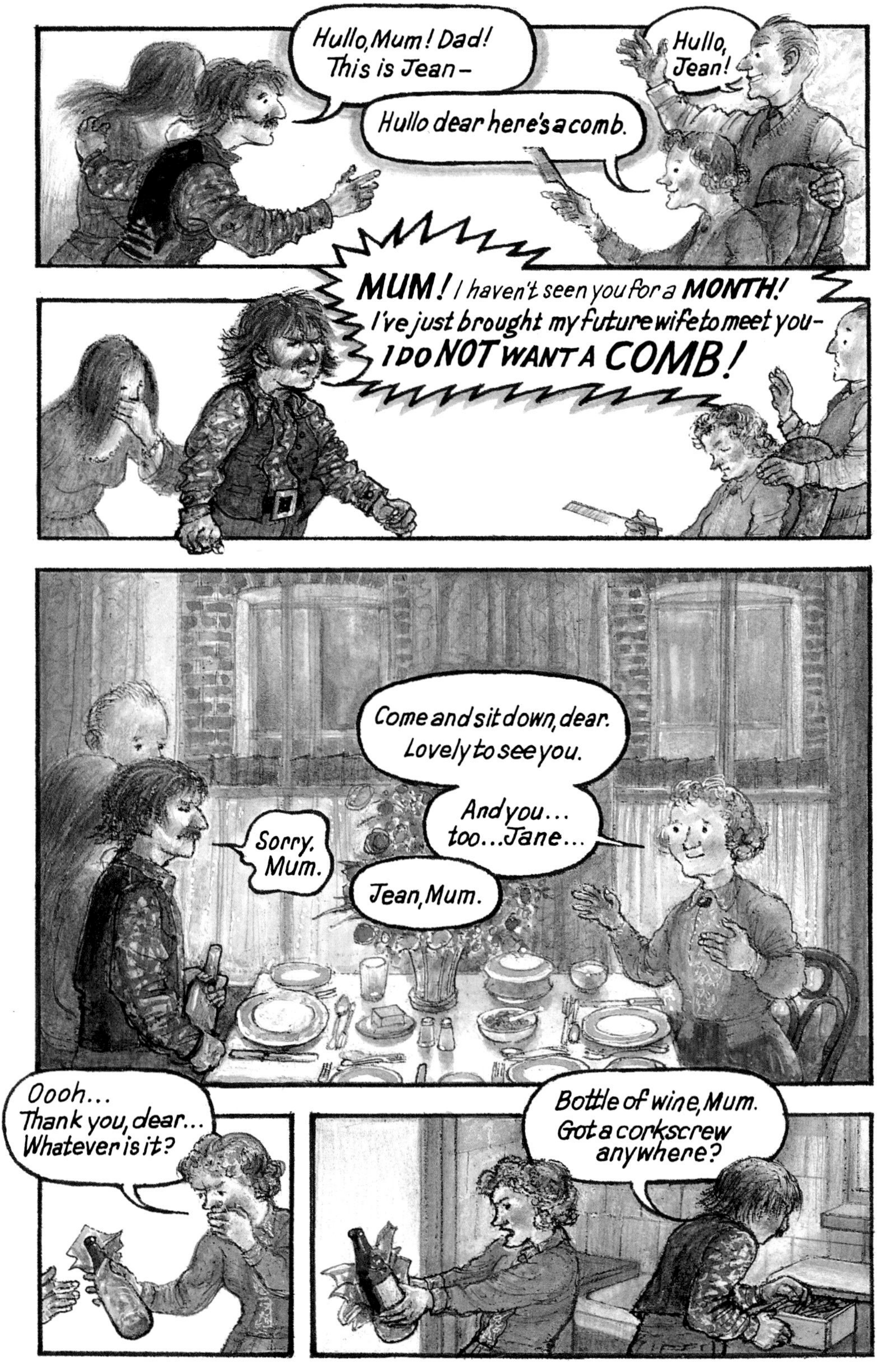

Hullo, Mum! Dad! This is Jean –
Hullo, Jean!
Hullo dear here's a comb.
MUM! I haven't seen you for a MONTH! I've just brought my future wife to meet you – I DO NOT WANT A COMB!
Come and sit down, dear. Lovely to see you.
And you... too... Jane...
Sorry, Mum.
Jean, Mum.
Oooh... Thank you, dear... Whatever is it?
Bottle of wine, Mum. Got a corkscrew anywhere?

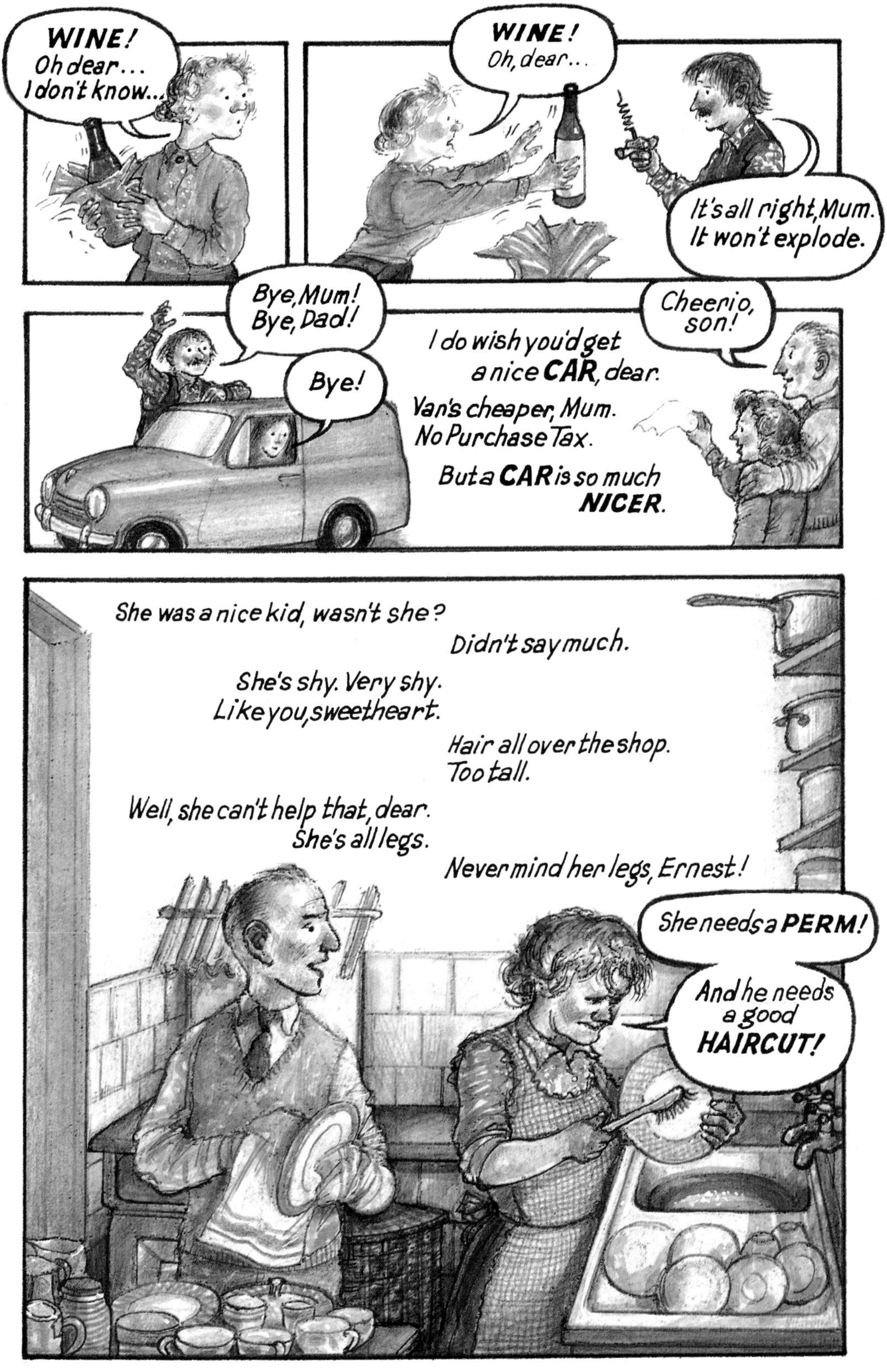
WINE! Oh dear... I don't know...
WINE! Oh, dear...
It's all right, Mum. It won't explode.
Bye, Mum! Bye, Dad!
Bye!
Cheerio, son!
I do wish you'd get a nice CAR, dear.
Van's cheaper, Mum. No Purchase Tax.
But a CAR is so much NICER.
She was a nice kid, wasn't she?
Didn't say much.
She's shy. Very shy. Like you, sweetheart.
Hair all over the shop. Too tall.
Well, she can't help that, dear. She's all legs.
Never mind her legs, Ernest!
She needs a PERM!
And he needs a good HAIRCUT!

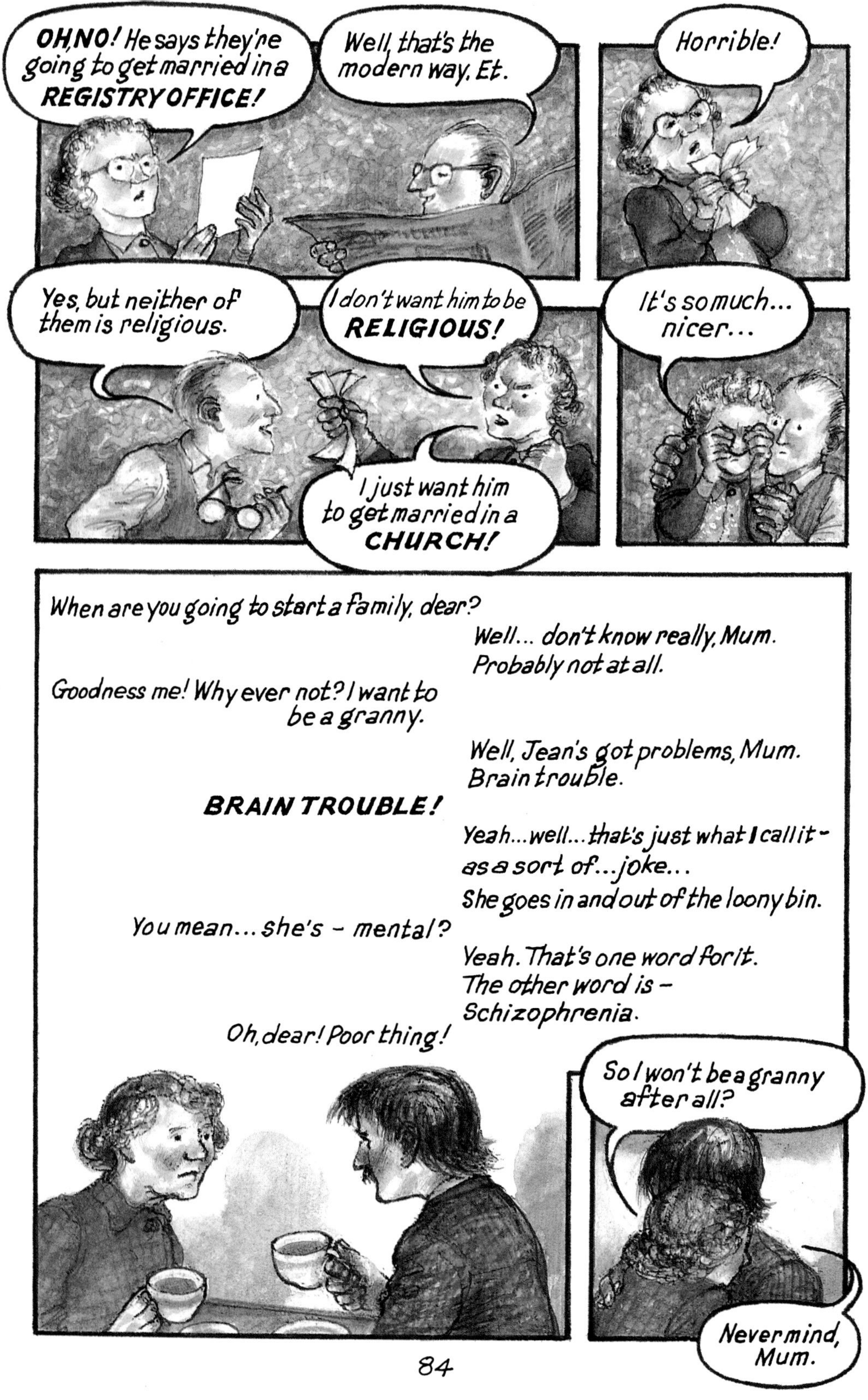

OH, NO! He says they're going to get married in a REGISTRY OFFICE!
Well, that's the modern way, Et.
Horrible!
Yes, but neither of them is religious.
I don't want him to be RELIGIOUS!
I just want him to get married in a CHURCH!
It's so much... nicer...
When are you going to start a family, dear?
Well... don't know really, Mum. Probably not at all.
Goodness me! Why ever not? I want to be a granny.
Well, Jean's got problems, Mum. Brain trouble.
BRAIN TROUBLE!
Yeah...well...that's just what I call it - as a sort of...joke...
She goes in and out of the loony bin.
You mean... she's - mental?
Yeah. That's one word for it. The other word is - Schizophrenia.
Oh, dear! Poor thing!
So I won't be a granny after all?
Never mind, Mum.

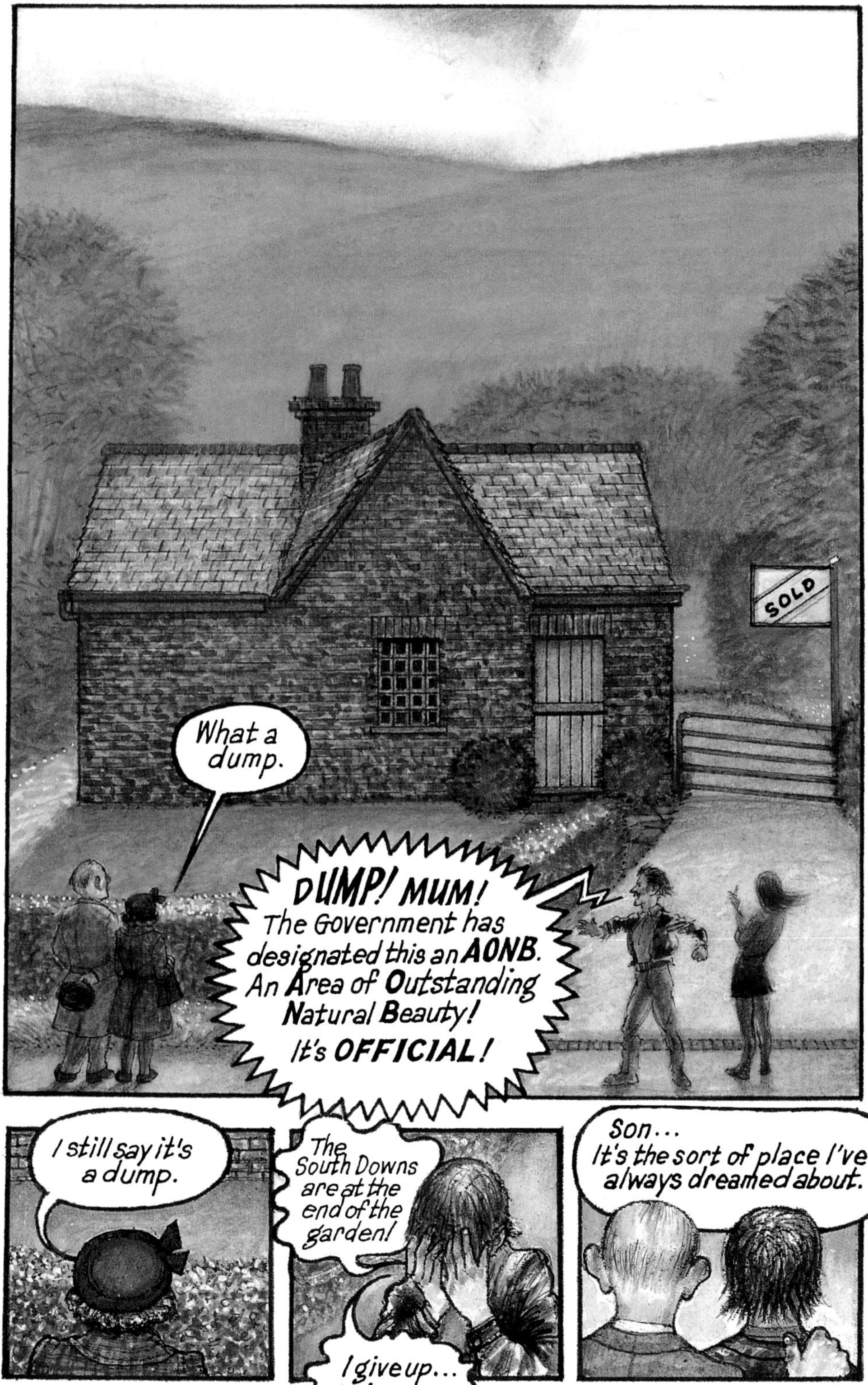
What a dump.
SOLD
DUMP! MUM! The Government has designated this an AONB. An Area of Outstanding Natural Beauty! It's OFFICIAL!
I still say it's a dump.
The South Downs are at the end of the garden!
I give up... I give up...
Son... It's the sort of place I've always dreamed about.

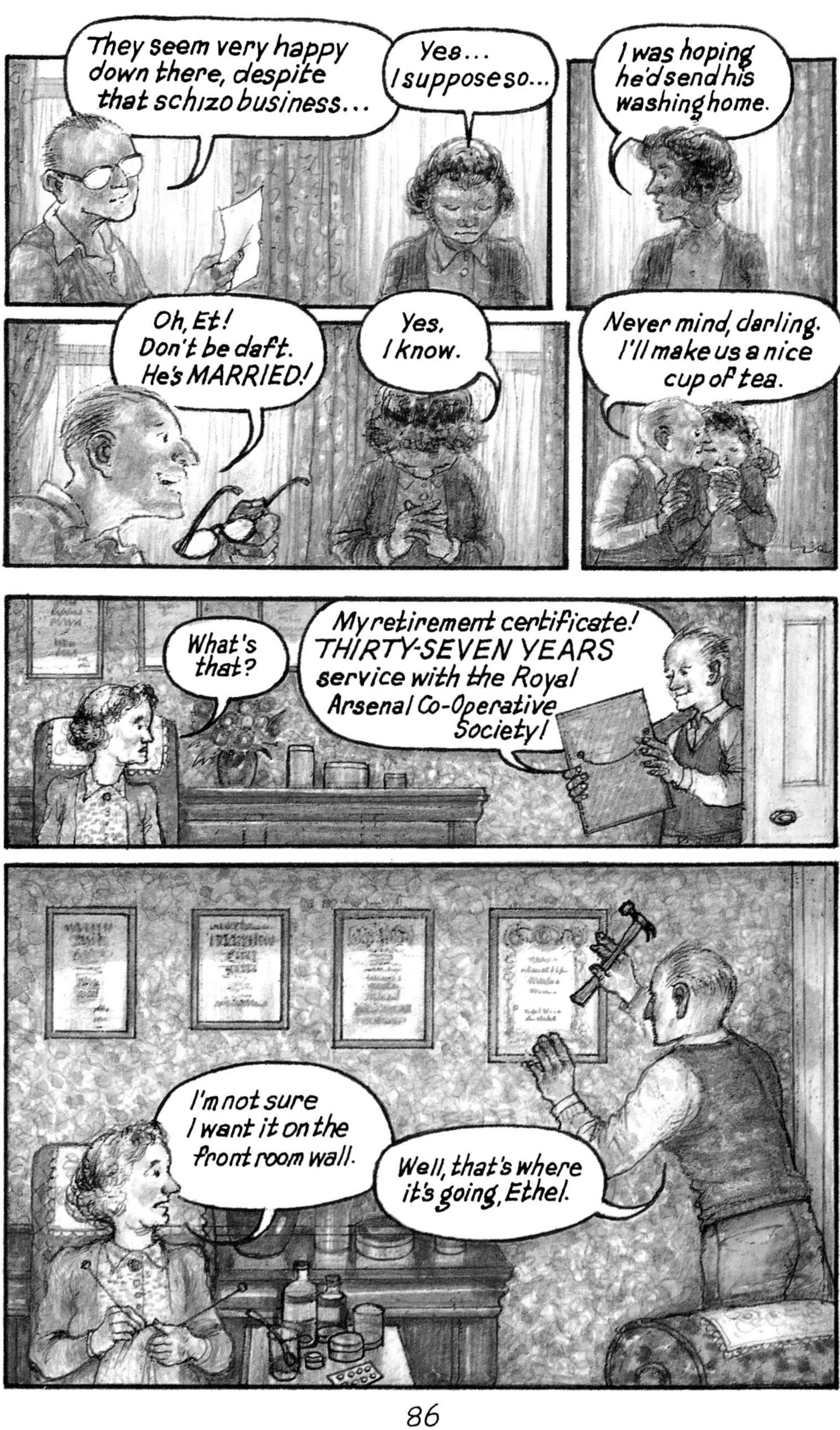
They seem very happy down there, despite that schizo business...
Yes... I suppose so...
I was hoping he'd send his washing home.
Oh, Et! Don't be daft. He's MARRIED!
Yes. I know.
Never mind, darling. I'll make us a nice cup of tea.
What's that?
My retirement certificate! THIRTY-SEVEN YEARS service with the Royal Arsenal Co-Operative Society!
I'm not sure I want it on the front room wall.
Well, that's where it's going, Ethel.

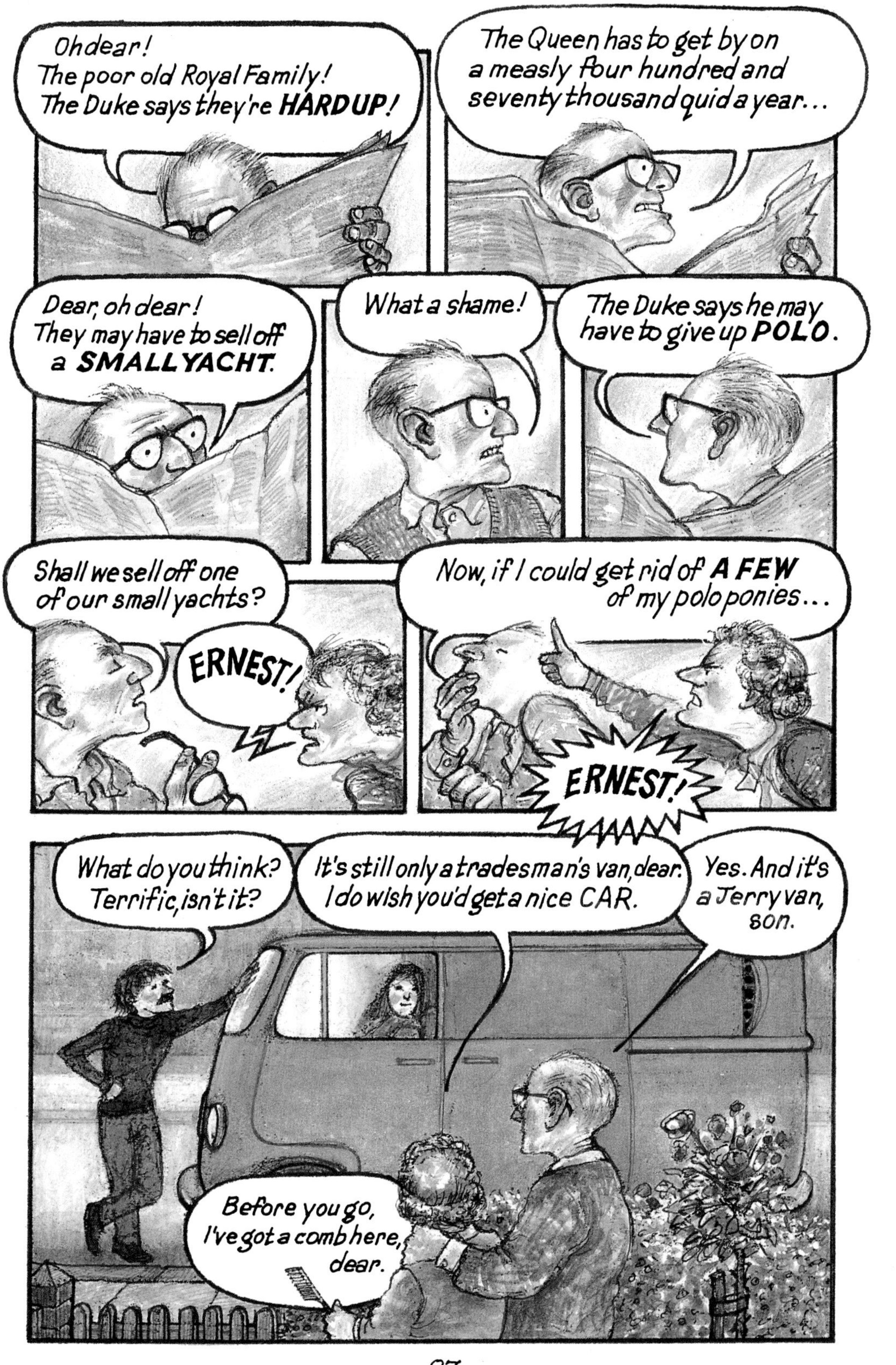
Oh dear!
The poor old Royal Family!
The Duke says they're **HARD UP**!
The Queen has to get by on a measly four hundred and seventy thousand quid a year...
Dear, oh dear!
They may have to sell off a **SMALL YACHT**.
What a shame!
The Duke says he may have to give up **POLO**.
Shall we sell off one of our small yachts?
ERNEST!
Now, if I could get rid of **A FEW** of my polo ponies...
ERNEST!
What do you think? Terrific, isn't it?
It's still only a tradesman's van, dear. I do wish you'd get a nice CAR.
Yes. And it's a Jerry van, son.
Before you go, I've got a comb here, dear.

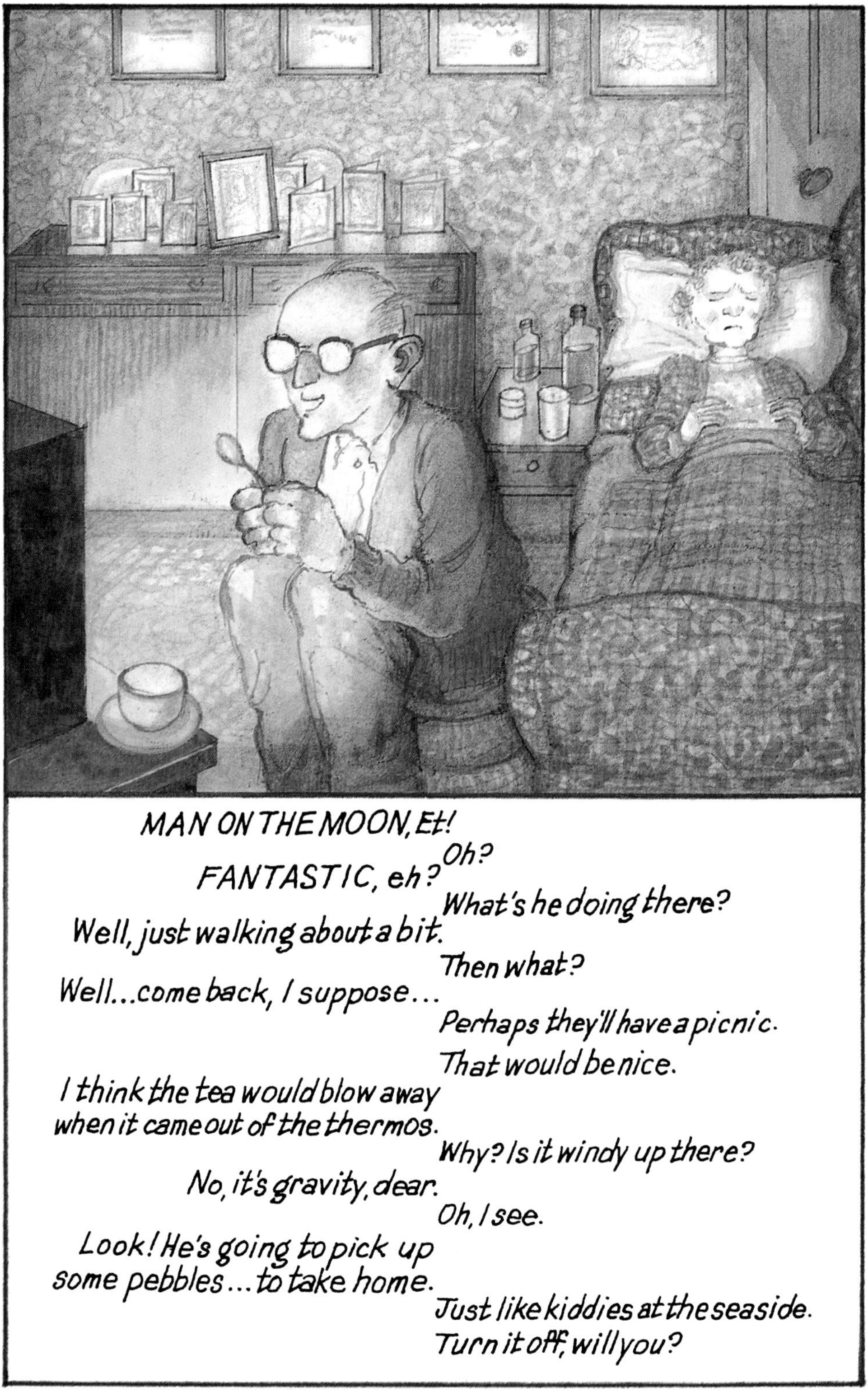
MAN ON THE MOON, Et!
Oh?
FANTASTIC, eh?
What's he doing there?
Well, just walking about a bit.
Then what?
Well...come back, I suppose...
Perhaps they'll have a picnic.
That would be nice.
I think the tea would blow away when it came out of the thermos.
Why? Is it windy up there?
No, it's gravity, dear.
Oh, I see.
Look! He's going to pick up some pebbles ... to take home.
Just like kiddies at the seaside.
Turn it off, will you?

1970
~
1971

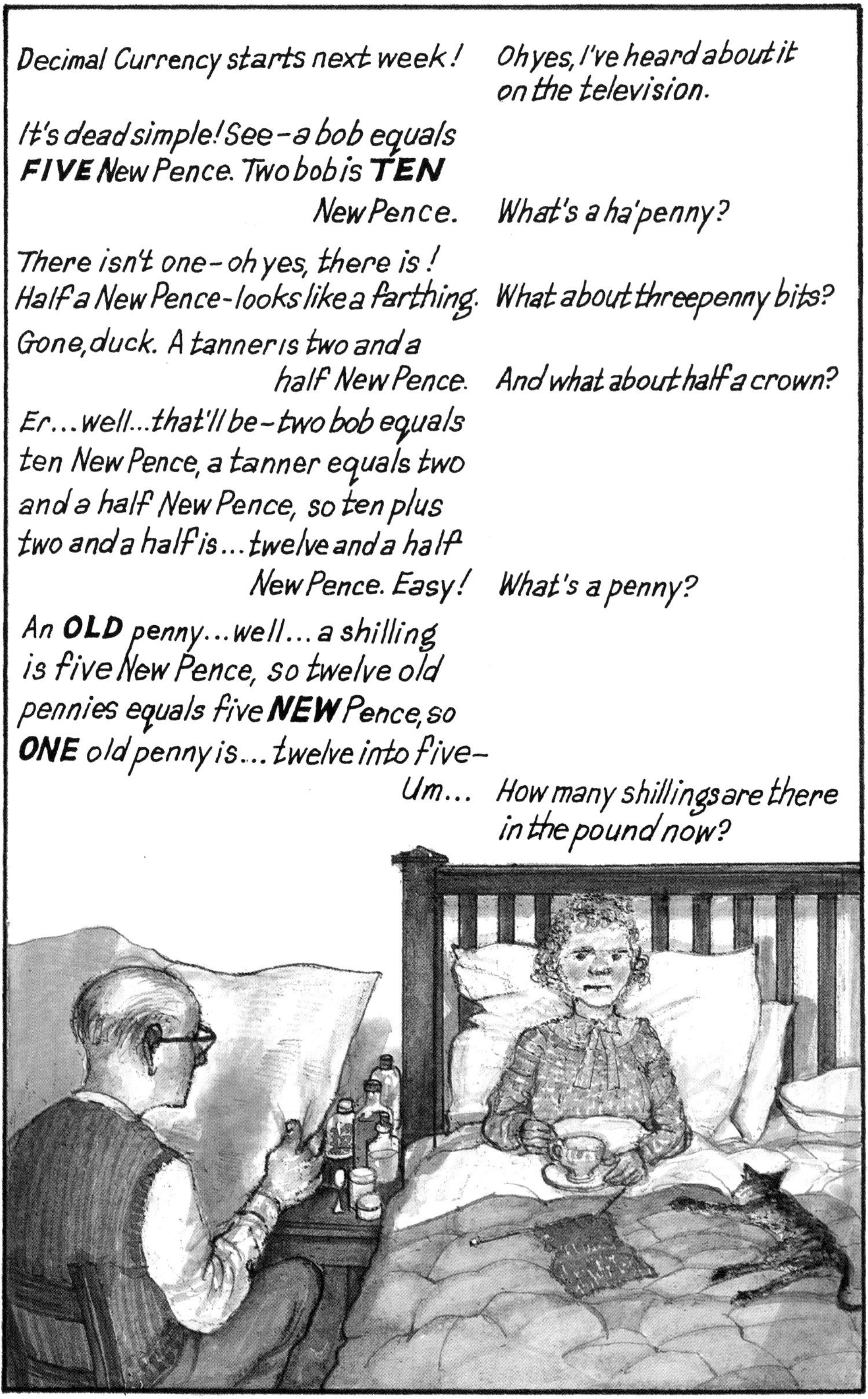
Decimal Currency starts next week!
Oh yes, I've heard about it on the television.
It's dead simple! See – a bob equals FIVE New Pence. Two bob is TEN New Pence.
What's a ha'penny?
There isn't one – oh yes, there is! Half a New Pence – looks like a farthing.
What about threepenny bits?
Gone, duck. A tanner is two and a half New Pence.
And what about half a crown?
Er... well... that'll be – two bob equals ten New Pence, a tanner equals two and a half New Pence, so ten plus two and a half is... twelve and a half New Pence. Easy!
What's a penny?
An OLD penny... well... a shilling is five New Pence, so twelve old pennies equals five NEW Pence, so ONE old penny is.... twelve into five – Um...
How many shillings are there in the pound now?

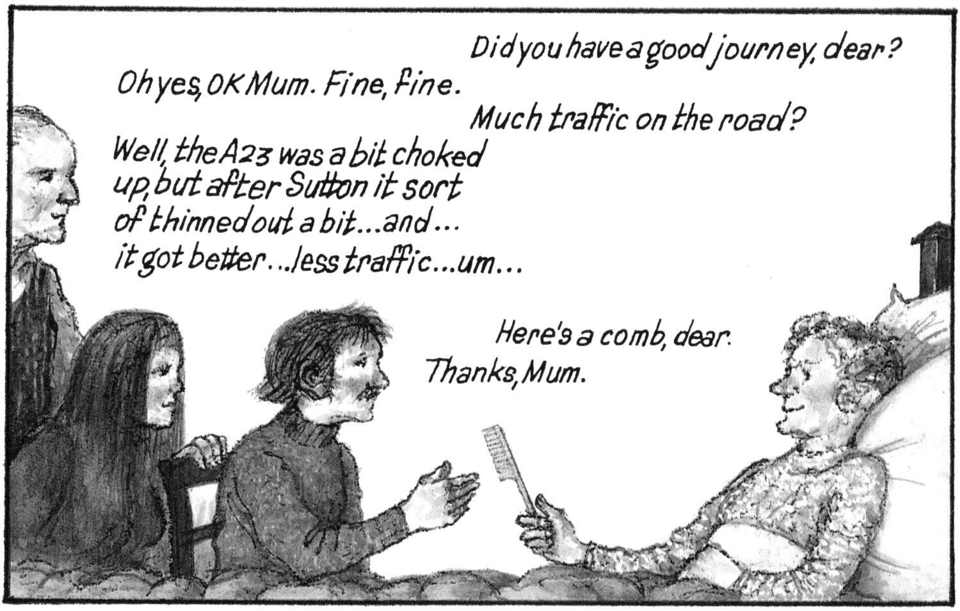
Did you have a good journey, dear?
Oh yes, OK Mum. Fine, fine.
Much traffic on the road?
Well, the A23 was a bit choked up, but after Sutton it sort of thinned out a bit...and... it got better...less traffic...um...
Here's a comb, dear.
Thanks, Mum.

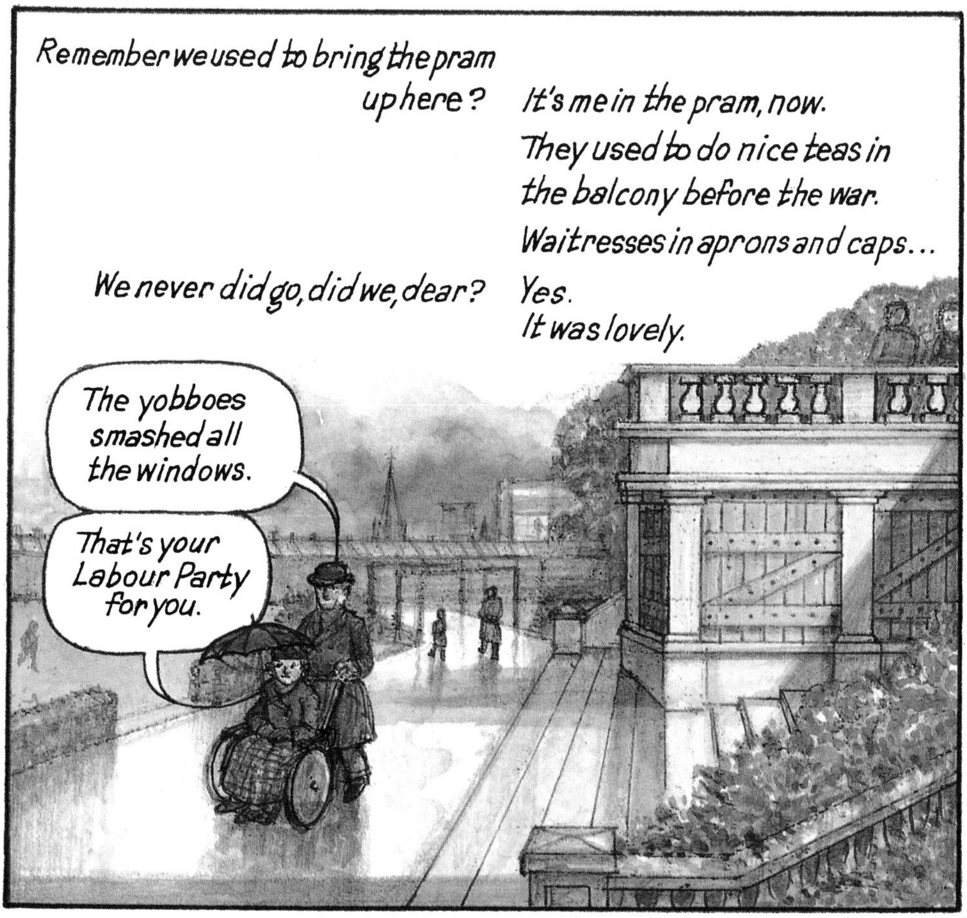
Remember we used to bring the pram up here?
It's me in the pram, now.
They used to do nice teas in the balcony before the war.
Waitresses in aprons and caps...
We never did go, did we, dear?
Yes.
It was lovely.
The yobboes smashed all the windows.
That's your Labour Party for you.

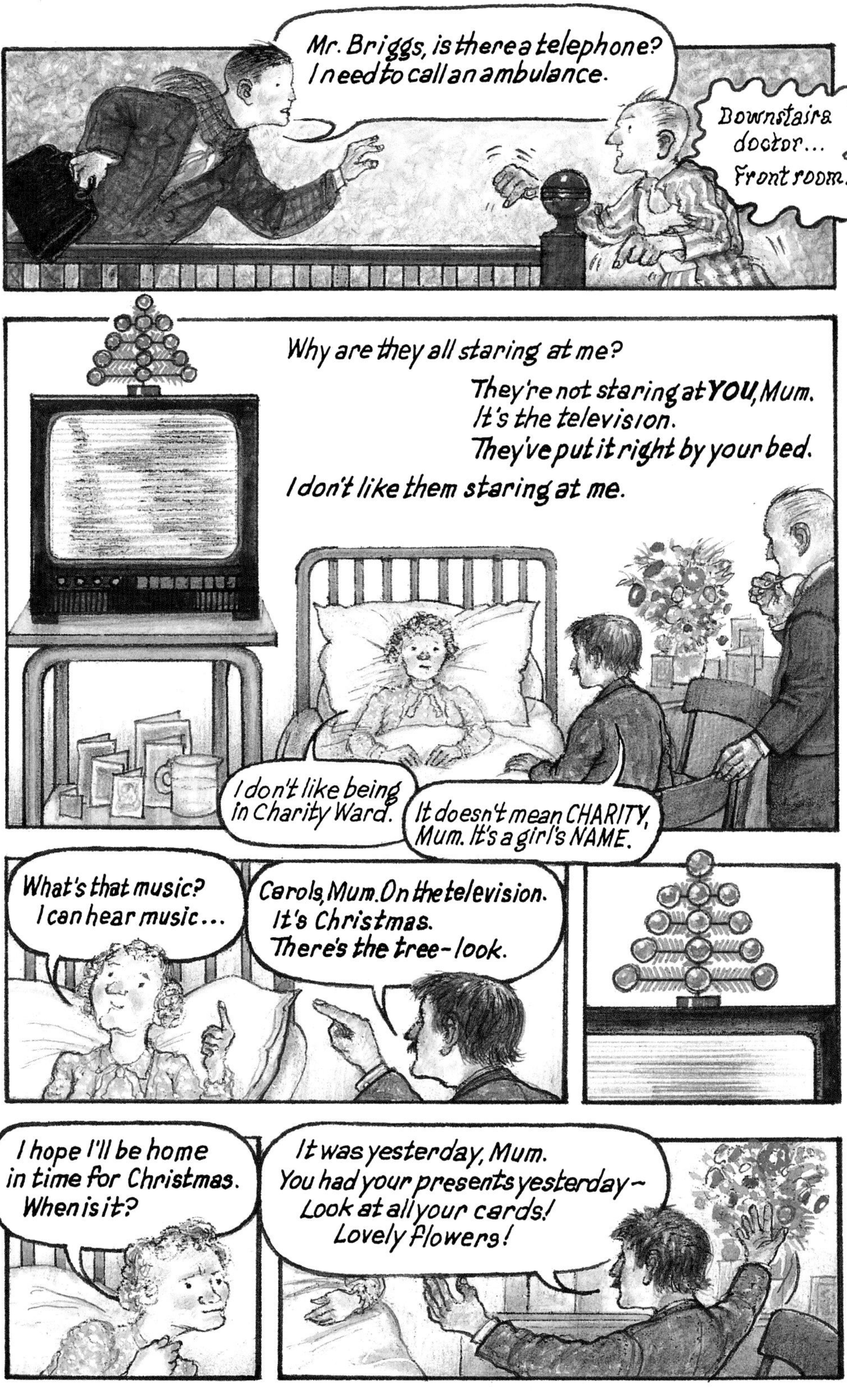
Mr. Briggs, is there a telephone? I need to call an ambulance.
Downstairs doctor... Front room.
Why are they all staring at me?
They're not staring at YOU, Mum. It's the television. They've put it right by your bed.
I don't like them staring at me.
I don't like being in Charity Ward.
It doesn't mean CHARITY, Mum. It's a girl's NAME.
What's that music? I can hear music...
Carols, Mum. On the television. It's Christmas. There's the tree - look.
I hope I'll be home in time for Christmas. When is it?
It was yesterday, Mum. You had your presents yesterday - Look at all your cards! Lovely flowers!

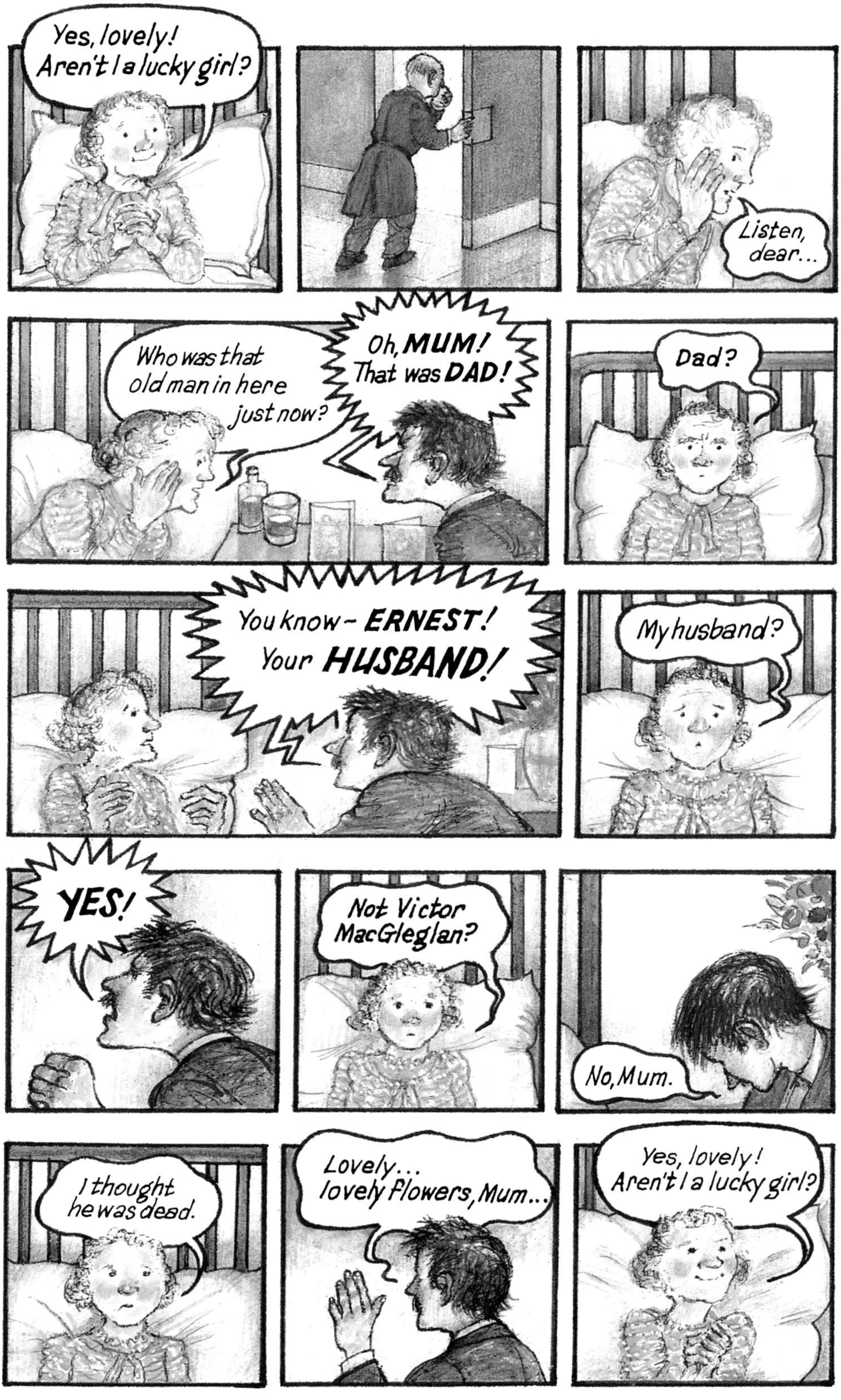
Yes, lovely! Aren't I a lucky girl?
Listen, dear...
Who was that old man in here just now?
Oh, MUM! That was DAD!
Dad?
You know - ERNEST! Your HUSBAND!
My husband?
YES!
Not Victor MacGleglan?
No, Mum.
I thought he was dead.
Lovely... lovely flowers, Mum...
Yes, lovely! Aren't I a lucky girl?

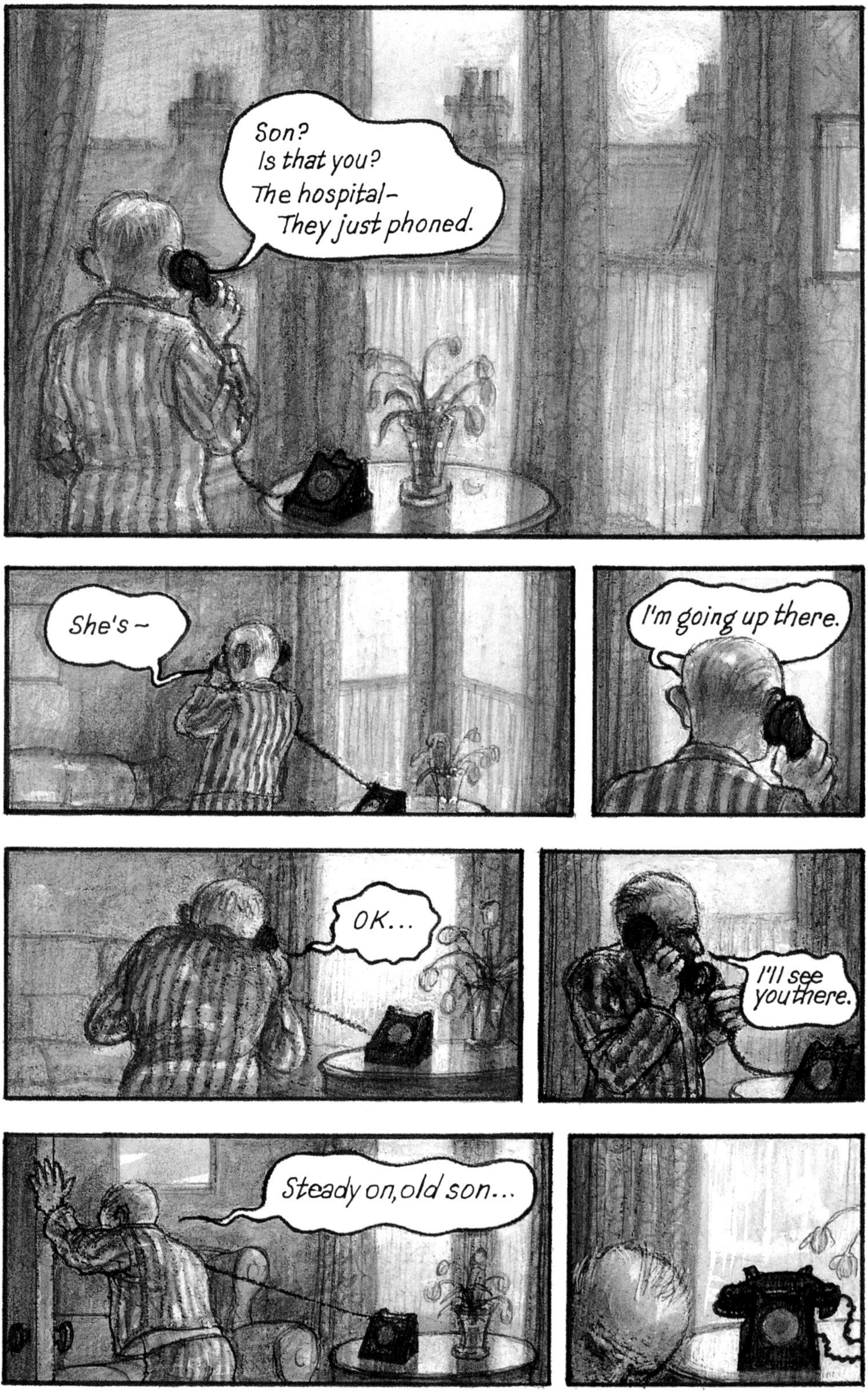
Son?
Is that you?
The hospital-
They just phoned.
She's ~
I'm going up there.
OK...
I'll see you there.
Steady on, old son...

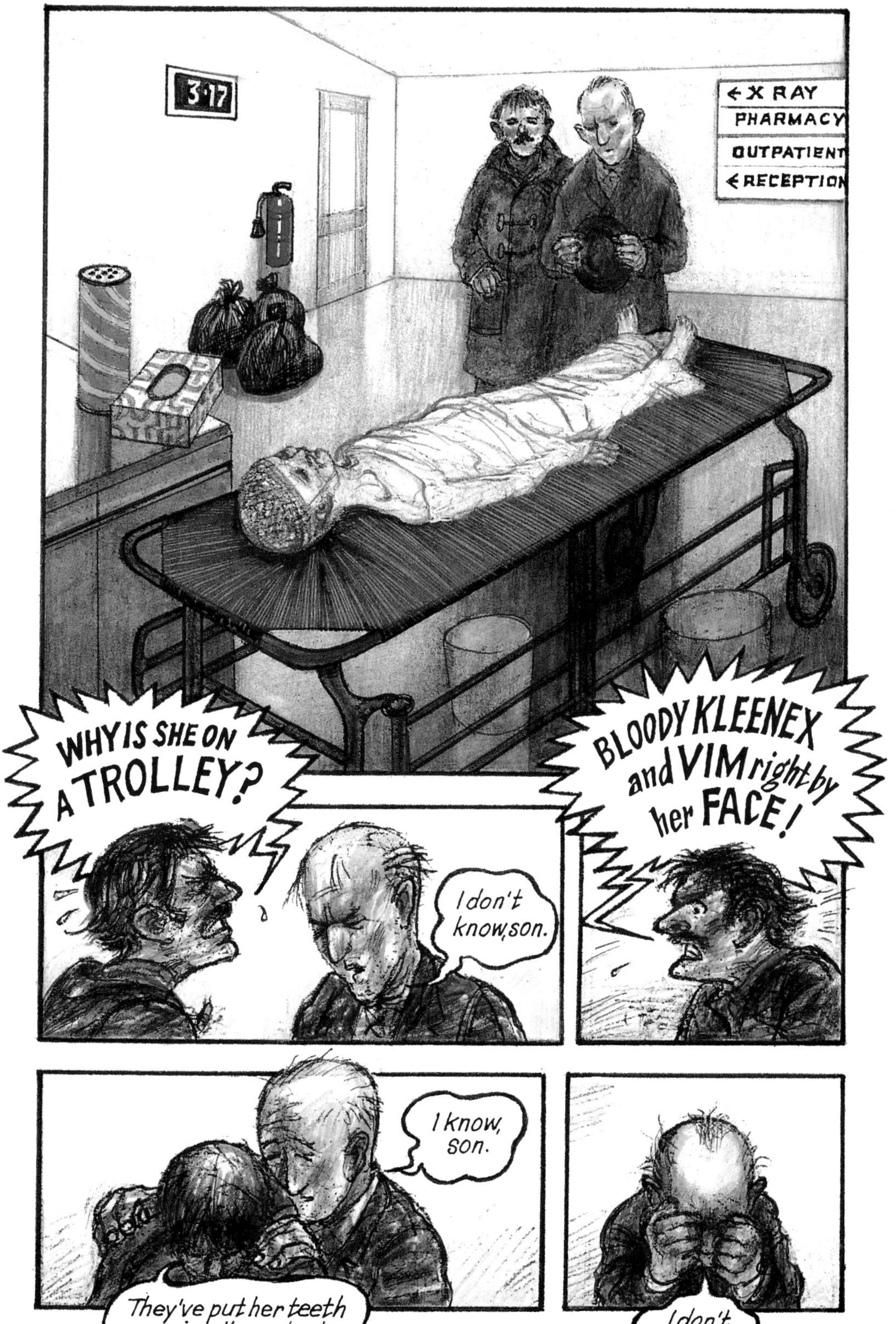
3·17
X RAY
PHARMACY
OUTPATIENT
WHY IS SHE ON A TROLLEY?
I don't know, son.
BLOODY KLEENEX and VIM right by her FACE!
I know, son.
They've put her teeth in all crooked.
I don't know...

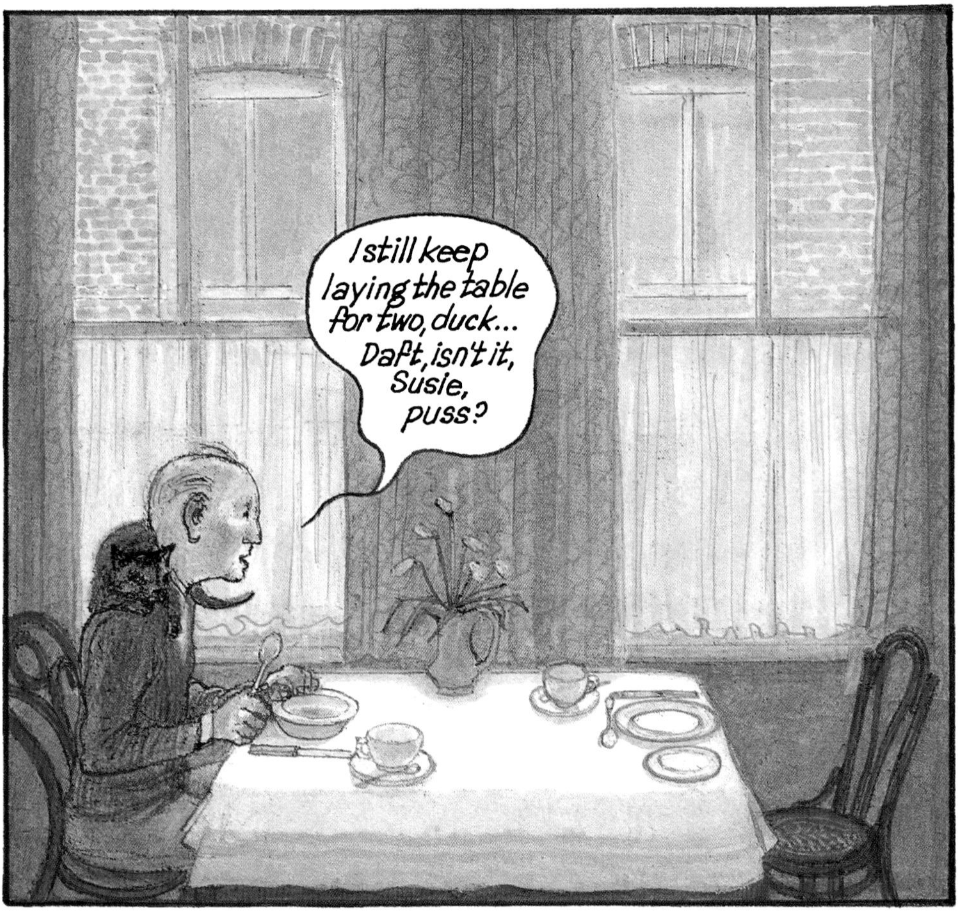
I still keep laying the table for two, duck... Daft, isn't it, Susie, puss?

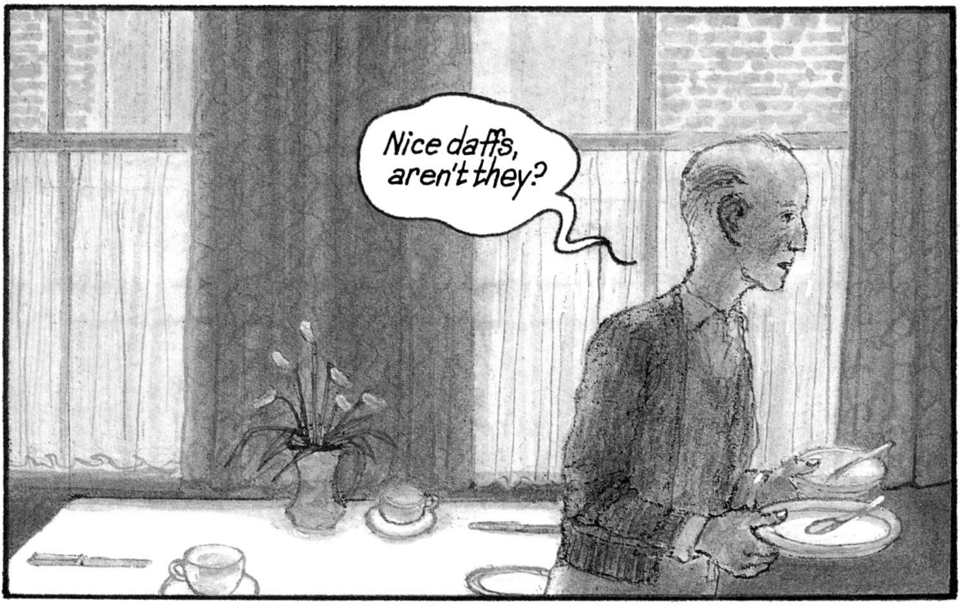
Nice daffs, aren't they?

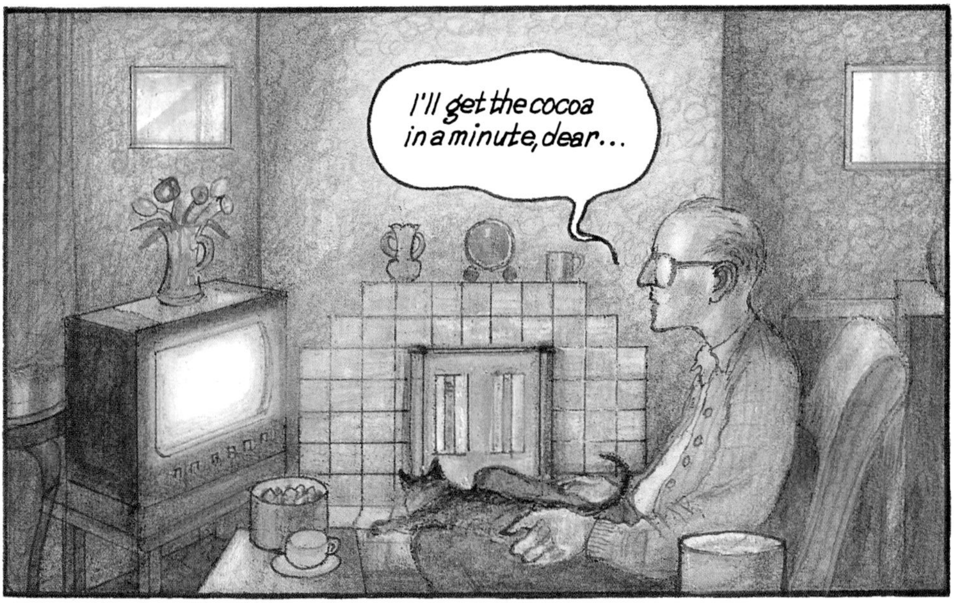
I'll get the cocoa in a minute, dear...

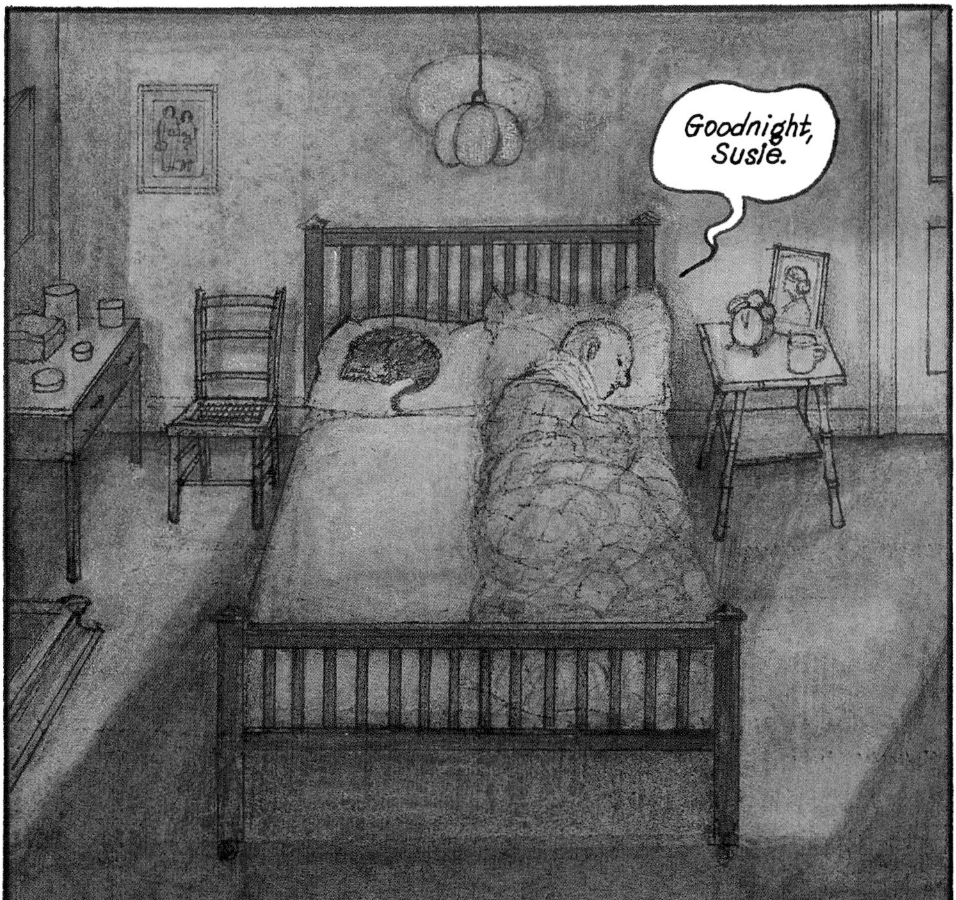
Goodnight, Susie.

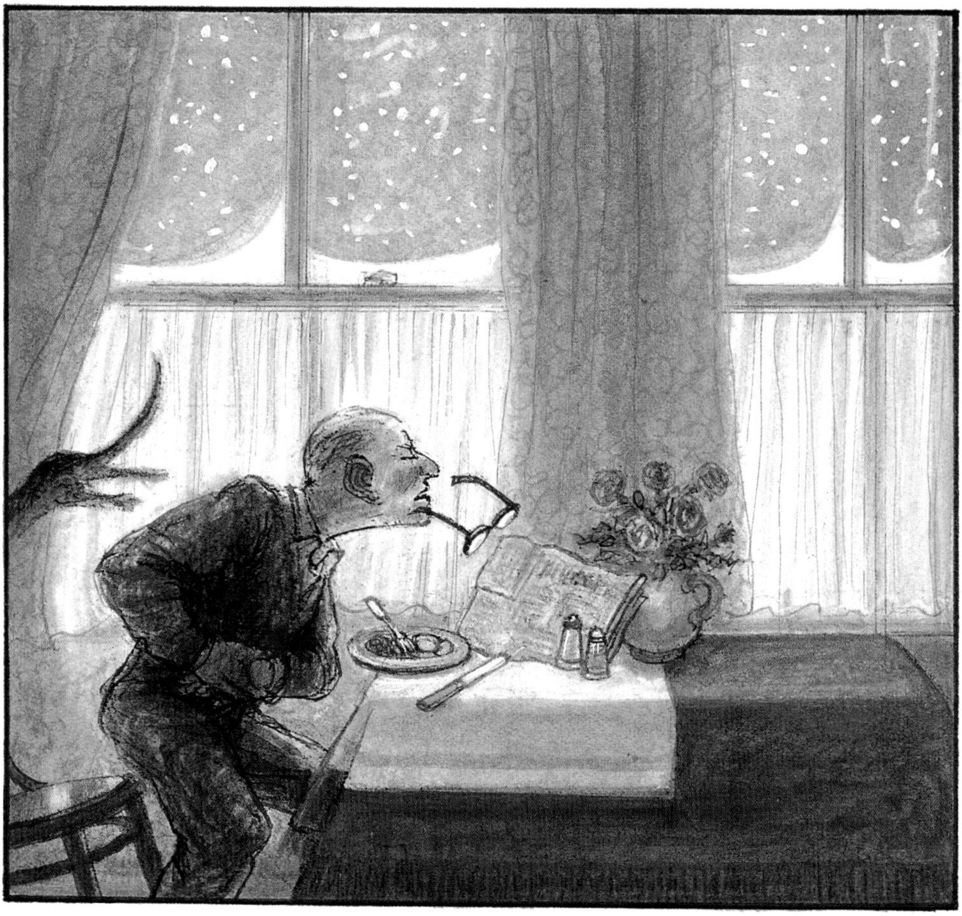

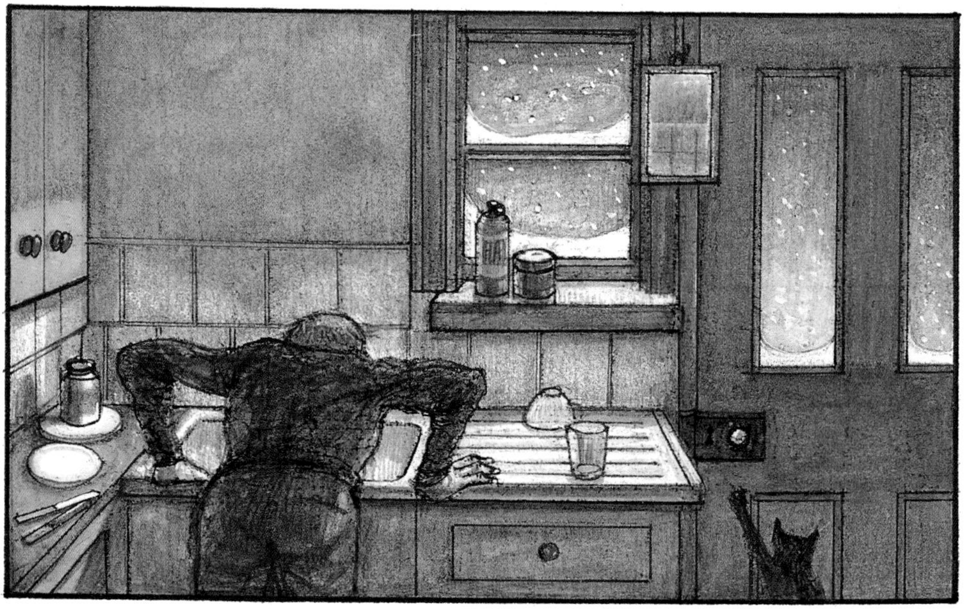

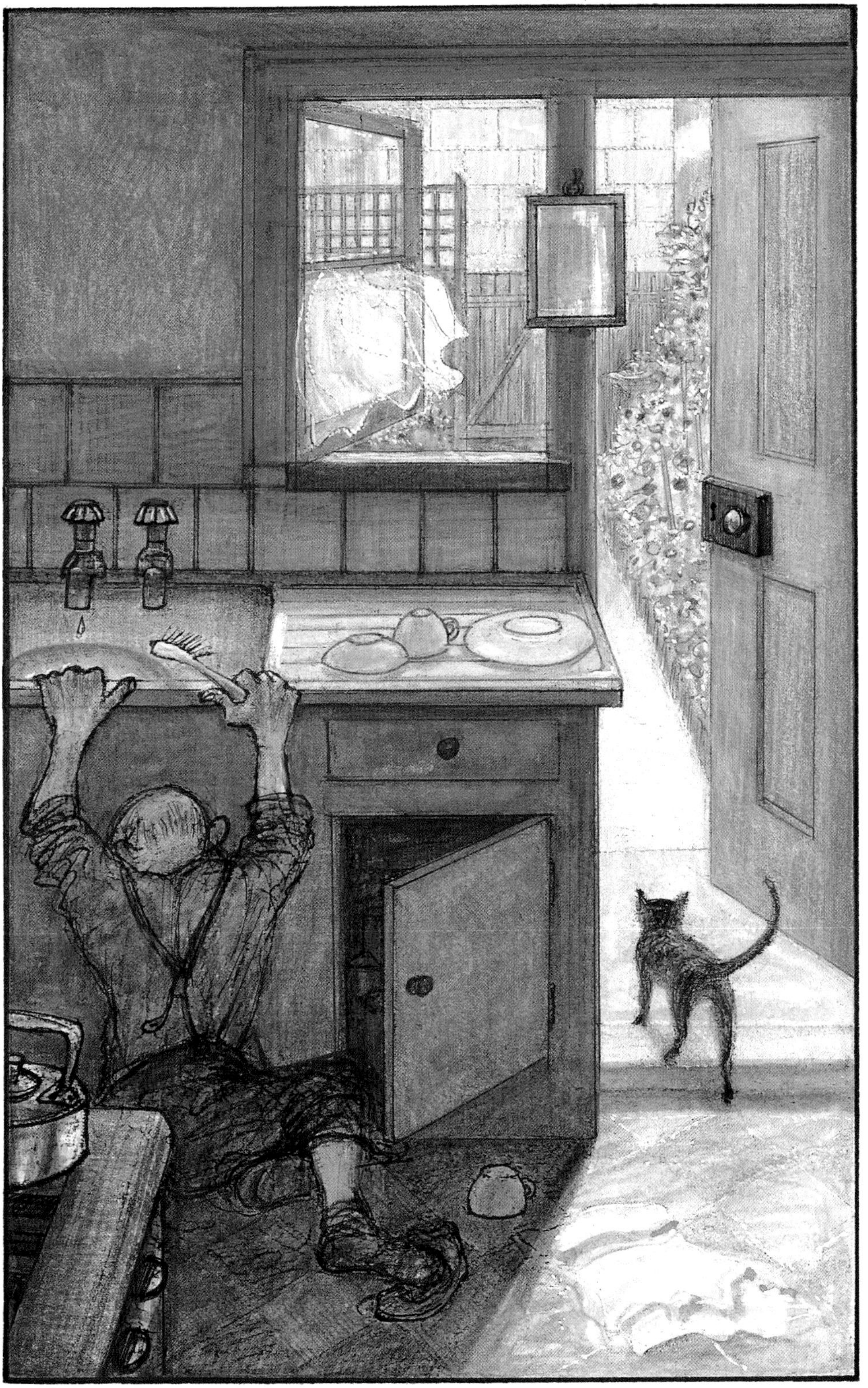

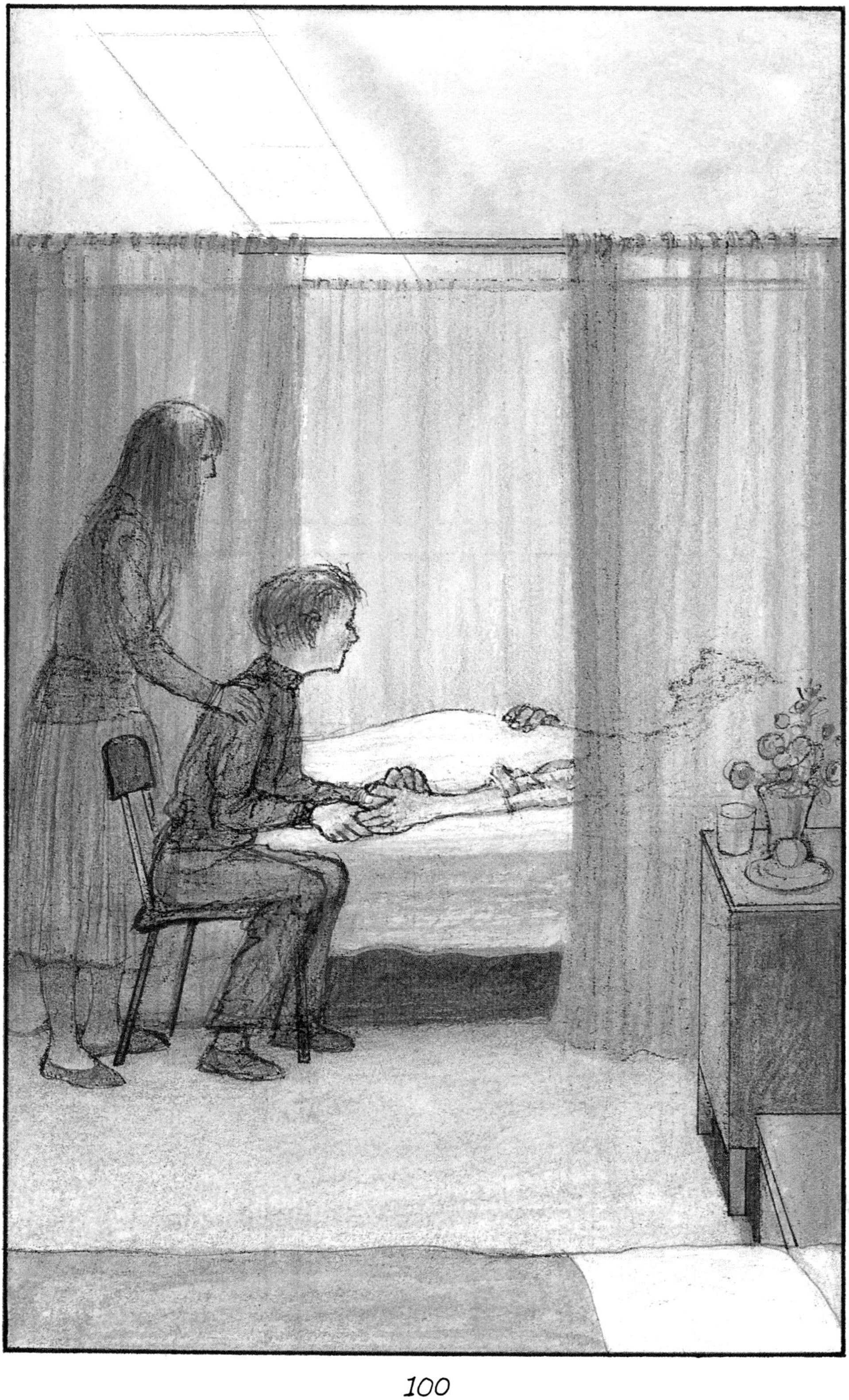

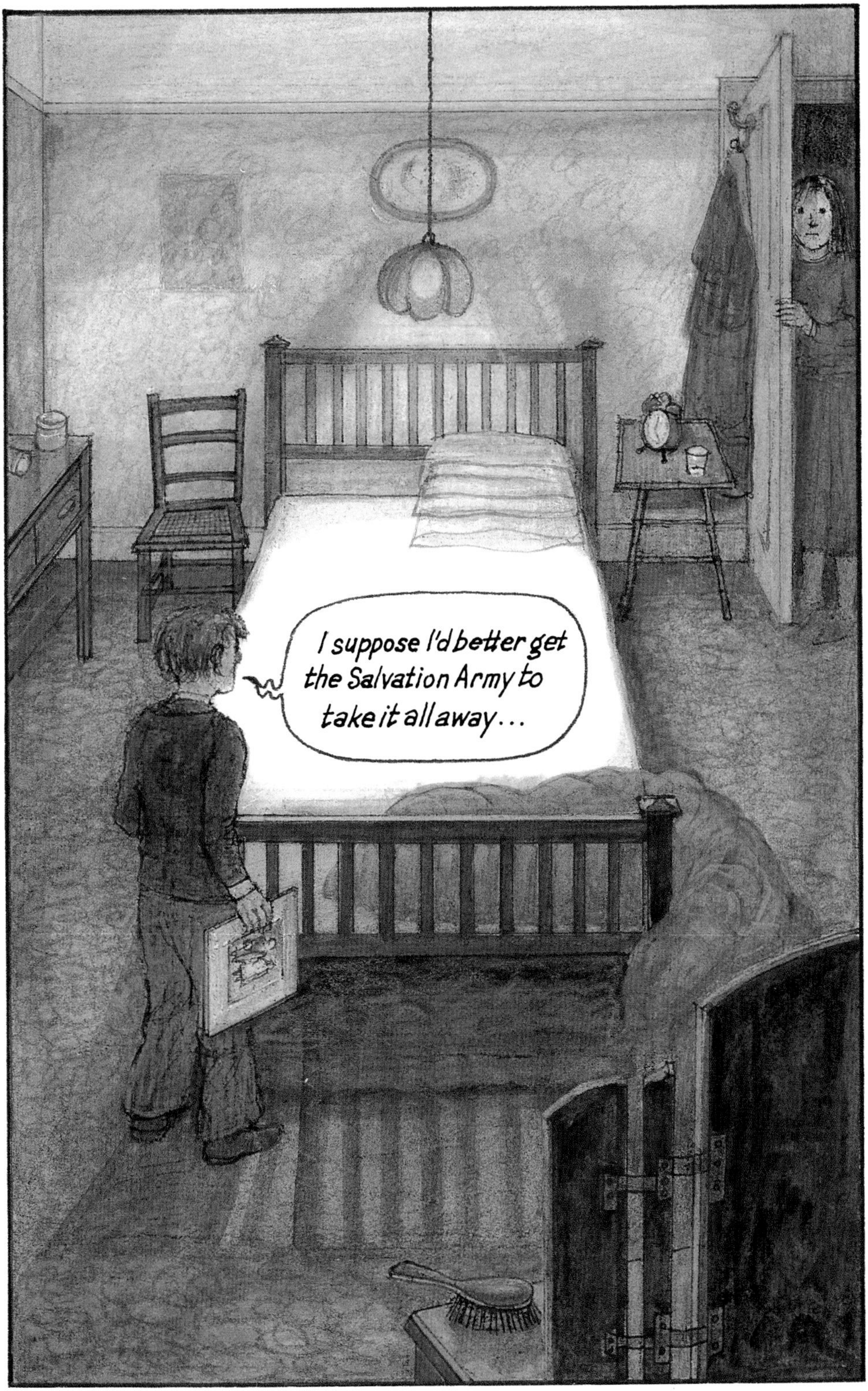
I suppose I'd better get the Salvation Army to take it all away...

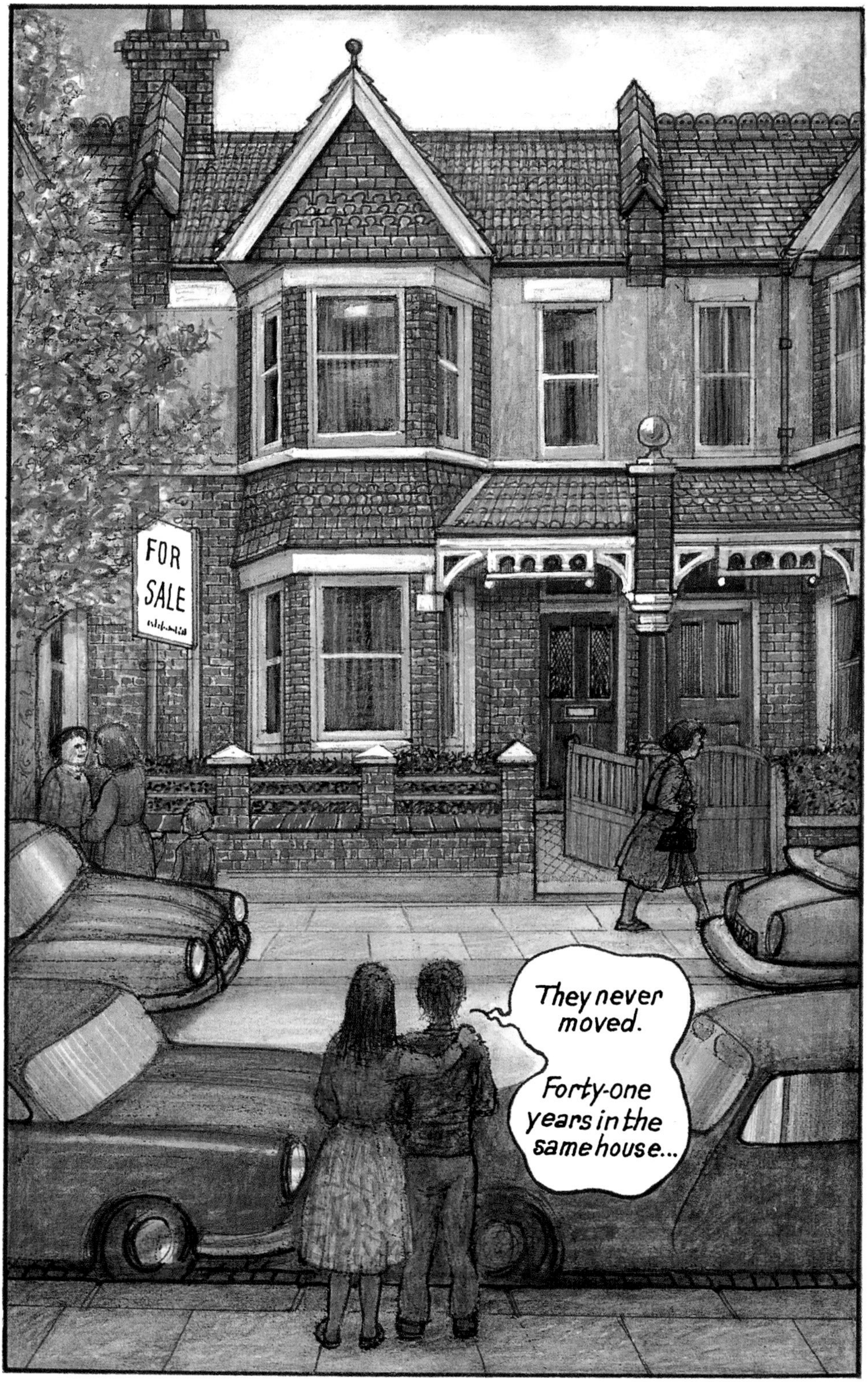
FOR SALE
They never moved.
Forty-one years in the same house...

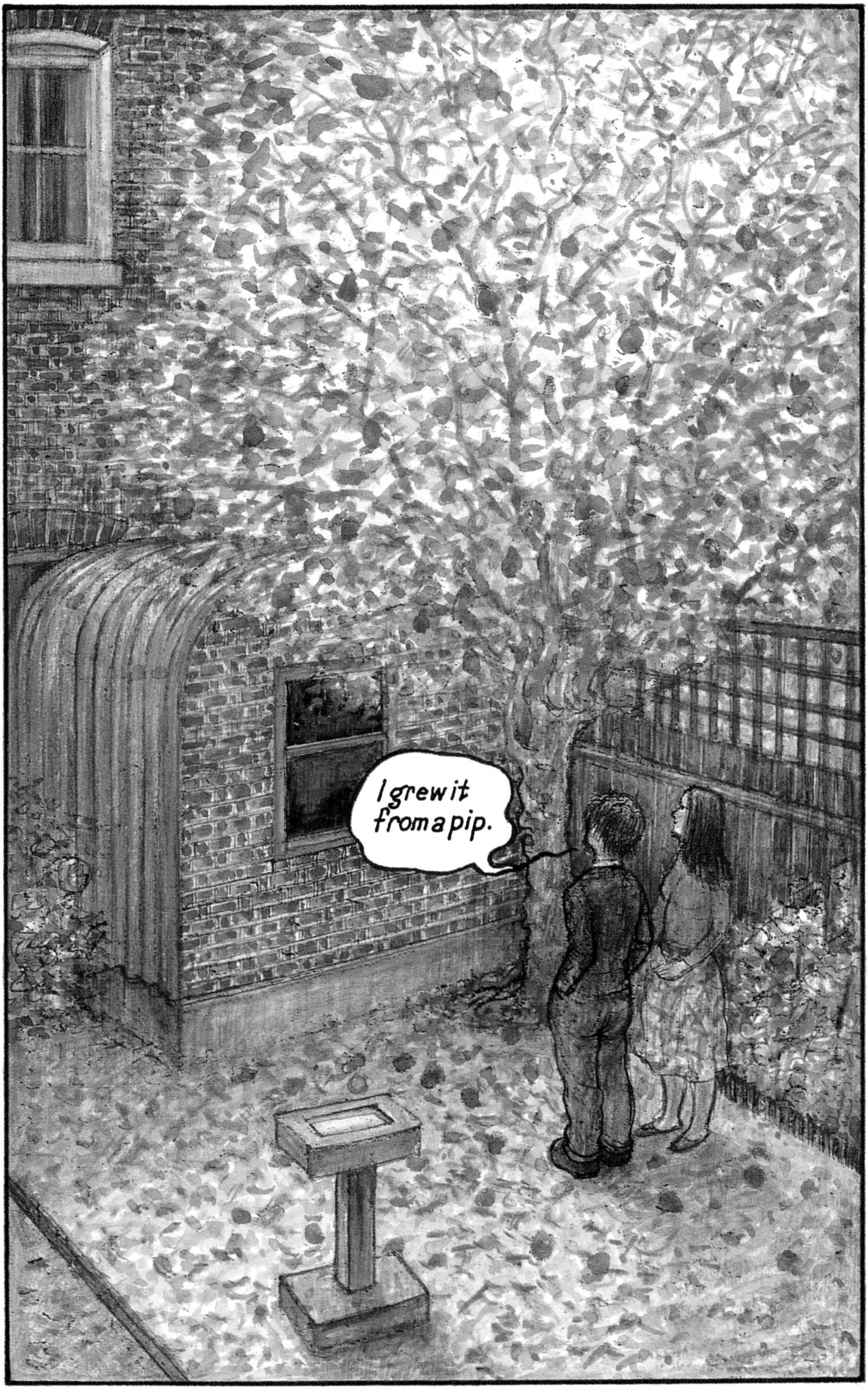
I grew it from a pip.

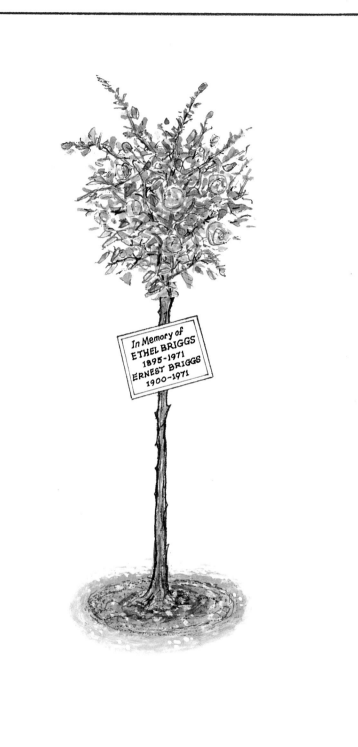

In Memory of
ETHEL BRIGGS
1895-1971
ERNEST BRIGGS
1900-1971